MONTESSORI IN ACTION

MONTESSORI IN ACTION

Building Resilient Montessori Schools

ELIZABETH G. SLADE

JB JOSSEY-BASS™

A Wiley Brand

Published by John Wiley & Sons, Inc., Hoboken, New Jersey.
Published simultaneously in Canada.

For general information on our other products and services or for technical support, please contact our Customer Care Department within the United States at (800) 762-2974, outside the United States at (317) 572-3993 or fax (317) 572-4002.

Wiley also publishes its books in a variety of electronic formats. Some content that appears in print may not be available in electronic formats. For more information about Wiley products, visit our web site at www.wiley.com.

Library of Congress Cataloging-in-Publication Data is Available:

ISBN 9781119763123 (paperback)
ISBN 9781119764953 (ePDF)
ISBN 9781119763130 (ePub)

Cover Design: Wiley
Cover Image:©TetianaLynnyk/Shutterstock
SKY10027785_062321

For Bella
Who prompts me daily toward the work
of finding and making meaning.

Contents

Acknowledgments

This work was born out of the experience of working with many amazing people in my time as a school-based Montessorian, and I am grateful for their commitment and drive. There are three school leaders during that time who offered me a chance to bring my full self to the work: Alan Feldman, Analida Munera, and John Freeman. You shaped my thinking about bringing the work of Montessori to the whole school, and I learned a great deal from each of you. Alan, thank you for sharing One School, Honest Talk, and Systems to support what we do as a frame for how we all might create something sturdier together. Analida, thank you for the opportunity to explore the yet unnamed parts of a whole school Montessori method. John, thank you for your partnership in implementing visions and for taking many big leaps together.

There were also three extraordinary Montessorians who walked alongside me during that time: Sandra Wyner Andrew, Gretchen Courage, and Uma Ramani. You were collaborators in developing this work, as you each brought the long arc of your experience and love of the method into the public sector. Thank you for the coaching you offered me regularly and for holding such a clear vision even in times of chaos.

I am humbled by the hard work done daily by public Montessori teachers and grateful for the trust of those I worked with over the years. Thank you for continuing to return to the essence of our calling: to serve the child.

In addition, there were many learners along the way who showed me what was needed and some who patiently coached me, including Jaquan, Maria, Edgar, Osvaldo, Mya, Dreshaun, and Kayla. Your willingness to engage in honest talk supported my learning and led to the big idea of sharing it widely.

I want to acknowledge the great impact working for the National Center for Montessori in the Public Sector (NCMPS) for six important years had on me. Thank you to Jackie Cossentino and Keith Whitescarver for giving me the opportunity to take these ideas to a national scale, offering them to school leaders and public Montessori schools of various means and in various settings. Thank you to the team at NCMPS, who engaged in ongoing conversations about the work with "strong beliefs, lightly held."

There have been many school collaborators along the way but three whose ears perked up and who boldly implemented these ideas from the start and thus further developed them. Thank you to these three original school collaborators who listened, trusted, questioned, refined, and made better almost everything in this book: Michelle Boyle, Megan Hubbard, and Hannah Richardson. We worked closely together for five years, enjoying annual summer retreats to reflect and improve upon what had been implemented the year before. I learned an enormous amount through our work together, and these ideas would have remained just that without your determination and hard work.

Katie Rucker, Peggy Johnson, and Kisha Young and the full staff at Moore Montessori are also collaborators who started their school based on the whole school Montessori method and continue to forward the work each day with children, staff, and families. Thank you for your big hearts and strong push to reach every child, reflect, regroup, shore each other up, and go back to make it stronger so that everyone might thrive.

My great gratitude goes out to the original think tank that resulted in the development of the system of justness – Genevieve D'Cruz, Bobby Johnson, and Allison Jones – as well as the practitioners I worked alongside in schools – Gail Ameral, Marla Dakin, and Luis Lumpris. Your quiet, consistent, and ongoing work to create equitable education through your daily work with key children was inspiring and the work grew from your gifts and insights.

The words and pages became a book with help from Christine O'Connor, Tom Dinse, Kristi Bennett, Mackenzie Thompson, Riley Harding, and the whole team at Jossey-Bass/Wiley. In addition, Katie Brown supported the ongoing research needed to make the work more robust.

I was fortunate to have some generous readers who spent time with this book as it was forming. Thank you to Michelle Boyle, Natalie Celeste, Teresa Chan, Alan Feldman, Allison Jones, Jacqui Miller, Jana Morgan Herman, Isaac Price-Slade, Hannah Richardson, and Sandra Wyner Andrew for your thoughtful review of these pages and for your suggestions to strengthen and improve them.

I'd also like to acknowledge the love and faith of my family as I gave precious minutes of our family time to various elements of the work over the course of my children's younger years. You spent summer hours scootering in empty schools, salvaged materials from dumpsters, cut laminated materials, and generously shared me with the work. May I return the favor as you find your life's work and turn your energy toward it.

Finally, this book would not exist without My Dear Associate, who saw me through Bella's death and steadied me to continue the work when I wasn't sure I would be able to. Your passion for creating an accessible, powerful Montessori experience for everyone inspired me to get back up. Your vision for what was possible moved me out of my comfort zone and deeper into making it real. Your belief in human flourishing continues to motivate me daily.

Land Acknowledgment

The ideas shared in this book were born and cultivated in western Massachusetts, home to the Agawam and the Nonotuck, two of many Indigenous groups from Kwinitekwa, the Connecticut River Valley. This book was largely written in Belfast, Maine, overlooking the Penobscot Bay, home to the Penobscot tribe of Abenaki people. "The federal government's Indian Removal policies wrenched many Native peoples from our homelands. It separated us from our traditional knowledge and lifeways, the bones of our ancestors, our sustaining plants – but even this did not extinguish identity," writes Robin Wall Kimmerer in her extraordinary book *Braiding Sweetgrass*. This land acknowledgment is placed here as a way to reconnect with the bones of our ancestors, to honor the land we inhabit, and to remind us to illuminate the identities of all those in our communities. I am grateful to the land and all that it has offered me in support of this work, to the Indigenous people who cared for it, and in particular to the wise Venerable Dhyani Ywahoo, who has guided and reminded me that we are all interconnected.

About the Author

Elizabeth Slade has been a Montessori educator for 35 years. She worked in both Springfield Public Schools and Hartford Public Schools building public Montessori programs, implementing systems to support all children, and developing the art of Montessori coaching. For six years, she worked at the National Center for Montessori in the Public Sector supporting school start-ups, designing Child Study trainings, and bringing the Montessori coaching method to hundreds of schools across the country. Elizabeth is a founder of Public Montessori in Action, a nonprofit organization with a mission to ensure fully implemented Montessori for children, families, and educators of the global majority.

Preface

For the past 35 years I have lived inside the world of Montessori, in independent and public schools, in rural and urban areas. I found ground there that has formed me into the person I've become, and it continues to change me. I imagine by the time this book is in print I will be yet another iteration of myself with revisions to what I've shared here and still more ideas sprouting. This is the nature of impermanence and the beauty of having spent a life aligned with a method that encourages self-discovery and a commitment to bringing what we have to emerging conundrums.

My Montessori journey began in Washington, D.C., in 1986 when I entered the Washington Montessori Institute and found a new way of education – one that spoke to me as a diverse learner and made sense as a way to honor the dignity of each person. I went on to teach 6–12-year-olds in Montessori parent–teacher co-ops for the next 13 years. The students of that time taught me a great deal about learning. My training prepared me to use observation as a basis for adjusting my approach to everything, so I watched and learned. I learned about building and being part of a community, about the power of honest and open conversations and of the importance of systems to guide us in our work. The children who taught me these early lessons have their signatures in much of the work shared.

In 1999, the first public Montessori school – Alfred Zanetti School – opened in my home state of Massachusetts, and I was then introduced into a wider world of Montessori implementation. I was invited to support district teachers with six weeks of Montessori training as they worked to begin Montessori classrooms in a school that had previously been a traditional K–5 program. The Zanetti school ended the previous year in June as a standard district school and opened in August as a Montessori school with multi-age classrooms and hands-on materials spanning children's house, lower elementary, and upper elementary.

The whole community was in the midst of a radical shift. When I think back on those early days, I see now my role as a translator supporting the transition from an old way of being into a new way of being for adults and children alike. I also see that an enormous amount of energy was spent on inventing the wheel. Unlike in my career as a classroom teacher, when I had shifted schools and was able to bring the knowledge forward to the next setting with established systems in place, in this situation we had no schoolwide systems to rely on: we were starting from scratch.

Within three years the school had grown an adolescent program and had a waiting list in the hundreds. This prompted the superintendent to convert a second district school to a Montessori school: the Gerena Community School. The principal, Analida Munera, and I shifted to begin the second school while our colleague Sandra Wyner Andrew remained as principal of Zanetti. Gerena was a larger school with an ever-changing student population; because it was in an affordable neighborhood, families arriving from the Dominican Republic or Puerto Rico would move into homes there and then relocate when their situation improved. Gerena was also built to reunite two neighborhoods divided by the construction of Interstate 91 and so had a public walkway tunnel running through its center. This construction, despite its many liabilities, along with families' determination and outspokenness showed me the importance of including the community in the work and life of the school.

The learners at Zanetti and Gerena taught me a great deal in those years. Their insights and frequent, often immediate, feedback about the school allowed for the development of more inclusive ways of being. They were the inspiration for the Seamless Transitions work as well as many of the other systems, structures, and practices shared ahead.

When a new superintendent arrived in the district and redistributed the Montessori leadership into traditional programs across the city, I began my work in Hartford public schools. What initially brought me there was the child study process, which I implemented at CREC Montessori Magnet along with Jackie Cossentio and Gretchen Hall. The experience of taking something that had originated as a system in Springfield and implementing it in a new setting helped me understand the power of creating shared language and systems across schools and districts.

From there I brought the child study process to the two other public Montessori schools in the district, which quickly led to a permanent position at Annie Fisher Montessori School as an elementary coach. My work there with

John Freeman, the principal, and Uma Ramani, the primary coach, allowed for an opportunity to implement the work begun in Springfield as well as to collaborate and co-create other missing components necessary to strengthen, support, and guide the work. I had not yet had the experience of working with other Montessori trained leaders with such clear vision and boundless passion for the work and this allowed us to move into full implementation of the method. Up until that time, my work was shaped by the demands of the district and the need to comply with external changes which often meant restrictions or requirements that did not serve the Montessori classrooms. Up until that time, I had known only compromise and the repeated experience of salvaging essential pieces of the program from the influx of new regulations. As a team at Annie Fisher, we focused all of our energy on full implementation of the method without compromise as an opportunity to see if in fact it would create the results we knew were possible. And it did. In our final year together as a team the third and sixth graders at the school were outperforming their district peers.

When I was recruited by the National Center for Montessori in the Public Sector, I joined the team, certain that this work could translate and spent the next six years sharing and implementing the tools, structures, and methods that had grown over the previous 14 years working in New England public Montessori schools.

The six years I spent traveling to schools across the nation brought me to work with some extraordinary people in our wider Montessori community: hard-working, determined educators who held a shared vision for fully implementing the method in a public setting with free access for children and families. The work has been developed together. The work will continue to be developed together, now including you.

PART I

Introduction

This is what is intended by education as a help to life; an education from birth that brings about a revolution: a revolution that eliminates every violence, a revolution in which everyone will be attracted towards a common center.

—Dr. Montessori, *The Absorbent Mind*

An introduction is a welcome, intentional way of meeting the new through a connector. As you open this book you are meeting some new ideas and for some perhaps even a new world: the world of implementing Montessori education. Welcome to the revolution! For over 100 years, astute observers of children have known that humans are natural learners, that creativity is as common as dirt, that genius resides in every child, and that when given the chance to flourish the potential for humans to innovate and move ideas forward is infinite. Whether you are an experienced Montessori practitioner or Montessori supporter or just coming to know about this method, you are invited to join the community of educators, families, and advocates for children – a community that holds this truth at its center.

The conventional and prevalent method of education in the United States over these same 100 years posits that learning happens because of the information presented by the teacher to a child. By contrast, the Montessori method emphasizes the child's interactions with a carefully prepared environment as an aid to life. This features individual learning over whole-group instruction and fosters intrinsic motivation, opportunities for concentration and independence, and the development of executive functioning skills. Although the impact of the method, when well implemented, has been researched and written about, the components of how to effectively implement Montessori at the school level, particularly in the public sector, have yet to be fully clarified. That is the direct aim of this work. This book is meant to serve those who are implementing Montessori: teachers, coaches, school leaders, district officials, or those who would like to begin a Montessori program. It can also be insightful for families wanting to know what goes on behind the scenes at their child's Montessori school.

Dr. Maria Montessori designed her schools to serve all children, but for historical reasons Montessori schools have often been largely reserved for the elite. Although this was neither Montessori's mission nor the context in which the method was initially developed, the majority of Montessori programs in this country are independent schools largely serving families with the means to pay for the tuition-based programs. There has consequently been no shared method for how to build sustainable Montessori institutions in the public sector. A complex and holistic model like Montessori goes against the grain of our current public education system – one designed to avoid complexity. The Montessori model requires unique autonomies and attention to structures for schools to outlast the passionate people and communities that come together to build them.

Therefore, when public school districts elect to open a district, magnet, or charter Montessori program and, in the absence of guidance, develop the school based on the needs of the other schools in the district, the foundation for the program is already working against its very nature. With a steady growth of public Montessori in this country over the past four decades and a significant rise in recent years,[3] this is a growing concern. Now that there are many more schools opening, we need a unified approach to propel the work forward. At its best, the Montessori method itself is unified by a shared understanding of a rigorous approach to personalized learning grounded in carefully chosen materials and the development of community in the classroom. This means children around the world are using the same materials in the same way to move their learning forward. This is an enormous strength that is often compromised in the public sector by the wide variation in the application of the method. If we can come together and share an implementation approach, this will allow for consistency across schools that will then offer equitable Montessori programs to children regardless of background and location. The whole school Montessori method presented in this book is a cohesive approach to implementing Montessori that will build resilient and lasting schools, allowing them to provide high-quality education for children and families over time.

Montessori educators go through extensive training to understand both philosophy and materials. This means a trained person could go into any Montessori school in the world and locate any Montessori material of their choice. A non–Montessori trained head of school once watched this occur as a visiting presenter requested the constructive triangle box to use in an evening presentation after all the teachers were gone. Not knowing what she needed or where to find it himself, the head of school led her to a nearby classroom. The Montessori presenter stood at the door, surveyed the room, realized it was a primary classroom, located and crossed to the sensorial shelf, and picked up the material. He was astounded. "Have you been here before?" he asked. When she shook her head, he asked, "How did you do that?" as though it were a magic trick.

This is a magic trick we need to be able to do with whole schools. We need to all be so familiar with the shared structures of a Montessori school that we can fluidly step in and keep the strong Montessori classrooms going, keep the vibrant community connected, and continue to serve all children and adults well. What slows us down, often to a halt, in public Montessori schools is the lack of cohesive shared structures that become known and easily used by everyone, fostering independence and a greater sense of agency for all. Instead, each school is innovating its own way, with much reinvention of the wheel and some missing pieces, leaving them vulnerable to systemic disorder that may ultimately threaten the success of the program.

At the writing of this book there are 557 public Montessori schools in the United States[2] serving over 150,000 children and growing. In the world of public education, however, Montessori schools are vulnerable to starting and then closing, leaving their materials locked in storage rooms – or worse, in district dumpsters – as they return to a conventional model. This cycle continues, with another school opening elsewhere with the same hopes and promises as the one closed just before it. The pages ahead are less about exploring the underlying causes and more focused on offering an approach that will create healthy environments for all Montessori schools that allow them to thrive.

A school district is a biome, and often Montessori programs are formed within them without considering the distinctive conditions necessary to keep them alive. Districts invest an enormous sum in Montessori teacher education, child-sized furniture, Montessori materials, and the resources to launch a unique program of hands-on learning. They do this all without altering the systems and structures the school is expected to function within, forcing a model that is at its core about society by cohesion and personalization of work in a system designed for competition and conformity. These district structures can range from the use of letter-grade report cards to required learning blocks of time each day to the purchase and distribution of workbooks across grade levels to prescribed time designated for "test prep." Each small element must be negotiated to preserve the health of the program, and much time and energy is spent in translation.

Many schools open with a solid vision and have early success cultivating a strong teaching community, bringing families together, reaching children, and serving their unique needs. These early days are full of energy, and often these schools generate waiting lists. However, what happens next is often the result of something there all along that has taken time to come to light: the unique ecosystem of the Montessori school is not being served within the biome of the larger school district. Thus, it begins to slowly decline in ways such as losing the three-year cycle that is a hallmark of this multiyear pedagogy of patience.

This deterioratin is often due to the pressures from annual assessment expectations that public schools are held to. Gains in Montessori elementary classrooms are noted at the end of a three-year cycle as children complete a sequence of lessons, become conversant with assessment terminology, and bring a greater application of abstract skills rather than at preset age requirements. This grace allows learners to build confidence as they move toward mastery rather than experiencing a rush to catch up or pressure to get answers correct regardless of whether they have ownership over the concepts. Rather than temporary recall resulting from preparing for a test, the goal in a Montessori program is a love of learning that results in permanent understanding and skill mastery.

At first, this decline is invisible. Then, when vital people at the school, who have been managing the dissonance, begin to leave, the deterioration becomes more rapid. Sometimes these schools keep their Montessori name but become traditionalized over time as teachers are hired without Montessori training and, lacking the knowledge of how to use them, Montessori materials begin to leave the classroom. Now the school is still considered a public Montessori school, yet it is not fully implementing the method. When the outcome begin to decline, then, it appears to be the result of the method rather than the hybrid approach to educating children.

This book is about how to support Montessori schools in becoming resilient – withstanding or recovering from difficult circumstances – which means acknowledging that choosing to be a part of a public Montessori school means accepting challenging conditions. Resilient Montessori schools are prepared to respond to the difficult conditions that surround public education in this country and stand solidly for what is best for children. Resilient Montessori schools pull together as a community to openly acknowledge the unique needs of the program and then advocate for them to be met within the larger landscape. Resilient Montessori schools hold clear their designer's original vision and are unwavering in the commitment to implement it fully while knowing that a large amount of creativity and innovation will be needed every day to fulfill this.

Like the method itself, we begin the learning process with a *direct aim* that gives us a sense of what we will know and be able to do once we are done.

Direct Aim:

  Know

    that the whole-school Montessori method (One School, Honest Talk, and Strong Systems) will increase access to Montessori for every person in your community

    that the core elements within the method are essential for implementation

  Do

    + unification moves that matter

    + honest conversations that lean into what is uncomfortable rather than avoid it

    + strong systems to support resilience, equity, and full Montessori implementation

---

In 1917, Dr. Montessori said in a lecture in Amsterdam, "We are the sowers – our children are those who reap. To labour that future generations may be better and nobler than we are – that is the task without egotism and without pride. Let us unite in this work then."[1] Here is a call for us to unite in this work and build equitable, resilient schools together through the vision of the whole school as a Montessori prepared environment, the shared value of honest conversations, and consistent use of coherent systems and structures.

In the past decade, I've had the opportunity to work in Montessori schools across the country and have met and collaborated with many talented school practitioners along the way. Many have implemented parts of the whole school Montessori method shared here, which has evolved and refined the ideas. In doing so, they have contributed to this book through their insight and knowledge of what is needed to truly serve each child while holding the larger framework of education in today's world. It is with great gratitude to all those who have contributed to a deeper understanding of how to implement the approach that I offer this work forward to you now.

Note about terms:

There is a wide variety of language used in Montessori schools. Here is a list of terms used in this book with guidance to ensure all readers are clear.

- **Primary**: Classrooms for children ages 3–6 years. Synonyms: early childhood, children's house
- **Lower elementary**: Classrooms for children ages 6–9 years. Synonyms: EI
- **Upper elementary**: Classrooms for children ages 9–12 years. Synonyms: EII
- **Adolescents**: Classrooms for students ages 12–18 years. Synonyms: middle school, high school, secondary
- **Key children**: Children who present atypically in the classroom and may need extra support or alterations in the learning environment. By their very nature they provide keys for our own personal transformation. Synonyms: behavior problems, high flyers, sped kids
- **Teacher, guide**: Used interchangeably throughout the book to mean the classroom adult who is trained in Montessori and leading the class
- **Assistants:** The other adult in the classroom working in support of the guide. Synonyms: paraprofessional, teaching assistant (TA)
- **Children, learners, students**: Used interchangeably throughout the book

---

NOTES

1. *Everyman,* June 1, 1917. Reprinted in *Maria Montessori – An Anthology,* AMI.
2. Mira Debs. *Diverse Families, Desirable Schools: Public Montessori in the Era of School Choice.* Cambridge, MA: Harvard Education Press, 2019.
3. Montessori Census, available at https://www.montessoricensus.org/

Chapter 1
Why Build a Resilient School?

Either education contributes to a movement of universal liberation by showing the way to defend and raise humanity or it becomes like one of those organs which have shriveled up by not being used during the evolution of the organism.

—Maria Montessori, *The Formation of Man*

There are three main reasons to build resilient schools: the children, the adults, and the wider community. The people who rely on schools as an equitable place for education, and who dream of an environment prepared for dignity in learning, all benefit from schools that are lasting.

CHILDREN AND FAMILIES

Children are at the heart of why schools exist, so creating lasting environments for them is a natural priority. Yet for public Montessori schools there is another element: our commitment to the three-year cycle. In Montessori schools, classrooms are designed to follow the developmental needs of the learner and so hold three ages. The primary classroom, for example, holds 3–6-year-olds who are in what Maria Montessori defined as the first plane of development. This is what she called the absorbent mind stage, where children learn through their senses. Those environments have four basic areas of study: practical life, sensorial, language, and mathematics. Classrooms, outfitted with furniture sized for the child of that age, are intended to provide a safe, culturally relevant learning environment that allows for freedom of movement and guided by the same adults for all three years. In this way the child becomes known by the adults – their individual style, preferences, gifts, struggles, and interests. All of these allow the Montessori-trained adult to tailor a learning program that will support learners in reaching their highest potential.

In addition, the three-year cycle allows the school-based adults to come to know the child's family and to build a lasting connection that develops over time. These trusting relationships serve to unite the adults around the growth and development of the child, allowing the family to rely on and collaborate with the school-based adults promoting an even greater sense of cohesion. This in turn further supports the child as there is a connection between home and school to see them through whatever events happen in their family life, once again allowing the child to thrive.

SCHOOL-BASED ADULTS

School-based adults also benefit from the meaningful relationships built over the three-year cycle as they become known and seen by both the families they serve and a stable group of colleagues. As an important person in the child's life, they are often kept in touch with, revisited, and even invited to graduations and – if they teach long enough – weddings. They also benefit from an unwavering school community; as people who are committed to Montessori they need public programs where they can work for years. As a member of a staff they are an important person in the school community both coaching and being coached by others as they grow into and through the work together.

Their own personal milestones such as having children, losing loved ones, and buying a house are shared and celebrated, allowing a closeness to form over time that offers a network of support both in and out of school. School-based adults benefit from an unwavering school community; as people who are committed to Montessori they need public programs where they can settle in and stay.

THE WIDER COMMUNITY

The wider community in the world of education also needs resilient schools with a cohesive curriculum, reasonable assessment expectations, and dedicated staff. The vision is to offer a Montessori to the wider community that values each child – to create schools where families can send their child knowing they will be seen and responded to with an education that suits both their developmental needs and their individual needs. Because our national educational system is stressed and struggling, it is ever more important that we build lasting Montessori schools. This is a critical call for social change and one that will have a lasting impact on our world when diverse groups of children are educated to believe in their own ability to make a difference in the world.

There will be a lasting impact when groups of children grow up valuing themselves and each other, with the ability to collaborate and build greatness together. This is the goal of public education in our country that is buried deep inside public policy but has led to misguided ideas of how we measure success. If we are to align and unite in this work, we must be willing to push into public policies that threaten Montessori programs. We must be willing to support the larger educational model in finding new ways, not as a subversive act but as an act of leadership. With over 100 years of experience in a time-tested method, we have what is needed to turn this country's education system around.

This begins in our own schools, leading by example, thus impacting the system simply by being a part of it. For instance, there is a public Montessori school principal in North Carolina whose state official is asking her about the nautilus approach – the unique Montessori alternative to a discipline policy that you will learn more about in Part Three. The state official visited the school and was impressed by the low discipline numbers and the system that protects against implicit bias by carefully collecting and watching data to ensure there is not an overreferral of children of the global minority. They wanted to hear more about a system based on proactivity rather than reactivity. This one conversation is an opening and was initiated only as a result of the school's good standing.

Our influence can be small and gradual, like the method itself, impacting the larger system of education. However, this can occur only if our schools are still open, still high-functioning, fully implementing programs that offer strong outcomes for all learners. If we are to be change makers and influencers, we need a long track record based on constancy in the midst of the regular sea of change in public education.

The whole-school Montessori method offers this opportunity: to begin the task of creating sustainable programs that can serve as a vision for how school can be in today's world. Building a resilient school will serve not only your immediate community but also the wider community of education as we create a lasting model in a larger system. It will accomplish this through preserving the Montessori model that so often suffers when it enters the realm of public schools.

Resilient Montessori schools support children, adults, and the wider community. They allow children to live into their unmanifest potential, that they might come to know their unique contribution and make an impact on the world. Resilient Montessori schools allow adults to settle into a functioning school that supports them in doing the work they are called to do, daily implementing a method with visible results that further galvanize them to continue. Finally, it may be aspirational, yet the wider educational community is seeking leadership. In addition, as people who are working in a method used around the world for over a century, resilient Montessori schools could serve as models and proof points for education centered on children.

CORE ELEMENTS

Just as there are three reasons to build resilient Montessori schools (the children, the adults, and the wider community), there are also three core elements, or critical lenses, for viewing the work of building them:

- *Constructivism* at the root of the method
- *Equity* and its role in building resilient schools
- *Coaching* as a means by which to implement the whole-school Montessori method

These are explored in the next few chapters, laying the groundwork for reading the rest of the book. They are called *core elements* because they live at the core of the whole-school Montessori method not just as a way of thinking but also as a way of acting. Our understanding of these elements offers insight into ways to foster resilience and will generate energy to support implementation of the upcoming components of the whole-school Montessori method (see the next list). Understanding them will impact every decision made for the school.

Following a whole-to-parts sequence, each of the next three chapters opens with an exploration of the larger idea and then focuses specifically on how it applies to Montessori schools and the implementation of the whole-school Montessori method. These chapters are meant not to explore these topics exhaustively but instead to bring into view the invisible influences on schools through their presence or their absence. Constructivist thinking, equity, and coaching are integrated into an understanding of the larger concepts introduced next.

COMPONENTS

- One School
- Honest Talk
- Strong Systems

Each of the subsequent parts of the book are devoted to one of these components with chapters outlining what it means and how to begin in your school. Together they strengthen the school for it to weather the external changes in education and continue serving children and families. With these in place there develops an inviting world that people are drawn to and want to be a part of for the foreseeable future. For children this means their family or caregivers are content and will not move them to a different school in the midst of their three-year cycle and that their teacher will also be content and will be there for all three years. For school-based adults, this means a community where there are meaningful connections, they feel seen and valued, and their work feels consequential. They are part of a team that wants to be there doing this work, and therefore each year the team is able to grow stronger. For you, reader of this book, it means a way forward and a community of practice to support your work building a resilient school.

Figure 1.1 visually captures how the core elements live inside the components. Much like the layers of the earth, the core is at the center offering strength and power. Our earth's core, about the size of the moon, spins faster than the surface. "That solid inner core is growing slowly as the liquid iron in the core cools and crystallizes. This process helps power the churning motion of the liquid outer core, which in turn creates the magnetic field that surrounds Earth and helps protect the planet from harmful cosmic radiation. In other words, the inner core is pretty important."[1] The core is largely responsible for the earth being habitable. The core elements of the whole-school Montessori method serve the same function for the school.

The components of the whole-school Montessori method are on the surface. The One School component, the lithosphere, represents the ground beneath us, what holds us steady. The Honest Talk component is the hydrosphere, the fluid way we can be nourished through communication. Water and honest talk are something we all need, and when we have clean water and

The Whole School Montessori Method

Core Elements	Components
▨ constructivism	▨ one school
■ equity	■ honest talk
▨ coaching	▨ strong systems

Figure 1.1 How the Core Elements Live Inside the Components.

clear conversations we are healthier. The farthest layer out – the atmosphere – represents Strong Systems, or the air that touches everyone in the school allowing for respiration. Clean air allows us to breathe easily, as do clear systems. School systems, like air, are invisible, and we tend to notice them only when we don't have them.

NEW WORLD

These ideas are being shared in the midst of a world pandemic that is impacting schools around the globe, asking Montessori educators to create a multiage, hands-on method digitally for this new world. This is a challenge we must rise to as a community to preserve this unique method. In the process, it is also revealing which elements of the school are strong and which are floundering, nudging us toward a whole-school Montessori method that allows for unification across schools for this new world in which we find ourselves. Therefore, at the end of most sections there is discussion of new world considerations outlining how to implement each component under these new conditions.

SUMMARY

Montessori in Action: Building Resilient Montessori Schools is organized around three core elements and three components of the whole-school Montessori method. Part I holds the core elements, and Parts II–IV hold the components. Part IV shares action steps you can take, including a suggestion of a three-year cycle. What if you took three years to implement the whole-school Montessori method? What if you shared it with your team and took it on together to implement slowly and intentionally in spite of obstacles that may arise within the district, in spite of the innovations necessary to keep school running virtually? Imagine being able to enjoy the unfolding over time rather than expecting instant gratification. The Montessori method itself is a long game rather than a quick fix, which might be why it persists after more than 100 years. Taking the time to lay the foundation and build it over time means that your school will be there long after you have left, continuing to serve your community of learners with strong Montessori education.

Now imagine that 5000 other Montessori programs are prioritizing these same areas, implementing these same components. In three years' time, as people's lives changed and they relocated, they could work at a different

Montessori school using this whole-school Montessori method. They could walk into their new school and seamlessly begin to work in the new community while building relationships with staff, children, and families. With some orientation, beginning in their first week they could support the strength of the school like a magic trick. When this happens, schools will no longer be people dependent, losing steam when talented people leave, but rather will continue to thrive under the guidance of another person who shares and understands these common goals and the structures that support them. Then our Montessori schools will be resilient: they will be fortified and prepared to respond to, and recover from, stressors or difficult conditions, lasting beyond our lifetimes to serve countless generations of learners.

NOTE

1. Stephanie Pappas. "Earth's Core Is a Billion Years Old." *Live Science*, August 26, 2020. https://www.livescience.com/earth-core-billion-years-old.html

Chapter 2
Constructivist Thinking

We can imagine an adult society organized as a constructive society on the same lines as the children's – that is, along the lines of this naturally cohesive society. Attachment to other people is the first stage, bringing men to work together towards a common goal. It would be good for everyone if society could be constructed like this. But we cannot demand it; it must come from nature. If nature is the base, the construction will be superior, but without this base there can only be an artificial construction, one that breaks down easily.

—Maria Montessori, *1946 London Lectures*

If society by cohesion is one of our central ideas then understanding the construction of it is an important framework to explore. As Maria Montessori says in the epigraph for this chapter, having nature as the base will lead to a superior construction. And so she did just that: created a system of education based on nature. As a physician fascinated by biology, Montessori developed a system of education that is adaptive and functions with its environment. Different from many other approaches to education that are linear, Montessori built her method around nature, leveraging the child's relationship with the environment and the interdependence of all the parts. In her article "Montessori as an Alternative Early Childhood Education," Angeline S. Lillard writes about the dichotomy between approaching education as a linear process or more of a dynamic system: "Montessori was a systems thinker. Like Piaget (who attended at least one Montessori congress and was a President of the Swiss Montessori Society), her background was biological (in medicine), and she approached children with deep appreciation of the body and brain as physical entities responding to and with the environment."[1] Montessori classrooms were thus designed based on the prepared environment as an essential aspect of learning. The children learn from the environment filled with materials, meaningful tasks, plants, animals, and other people. They learn by actively doing rather than passively receiving information. There is a natural interdependence within the three-year cycle where everyone is learning with and from each other in a manner reminiscent of symbiosis in nature; children are not only free but also encouraged to collaborate. Supporting one another and learning together are expected parts of every day in a Montessori classroom.

Education today approaches the work of learning from a range of perspectives, two of which are behaviorist and constructivist. Before exploring the constructivist approach underlying the Montessori method, it's important to understand the behaviorist approach within which many educators were educated.

BEHAVIORIST APPROACH

Briefly, from an educational perspective, behaviorism, a term first used by John Watson in 1912 and further developed with B. F. Skinner, takes the stimulus–response relationship and applies it to learning. This is the idea that learning happens when there is a proper response to a stimulus, such as correct answers (proper response) to math problems on a worksheet (stimulus). The child then is merely reactive to the conditions in the environment without being expected to take an active role in discovery. The belief is that facts and information are separate from the learner and are something to be acquired. Behaviorism then is focused on the outward behavior or result, situating learning outside of the learner.

Many public schools continue to see the work of education from a behaviorist approach with the teacher central to the children's learning, without whom there would be no learning. Learning is evaluated through tests that illustrate whether the student is able to recall and give back the information they have been given. Motivation to engage in learning is largely external, relying on punishments, rewards, and praise from adults to move a child forward in their education.

CONSTRUCTIVIST APPROACH

By contrast, constructivism sees learning as creating meaning from experience. Constructivism has its roots in the work of contemporaries to Montessori. John Dewey, who published his philosophy of education in 1897, took issue with the rote learning of the time, instead promoting learning through real-life experiences: "True education comes through the stimulation of the child's own powers by the demands of the social situation in which he finds himself."[2] Jean Piaget used the term *constructivism* in 1967 connected to his theory positing that human intellect evolves through adaptation and organization and that human learning is a transformative process, meaning children do not learn in bits and pieces but rather make sense from whatever information they have and then revise as new information is acquired. Lev Vygotsky brought a social aspect to the theory investigating the development of children's reasoning when by themselves and with a "more competent other." He is known for establishing the zone of proximal development, illustrating the potential of working with another as opposed to entirely self-constructing.

Constructivist thinking rests then on the idea that learners acquire knowledge through active engagement. "Constructivism is an approach to teaching and learning based on the premise that cognition (learning) is the result of 'mental construction.' In other words, students learn by fitting new information together with what they already know. Constructivists believe that learning is affected by the context in which an idea is taught as well as by students' beliefs and attitudes."[3] The environment for learning thus plays a more important role, as it is through engaging with the environment that people learn and create an internal understanding of the world around them.

The Montessori method is a constructivist approach, one that builds the child's understanding and knowledge based on their experience rather than seeing them as empty vessels to be filled with information. Children are expected to engage with their environment as a vehicle for establishing and then refining their growing understanding of the world. Montessori classrooms for the very young shy away from fantasy (books with animals wearing aprons and washing dishes) and provide information that mirrors reality (plates break when dropped) to support this ongoing construction.

With children as active partners, the method relies on practitioners' understanding of and ability to implement the constructivist approach, though many themselves have been raised through a behaviorist approach. Often adults will come to learn about these two approaches in Montessori teacher training, and for many it explains why they are drawn to this alternative method – one based not on punishments and rewards but on satisfying a natural desire to learn. In training, this is part of the philosophy or theory portion and therefore begins as an abstraction, which for many trainees is not concretized during their course of study. The opportunity for connection between theory and practice then comes in their first teaching experience.

FROM THEORY TO PRACTICE

Once in the classroom, teachers are implementing the theory as the creators of structures within their learning environment. Without clarity about how to take it from theory to practice, the classroom structures implemented by the teacher can follow an unconsciously behaviorist approach, reflecting their own childhood school experience.

Here's a common scenario one might observe in a primary classroom: A child at the snack table enjoys the apple slices they are eating. When they are done they take their plate and serve themselves more slices, returning to the snack table to eat the additional slices. Another child waiting for a snack goes and reports the consumption of the additional slices to a classroom adult.

The expectation in many classrooms is that each child has one snack with an established portion, often with a sign or picture showing children what's expected (i.e., two apple slices). There are many ways adults might respond to this situation based on the age of the child, the time of year, the moment in time in the classroom, with too many variations to include here. For the sake of understanding the contrast in the two educational approaches, let's look at two classroom procedures that fall into those.

- *Unconsciously behaviorist:* The classroom adult approaches as the last bite of the additional slices is being enjoyed and tells the child they cannot have snack tomorrow since they had two servings today.

- *Consciously constructivist:* The classroom adult approaches as the last bite of the additional slices is being enjoyed and says to the child, "It looks like you enjoyed your snack." The child nods, smiling. The adult asks, "Did you know that there are only enough slices for each child to have two?" The child stops smiling. The adult says, "Let me show you how we know that." She takes the child and shows them the picture, reviewing how to interpret it.

In this scenario, the response of the classroom adult informs how the child will feel, which links to identity formation and self-confidence. Montessori acknowledges that prior to normalization the adult is quite directive, supporting the child in making choices until they show signs of impulse control; however, *how* teachers do this matters. In the unconsciously behaviorist approach, the response comes as punishment. The emphasis is on changing the child's behavior rather than on understanding it. In the consciously constructivist approach, the response comes as engagement and inclusion into the procedures of the classroom. This high-contrast example draws attention to the impact of these approaches on the child and their growing sense of agency in the primary classroom.

Now here's a common scenario one might observe in an elementary classroom: A child completes work with the grammar box material and then carefully returns the grammar box, the filler box, and the box of grammar symbols to their rightful places, putting away each colored pencil and their clipboard and storing the finished work in its proper location. They then get a drink of water and are invited to join some peers who are about to get out the long division material. What they don't realize is that, in their joy completing the last task, they neglected to roll up their rug.

In elementary classrooms, as in primary classrooms, there is the expectation that each learner completes a work cycle, putting everything away prior to starting the next task. That said, there are a range of situations that may alter that based on circumstances, with the highest goal being to develop a community of learners. For the sake of looking at the two approaches and how they may creep into common practice, let's imagine this common scene from the perspective of two classrooms.

- *Unconsciously behaviorist:* Another child is looking for a spot to unroll a rug and sees the abandoned one taking up space. They report this to one of the classroom adults, who remembers the child doing the grammar box there. The adult tracks the child down in the midst of a complicated division exchange. "You need to go roll up your rug," the adult tells the child. The child, focused on counting beads, loses track as they switch to focus on the request of the adult.

- *Consciously constructivist:* Another child is looking for a spot to unroll a rug and sees the abandoned one taking up space. They report this to one of the classroom adults, who looks to see what has become of the child Who was doing a grammar box there. The adult observes them deeply engaged in the work of division with two peers. The adult asks the reporting child, "What should we do about that?" The child thinks for a minute and then offers, "Roll it up?" The adult agrees and observes the child for a minute to see if the child will realize they can use the rug that is out or if they will roll it up and roll out the rug they originally selected.

In this scenario the classroom norms set the tone for how the learners will engage with both their environment and each other. In the unconsciously behaviorist response, the system of individual responsibility can lead to children learning to police one another, without attention to or value of engagement. This can amplify fissures in the classroom community as children lay blame and abdicate responsibility rather than contributing.

In the consciously constructivist approach, engagement is protected, and children learn both to take ownership for their environment and a sense of collective responsibility. Now it is no longer focused on whose fault it is but instead on what needs to be done. These two different responses shape the elementary child's emerging sense of what it means to be in a community and their first experience of what Montessori referred to as a practice society. Is this a society with a linear approach or one based on interdependence? And when they move into the world how will this impact their behavior when they see litter on the ground or someone who needs help with packages?

There are hundreds of small decisions a new teacher must make to set up their multiage learning environment, and without an understanding of how to implement the constructivist approach, their own default thinking will often be the driver. Without guidance and reflection on these decisions, the classroom can be using Montessori materials without the benefit of full implementation of the method.

Lillard draws our attention to this conundrum in the opening chapter of *The Science Behind the Genius*:

> When they begin teaching, the superficiality of their understanding [of constructivism] becomes apparent, and they take up the traditional methods used by their own elementary and high school teachers. Traditional teaching fits both a teacher's memory and the culturally dominant view of what school is, and teachers who have less understanding of alternatives will naturally fall back on it.[4]

This underscores the very real possibility that Montessori teachers may be creating the procedures and routines in their classrooms based on old ideas, out of old ways of thinking. In addition, they may be responding to children, "grading" or disciplining children based on the view of the dominant culture as they sort out the dynamics of working within the larger public school system.

WHOLE-SCHOOL MONTESSORI CONSTRUCTIVISM

This thinking doesn't simply inform what is happening in classrooms separate from the way the rest of the school runs. As one ecosystem, there also needs to be a synchronized understanding and use of the same framework. So when we are working to implement the Montessori method across the whole school, understanding the distinction between these two educational approaches and activating a commitment to using a constructivist approach becomes the shared frame. This tension can be felt everywhere – from district-level meetings to negotiating the structure of individualized education plans and implementation of special education services. There will be tension between the systems alongside the complete clarity that the school has adopted a constructivist approach. This means phasing out programs that include prizes or awards, creating new rubrics for report cards, avoiding practices such as sticker charts or work plans, and countless other possibilities that arise within schools.

With this commitment we understand that learning is a natural drive of being human and that we do best without punishments and rewards. So how might we create a school that follows that approach with families and staff? If we understand that intrinsic motivation is the driving force for our actions, then how might we tap into what moves the people in our community? If we understand the value and importance of supporting real change in understanding (cognition) rather than looking simply for a change in behavior (compliance), how does that shape our policies and practices school-wide?

Lillard points out, "Superficial insertions of research-supported methods do not penetrate the underlying models on which schools are based. Deeper change, implementing more realistic models of the child and the school, is necessary to improve schooling" (n.d.). Deeper change must happen both in the classroom as well as through and across the whole school.

SUMMARY

Constructivist system thinking lives at the core of the whole-school Montessori method as it shapes all of our decisions and provides that magnetic field holding us to the earth. The resilient Montessori school then is a complex, adaptive system based on the practice of observation and the belief in each person's right to acquire knowledge through active engagement.

The Montessori method instructs us to use observation as a tool to adapt and modify, so in the biggest picture it can support the strength and survival of our ecosystem. If we are able to bring a constructivist lens to every aspect of the work in our schools and to observe for ways we transgress, then we are one step closer to full implementation. This means a commitment to regular observations in classrooms, at transition times, in meetings – across all parts of the school day and every interaction between members of the community to guide living into the method. Constructivist thinking is not something that stands alone in the classroom to be employed in adult interactions with learners alone but something for everyone to hold as a core element of the work.

From this place of owning constructivism as a community, the environment becomes one that will allow the components of the whole-school Montessori method to solidify. Once they do, their strength can support the growth of a school that will flourish. It will flourish, and it will last. Then there will be a naturally cohesive society – one where people are working together toward a common goal. When this occurs, there is a strength that protects the school from erosion and allows it to weather changes while still holding true to the method-the original commitment to allowing learning as a natural, transformative process that is every person's birthright.

NOTES

1. Angeline S. Lillard. "Montessori as an Alternative Early Childhood Education." *Early Child Development and Care*. doi: 10.1080/03004430.2020.1832998, 2020.
2. John Dewey. "My Pedagogic Creed." *School Journal*, 1897.

3. Steve Olusegun. "Constructivism Learning Theory: A Paradigm for Teaching and Learning." *IOSR Journal of Research & Method in Education (IOSR-JRME).* e-ISSN: 2320–7388, p-ISSN: 2320–737X Volume 5, Issue 6 Ver. I (Nov.–Dec. 2015), pp. 66–70.
4. Lillard, A. S. (2005). Montessori: The Science Behind the Genius. New York: Oxford University Press.

Chapter 3
Equity

Among the revelations the child has brought us, there is one of fundamental importance, the phenomenon of normalization through work. Thousands and thousands of experiences among children of every race enable us to state that this phenomenon is the most certain datum verified in psychology or education. It is certain that the child's attitude towards work represents a vital instinct; for without work his personality cannot organize itself. . . . Man builds himself through working, working with his hands, but using his hands as the instruments of his ego, the organ of his individual mind and will, which shapes its own existence face to face with its environment.

—Maria Montessori, *The Secret of Childhood*

Equity lives as a critical element of this conversation and this book. In recent years, equity in education – particularly racial equity – has come to the forefront of the conversation, alerting educators to the impact of implicit bias and their role in forwarding a dominant cultural view in the classroom.

OVERVIEW

The Organisation for Economic Co-Operation and Development (OECD) highlights two aspects of equity – or the lack thereof – that influence educational outcomes.[1] The first is fairness: looking at how both personal and socially constructed circumstances are barriers for children in reaching their full potential. The other is from an inclusion perspective: the importance of ensuring that children's varying needs are met. In this conversation, we open a wider view to envision manifesting both of these aspects of equity for adults in the community, in addition to the children. How can our schools become fairer and more inclusive for all members: children, families, and school-based adults? What barriers exist in the way we function that limit people's sense of involvement, dignity, and agency? How are we aware of and respectful of the varying needs within the community? What is our relationship with power, and are we consciously sharing it?

First, if we are committed to an education for peace, then we must ensure that we are making the Montessori method available to all children and educators. We must be able to talk openly so that we are then able to widen our perspectives and be of greater service to one another, particularly to children and educators of the global majority.[2] Maria Montessori writes in *Education and Peace*, "A great work must be undertaken. An extremely important social task lies before us; actuating man's value, allowing him to attain the maximum development of his energies, truly preparing him to bring about a different form of human society on a higher plane." Here she acknowledges value and the attainment of maximum development as aspects of our preparation. Zaretta Hammond, in her book *Culturally Responsive Teaching and the Brain*, explains, "To understand structural racialization, we have to move beyond one-dimensional, linear explanations of inequity in society and education. We have to entertain the idea that a series of seemingly benign or supposedly well-intended policies actually create a negative cumulative and reinforcing effect that supports, rather than dismantles, the status quo within institutions."[3]

What are the policies in your school that may keep a status quo within your community of educators? Do all staff members in public Montessori programs see themselves as capable, productive contributors, or is there a racial disparity in self-perception based on unspoken messages? Are all the Montessori trained teachers in the school white and all the assistants people of the global majority? What is the power-sharing structure that ensures everyone is comfortable speaking their concerns and observations for the benefit of the whole school? The onboarding system, including hiring and orientation, will either align with the dominant narrative, offering lower-paying positions to people of the global majority, or correct it, offering role models of all races for the children in all classrooms.

This chapter explores these ideas: the social task of allowing everyone maximum development and the hidden or unexamined attitudes and policies that keep structural racism in place.

SHARED COMMITMENT

"Degree of ownership" is another meaning of the word *equity* and a good one to frame how school communities might ideally function to allow maximum development for all – that everyone has the same degree of ownership in the work. From here we are able to build school communities that offer respect to all members and therefore inspire a shared commitment to the mission of the school.

A place to begin this work is to get a baseline for where you are with this right now. There are many resources[4] out there for reviewing your school's place on the continuum for becoming an equitable organization and many resources for taking stock of where you are personally. The Montessori community has mobilized to provide support for moving forward in our classrooms,[5] and this is an invitation to take a wider view and see your whole school through this lens.

One starting place is to consider your community's say–do gap, which is the space between what we communicate and the actions we take. For example, we might have a stated intention to make the family organization a space for everyone but reflect that this governing body is made up mostly of people without day jobs in a district made up of mostly working-class families. It is only after we are willing to confront this kind of say–do gap that we can effectively move toward making the space more inclusive. Perhaps we have, without even realizing it, scheduled the family organization meeting for 10 o'clock on Monday morning when working families aren't able to participate, thus creating a governing body made up mostly of people who have a perspective that is not representative of the whole. Have we done this without a survey to discover the best time for families or without intentional recruitment to ensure the whole community is represented? This will impact the degree of ownership experienced and skew issues tackled, events planned, and resources delegated.[6] In the end, though we say we welcome everyone, we have made space only for some.

Your say–do gap speaks louder than any published mission statement or declaration around equity, so take the time to investigate: Are you really doing what you say? How do you know? What are the measures you are using to determine progress? Indicators of progress across each area of your school will help you to periodically take stock, and that alone speaks volumes to your community. For example, to help participation in your family organization, you might have a sign-in sheet at every meeting, every event, every point of contact with families. This data can then be reviewed to understand where the dominant involvement exists, looking at indicators such as race, free or reduced lunch, gender, and child's age. When you begin this practice you will have a baseline to understand who your dominant group is, such as white, non–free or reduced lunch, women caring for primary children. This will then direct your next steps in moving toward balanced involvement, one where there is parity in everyone's degree of ownership.

The next step is to look at the say–do gap within classrooms and the way it is connected to the gap in student achievement. Classroom say–do gaps contribute to an opportunity gap for learners that is only perpetuating the social racial stratification in the United States.

There is ample evidence of inequity in U.S. public schools, with a disproportionate number of discipline referrals for children of the global majority.[7] The U.S. Department of Education Office for Civil Rights found in their most recent data release that nationally, Black children are more than three times more likely to be suspended than their white peers (5% of white boys and 2% of white girls receive one or more out-of-school suspensions annually compared with 18% of Black boys and 10% of Black girls and 7% of Hispanic boys and 3% of Hispanic girls).[8] The school-to-prison pipeline[9] begins in preschool, where 48% of preschool children suspended more than once are Black. There are countless statistics of injustice emerging all the time[10] as we examine our school system through the lens of systemic racism.

In her book, *Teaching to Transgress*, bell hooks discusses teachers' inherited dominant teaching style that comes from an outdated model and the importance of not only recognizing it but also accepting that it needs to change: "Among educators there has to be an acknowledgment that any effort to transform institutions so that they reflect a multicultural standpoint must take into consideration the fears teachers have when asked to shift their paradigms."[11] It is time to take on the fear and close the say–do gap in classrooms.

Taking it on means leaning into the questions of why the students of color are overidentified as the source of discipline issues, why they are lagging in scores, and what needs to change in us to offer them a fully implemented Montessori education. Asking this question as One School will help to shift away from a reactive approach where the gap is tackled with traditional measures (e.g., skill and drill interventions out of the classroom setting) that move children further away from the method and the source of attaining their maximum potential.

If, as Montessori reminds us in *Spontaneous Activity in Education*, "Our care of the child should be governed, not by the desire 'to make him learn things,' but by the endeavor always to keep burning within him that light which is called intelligence," then we are further underserving our children of the global majority by disrupting their attitude toward work and neglecting the light burning within them. Instead, let us remember Montessori's insight that when there is an obstacle, first we check the environment, and then we check ourselves. What must we change in the environment and in ourselves – in the very way we are as teachers – to remove the barriers to the Montessori learning environments for all children?

With signs around the world at the writing of this book that read "Don't look away," it is time for us to look and talk honestly about how equity does and doesn't exist in our Montessori classrooms. As mentioned in the OECD report, it is the task of schools to address the needs of all learners. We can do this through an unflinching determination to change systemic racism by disrupting our own and each other's unconscious behavior.

Considering the individual work we must all do means offering your school community an ongoing willingness to move this work forward. If you are white, this may mean being wrong, self-correcting, giving the authority to another in the community rather than keeping it for yourself. For everyone, when we regularly empower different members of the wider community, we are supporting each person's degree of ownership in and commitment to the mission and vision of the school, thus bringing a greater degree of equity.

DOING THE WORK

What begins with One School thinking – preparing an environment that has a diverse teaching staff and an expectation of self-interrogation to uncover bias – is followed by talking honestly to open and strengthen the community as a whole. This is where school communities investigate and discuss the hidden or seemingly harmless attitudes and policies that keep structural racism in place.

How you approach this work will depend on your background, your racial identity, and your experience in the world as a racial being. As a white, cisgender woman who spent the majority of my adult life partnered with another woman and as the mother of three children, one with special needs, I bring my own perspective to the conversation. There are both blind spots and insights as a result of this intersectionality. Everyone will be entering this work from a different place and will need to take their own path. In that, there will likely be shared discomfort and the need to be brave in the face of tackling this work. It may mean being humble, making mistakes, and making repairs. It may mean speaking up when you'd rather let it pass or struggling to find the language to talk about something honestly. It will mean a willingness to feel uncomfortable while remaining committed to repairing mistakes with the goal of creating a diverse, empowered community.

For too long we have been tied to a fear that results in complacency. To take action, we must brave up and delve into topics we are less confident about and comfortable with. This is how we learn. The children in our schools model this every day. If you need to regain motivation, walk into any classroom and observe at any time of the day to see bravery in action and understand the urgent need for this work.

A resource for honest talk is Glenn Singleton's book *Courageous Conversations,* in which he offers an approach and tools for talking about race. "To exercise the passion, practice and persistence necessary to address racial achievement disparities, all members of the school community need to be able to talk about race in a safer, honest way."[12] Introducing a structured way into this work messages both that this work is of value in the community and that no one needs to figure it out on their own. The community will establish shared language and a known way of having important conversations.

The urgency for the start of open dialogue around race is the knowledge that racial identity begins in the first plane of development, when children are in the first six years of their lives. Children in primary are establishing who they are based on their race and culture. Lawrence Hirschfeld, in his research "Children's Developing Conceptions of Race," shows that 2-year-olds use racial categories to make sense of people's actions and that, by the end of the first plane, children of color are aware of their racial group and the negative stereotypes associated with it.[13]

As a result, adults' awareness of and willingness to talk about race in Montessori classrooms matters. Our ability to be conscious of children's race when offering affirmation or correction may be either supporting the dominant narrative or countering it. Our ability to respond to questions about race and to engage in ongoing conversations with learners in a way that normalizes it as a topic impacts their comfort and ease with one another and inside themselves.

Open and honest conversations are necessary to expose, examine, and revise the unspoken beliefs that are the drivers of inequity in the larger school community as well as in the classroom. Making a commitment to speaking up and engaging in conversations around disparities, slights, or microaggressions means a more unified school, one that will be more resilient and lasting.

RESTRUCTURING

Systems exist within a school to streamline and enhance the program. From the context of equity, what are the systems in place to support this both in and out of classrooms? What are the systems that without awareness are creating greater inequity for adults and children of the global majority?

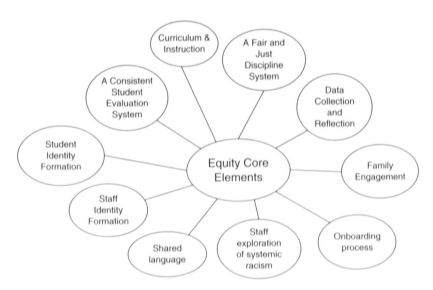

Figure 3.1 Montessori Equity Core Elements

Figure 3.1 shows core elements to be examined through an equity lens. Each area will need a system to guide the process and ensure the work begins and continues. To arrive at these systems, each one will require in-depth discussion to surface the hidden or unexplored assumptions driving the process. The single area of onboarding requires a review of areas such as hiring practices, pay scales, and professional development for the newly hired. Do these systems equally serve everyone, or have they gone unexamined and undiscussed? And from the classroom perspective, in the area of a fair and just discipline system, this leads to an important discussion of how we respond to children – what we perceive as a "problem" – as well as the system in place for moving children forward through lessons to ensure they are appropriately engaged and challenged.

In their dissertation, "An Examination of Culturally Relevant Pedagogy and Antibias Antiracist Curriculum in a Montessori Setting," Canzoneri-Golden and King looked at three public Montessori schools across the United States that were implementing antibias, antiracist (ABAR) curriculum and using culturally relevant pedagogy (CRP). One of their questions was whether this layer of work had an impact on both behavior referrals and student achievement.

> The high-stakes test scores and behavioral referrals continue to follow the national trends. The implication is teachers' biases could affect how children learn and the race of the child could impact decisions on how issues of behavior are perceived, interpreted, and recorded. Teachers often view Black children as less deserving because of the narrative of poverty, class, and educability associated with them. Racism is such an integral part of our history that racialized thinking and actions are seen as normal. Until racism is eradicated, there will continue to be academic and behavioral disparities.[14]

If Montessori education is to move toward greater acceptance within the realms of public education as a viable, effective, research-based curriculum and an alternative educational pedagogy for students of color, there has to be close examination of and a radical shift in the way we are implementing the Montessori method. As "An Examination of Culturally Relevant Pedagogy and Antibias-Antiracist Curriculum in a Montessori Setting" clearly points out, simply training teachers in CRP and ABAR work is not enough, but mere starting points with much more needed to address the inequities living in our classrooms and our schools. In other words, the work cannot be layered on top of what we are doing in schools; it must transform and forever alter what we are doing in schools to better serve a wider population. The restructuring of how we implement Montessori is an outgrowth of this. It arises from the application of an equity lens to all that we do.

We need shared systems for honestly evaluating our programs to ensure that, as children develop their identities, Montessori educators remain aware of the influence their unconscious bias is having on that process. We need shared systems for responding to struggling learners that prevent class-room adults from referring them out of the classroom and instead offers the support needed.

SUMMARY

Equity is a core element of the whole-school Montessori method. If we use the image of the layers of the earth, it would be the outer core surrounding the inner core of constructivist thinking. The outer core is the only liquid layer, and it is responsible for the magnetic field, which extends around the planet, sustaining life there. This is the power of our equity lens: to create an energy field that sustains life in our schools. Being aware of the importance of equity is at the core of the work.

The Montessori method is a revolutionary pedagogy that promises to transform the lives of children – and the world as a whole – in a radical manner. This is an aim that has been achieved for some students, some teachers, and some families, but not all. As we implement the whole-school Montessori method, the core element of equity is a critical lens. Without it, we see will only part of the picture and be unable to serve all students completely – as we intend.

NOTES

1. Simon Field, Małgorzata Kuczera, and Beatriz Pont. "No More Failures: Ten Steps to Equity in Education." *OECD*, 2007.
2. The term *global majority* refers to Black, indigenous, and people of color as they represent over 80% of the world's population.
3. Zaretta Hammond. *Culturally Responsive Teaching & the Brain: Promoting Authentic Engagement and Rigor Among Culturally and Linguistically Diverse Students.* Corwin, 2015.
4. Crossroads is one such resource: http://crossroadsantiracism.org.
5. See the work of Koren Clark of Knowthyself Inc. or Britt Hawthorne's work at https://britthawthorne.com.

6. Listen to *Nice White Parents,* reported by Channa Joffe-Walt and produced by Julie Snyder, July 2020, a five-part series by *Serial* and the *New York Times,* which offers more insights about how issues of equity in family engagement impact a school. https://www.nytimes.com/2020/07/23/podcasts/nice-white-parents-serial.html

7. Maithreyi Gopalan and Ashlyn Aiko Nelson. "Understanding the Racial Discipline Gap in Schools." Research article first published April 23, 2019. doi: 10.1177/2332858419844613

8. U.S. Department of Education Office for Civil Rights, 2016. Next data release scheduled for 2022.

9. Libby Nelson and Dara Lind. "The School to Prison Pipeline, Explained." Justice Policy Institute, February 24, 2015.

10. Read Erica L. Green, Mark Walker, and Eliza Shapiro. "A Battle for the Souls of Black Girls," *New York Times,* October 1, 2020.

11. bell hooks. *Teaching to Transgress: Education as the Practice of Freedom.* Routledge, 1994.

12. Glenn Singleton. *Courageous Conversations.* Corwin, 2015.

13. L. A. Hirschfeld. "Children's Developing Conceptions of Race." In S. M. Quintana and C. McKown (Eds.), *Handbook of Race, Racism, and the Developing Child* (pp. 37–54). Hoboken, NJ: John Wiley & Sons, 2008.

14. Canzoneri-Golden, Lucy and King, Juliet, "An Examination of Culturally Relevant Pedagogy and Antibias-Antiracist Curriculm in a Montessori Setting" (2020). Graduate-Level Student Theses, Dissertations, and Portfolios. 360. https://spiral.lynn.edu/etds/360.

Chapter 4
Coaching

There exists only one real biological manifestation: the living individual; and toward single individuals, one by one observed, education must direct itself.

—Maria Montessori, *Discovery of the Child*

In the discussion of why to invest energy in building resilient schools, one of the considerations is the adults. As part of the prepared environment of the Montessori school, adults are arguably the single most valuable component of a thriving school: their time, energy, gifts, skills, and commitment define the experience and outcomes for children. Much of this rests in the adult's ability to know and understand their role as a Montessori educator and to embrace the ever-evolving sense of themselves in that work.

TEACHER IDENTITY

There has been much general research done on the topic of identity and specifically teacher identity and how that links to teacher preparation. Montessori teacher preparation holds an articulated goal of transformation, and over the course of the training seeks personal transformation on the part of the participants, as they begin to shift their view of education to see a different approach in Montessori. This process, which begins in training, only becomes more complex and more tied to identity as teachers begin their work in the classroom. Parker Palmer writes, "The techniques I have mastered do not disappear, but neither do they suffice. Face to face with my students, only one resource is at my immediate command: my identity, my selfhood, my sense of this 'I' who teaches – without which I have no sense of the 'Thou' who learns."[1] Here, he is pointing out that skills and tools are not enough to prepare a person to work with children. There must also be the attention to the self. There must be self-reflection to come to know and trust oneself.

Linking that to the specific identity of being a Montessori teacher, Birgitte Malm writes in her article "Constructing Professional Identities: Montessori Teachers' Voices and Visions":

> Being able to call oneself a "Montessori teacher" and representing "Montessori education" is an essential aspect related to these teachers' professional identity. There is a sense of an implicit common identity, evident in the ways in which these teachers relate to their profession, a natural assumption concerning the philosophical implications associated with being a Montessori teacher.[2]

Through Montessori training there is an opportunity for people to begin a process of self-exploration that shifts their sense of their own identity, a process acknowledged by Montessori in her writing.

Olivia Christenson builds on this in her article "Montessori Identity in Dialogue":

> A social identity comes equipped with other people's expectations and opinions of our own behavior, knowledge, and beliefs. While such expectations can certainly be important in maintaining order, quality, and goals, they can also be harmful and cause negative reactions such as insecurity, guilt, and stress. Such explicit teacher qualities have the potential to evolve into a seemingly inflexible social identity that may prevent Montessori teachers from exploring and accepting other ways of being in a classroom.[3]

This observation describes the experience of many Montessori educators who enter the classroom and struggle to implement what they have learned in training. Without support, new teachers will often default to a more familiar approach to survive their first year in the classroom, accidentally further weakening the learners' experience.

Christenson then takes the idea further, making the connection between identity and implicit bias: "Implicit biases about student behavior and lifestyle, among other social markers of difference, are often harbored deep within both a social and a personal identity and can affect a teacher's self-conceptions and social perceptions, as well as the experiences of the students whom they teach."[4] Adults' attention to identity work – or lack thereof – then directly connects with the previous core element of equity. Without this work we will be unable to build equitable, thus resilient, schools.

Malm closes her article: "Tendencies towards continuity or change in education depend to a great extent on the ways in which teachers are able to critically reflect about how they think and what they do."[5]

The question then is who is holding the space for reflection and the continual construction of the adults, supporting the growth and development of their evolving identity as educators, and ensuring a Montessori environment that serves all learners in which everyone can expand into their full selves?

MONTESSORI COACHING

One answer is a trained Montessori coach. This is the person in the school with a background as a Montessori educator who is now working to support the adults in the building and to allow elements in the system to come into balance based on the coherence of One School, the opportunity for Honest Talk, and the infrastructure created through Strong Systems.

In other fields, coaching is often synonymous with giving feedback. Giving feedback means offering people a critique of their performance based on determined expectations or goals. It is often an aspect of evaluation. The Montessori coach is not the evaluator. They are there in support of the teacher's growth and development, offering observation as a source of information to support the adults in crafting their own course adjustments. Observation, listening to understand, and offering direction when needed help to inform decisions that will guide the direction of the school, which is an alive, everchanging ecosystem.

To appreciate its complexity, we must remember that Montessori is both a philosophy and a method. Practitioners share beliefs about human development and the aims of education as well as technical knowledge of the Montessori sequence of materials and lessons. Because Montessori was never a trademarked set of practices, there has evolved a variation in the way training centers prepare Montessori educators, and that translates to variability in teaching practices and technical proficiency. There are teachers in classrooms across the hall from each other with very different amounts of preparation for the job they have been hired to do, who may share the same goal but have different ideas about how to get there. This variance in public schools can impact the children with the least advocacy. Parity across classrooms is therefore a critical aim for schools that work to implement this unique model of education. It is our responsibility to offer a just education, and this is where the work of Montessori coaching comes in. With a Montessori coach, who is prepared through the Montessori Coaching Course,[6] teachers get the support they need to reach all children. Through the work of the coach they become interconnected, growing even stronger rather than operating in isolation or opposition.

The Coach's Work

There are six aspects of the coach's work, as shown in Figure 4.1.

- *Observation*: Does daily observations of the whole school in motion and weekly observations of every classroom
- *Individual coaching*: Holds one-on-one reflection meetings with Montessori guides
- *Team coaching*: Facilitates regular meetings with protocols for professional learning communities to collaborate around children, Montessori materials, their own practice, as well as other topics to support growth
- *Professional development*: Provides year-long interrelated professional development
- *System of justness*: Supports the ongoing implementation and school-wide consistency of responding to all learners.
- *Leadership*: Holds both the authority and agency to support the day-to-day experiences of children, families, and school-based adults

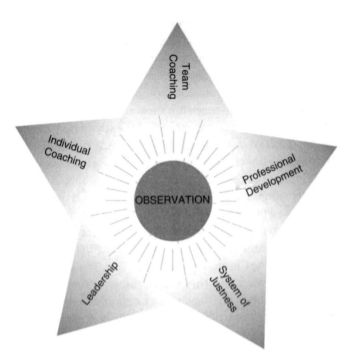

Figure 4.1 Work of the Montessori Coach.

The Montessori coach then is the person hired to work in service of the school's implementation of the method – both at the whole-school level and in classrooms – and in service of the adults so that they are better able to work to serve the children. They hold a strong understanding of the Montessori pedagogy and they work in three ways: (1) to support the implementation of the whole-school Montessori method; (2) to advocate for and ensure a strong implementation of the Montessori program; and (3) to support the transformation of the Montessori educator.

IMPLEMENTATION OF THE WHOLE-SCHOOL MONTESSORI METHOD

To support the implementation of the whole-school Montessori method, the Montessori coach holds the whole school as a prepared Montessori environment, where everyone is learning and growing all the time. As noted in

Figure 4.1, observation is at the heart of the coach's work, though now the whole school is the subject of daily observation as coaches observe everything from arrival dynamics between families, children, and teachers to hallway moments to the tenor in leadership meetings to dynamics of district walk-throughs. These observations provide information for the team about the Montessori program and the environment in which it is situated. This information then contributes to future planning across all aspects of the school from family engagement to hiring and professional development as a vehicle for making the system stronger. The coach brings the Montessori lens to every interaction, and every decision then is borne out of a constructivist approach. This advocacy, arising through observation, allows leadership to respond proactively in support of full implementation of the whole-school Montessori method.

For example, it is early September, and the new Montessori coach is observing an extended period of the youngest children having difficulty separating from their caregivers during the morning arrival process. This observation generates curiosity around why this is true. Closer observation over more days reveals that an increasing number of families are getting out of the car in the car line to give extended hugs and kisses. Some families who walked or took public transportation are entering through a different door. The staff member posted there is having a hard time supporting the transition and is allowing family members to carry their children into school. The separation struggles are then continuing at the classroom door. In addition, some families are parking and walking their children to the door but then having difficulty leaving their children. This is all happening in the midst of the buses arriving one by one with floods of excited children entering around them activating an unnecessary experience of chaos. The coach is aware of the need for more clarity around the process to simplify and streamline the procedure. Here is a whole-school Montessori moment!

The coach's first move is to connect with the primary team to discuss and understand the impact the current arrival plan is having on the children. From there they will be able to collaborate to create a tighter drop-off procedure that will allow children to have a more seamless transition into school each morning. A staff meeting is held, and the coach opens by framing the situation, its impact on the children, and the importance of fostering independence from the start of the school day and all the way through. The adults responsible for managing arrival then lead off the discussion, sharing the issues and their insights. The Montessori-trained teachers, who are typically in their classrooms to greet children at that time, are then able to participate in the brainstorming as the group works toward a stronger plan, including staggering arrival time, using only one entrance, and ensuring children walk into school on their own. Once this is determined, the group generates shared language to use to support families and children so that everyone receives the same message. This might be something like, "Thank you for saying goodbye at the door. We are ready to start a new day together – your class is waiting for you!" Extra adults volunteer to be at the doors for the first week of the new plan to support the children in saying goodbye.

A family meeting is then held, complete with coffee and muffins, and following a short explanation around the importance of fostering independence and building the child's confidence the revised drop-off procedure is reviewed in detail. Shared language is offered for family members to use with the children so that everyone is giving and receiving the same message: "You're ready for this new day. I will be right here at the end of it." That same day, a follow-up email goes out to the whole community outlining the goal (independence), agreements, shared language, and a message letting everyone know that starting the next day the new protocol will begin. In addition, there is contact information in case anyone who wasn't able to make the meeting has questions.

In this scenario, a common system glitch is observed, discussed, and analyzed, and a revision is created to support the rebalancing. Rather than being done unilaterally by one person, this is done as a school community holding the experience of the child at the center, seeking to increase the positive experience of school for everyone. Those in the school who have the greatest knowledge lead the community toward an approach that allows the whole system to work smoother and stronger. Such moves also serve to prevent splitting – a possibility, as Montessori guides are on the receiving end of a bumpy arrival process – and their daily work to settle children begins again each morning. That could easily slide into blame as the system is stressed without signs of relief. Instead, taking the extra time to meet and discuss as a community allows everyone to fully understand the issue and contribute to the solution. When the new arrival process begins, not only will everyone understand what it is and why each part is important, but they will also be more intrinsically invested in its success.

The Montessori coach is the activator of this process. Much like the classroom guide, the coach observes from a holistic view and takes action to support resolution. They take ownership of these school-wide elements and responsibilities for ensuring balance while involving others in the investigation and creation of solutions. They are seeing the whole school as a Montessori environment and infusing the method into all parts of the work using open, honest conversations and strengthening a system so everyone has the opportunity to focus on the children

STRONG IMPLEMENTATION OF THE MONTESSORI PROGRAM

Earlier in this chapter, the variation in teacher preparation was raised. A central role for the coach is to ensure a shared vision for Montessori implementation and to support the adults in developing the skills needed to do so. This is achieved through their central task of observation. More lies ahead on observation,[7] yet the weekly practice of sitting in every classroom using a shared tool through which to take notes creates an attunement.

The strong implementation of Montessori falls into two categories: philosophic and material. Implementation of the philosophy covers everything from having multiage grouping and an uninterrupted work period to the elimination of punishments and rewards and the careful balance of freedom and responsibility. The Montessori coach is able to observe each guide's implementation of the philosophy through the established procedures and routines, use of grace and courtesy, and the guiding expectations. Through conversation, the coach makes visible the invisible structures set up by the guide, which then allows them to consciously choose practices more aligned with the method.

Implementation of the materials covers everything from an inventory ensuring all classrooms are equitably equipped to training in the use of those materials to planning and delivery of lessons using all those materials. The Montessori coach is able to observe the classroom layout, the guide's lessons, and the children's use of materials as well as classroom recordkeeping to support each guide in strengthening their practice. This work cannot be undervalued, as it will determine the outcomes for the program. If there is no one in this role to calibrate and guide this part of the implementation, the school's success will once again be people dependent, meaning it relies solely on the skills and abilities of the individual teachers, which leads to varying results across classrooms. A family with triplets might then have three separate experiences of the school with three different outcomes for the children.

Instead, the consistent observation of classrooms, using an agreed upon tool, allows the coach to see regularly where the classrooms are working in sync and where more calibration is needed. They are also able to observe skill gaps or blind spots to raise in the one-on-one coaching sessions. Much more is discussed in subsequent chapters about how the coach does this, yet it's important that the community understands that this is the work of the Montessori coach. Everyone will grow in their practice as a result, and rather than being threatening or intimidating this can be exciting and rewarding. There is one other person on the planet who knows your classroom, your children, and your challenges as well as you do and is invested in your success and prepared to see you through to full implementation of your mutually chosen method. This resource for teachers means a lightening of the cognitive load where their struggles, their questions, and their confusion are shared with someone knowledgeable and confident. This loops us back to Vygotsky's zone of proximal development and the idea that the coach is the "more knowledgeable other" supporting the individualized growth of each teacher.

A scenario that illustrates the Montessori coach's ability to impact practice is one where the coach observes children in lower elementary staying in from recess. The coach then raises this observation at a lower elementary team meeting, and the subsequent discussion reveals that children who don't complete their work are then missing recess to complete it. Here is the awareness that punishment is being employed by some adults as a default response to a deeper issue. It is the Montessori coach's job to ensure the strongest Montessori implementation, so the conversation doesn't end there.

Instead of shutting the conversation down by declaring that punishments aren't used and the practice must stop, the coach pushes the discussion further, asking questions that lead the team to consider why children are not completing their work. Montessori reminds us when there is a concern to first look to the environment. What is set up in the environment to support children in completing follow-up work?

From this next part of the conversation, the coach comes to understand that teachers have a variety of work accountability systems for their students across the lower elementary classrooms. Out of six lower elementary classrooms, only two of them have mature systems the children know and understand how to use, leading them to successfully meet deadlines for follow-up work and to have time regularly to engage in Big Work. Two of the classrooms have systems that don't appear to be working and are generating mixed results: some children completing work often, some children completing work sometimes, and others rarely able to complete work. And the last two classrooms have no systems at all: one teacher is excited to be hearing about systems, and the other one is uninterested. The teachers themselves are able to make the connection that the classrooms where children are missing recess as punishment for not completing work are the same classrooms where there are no systems in place to support the independent completion of work. These are mostly 6- and 7-year-old children, who have not yet acquired time management skills, who are being left without support for how to get their work done and then penalized for not completing it.

The Montessori coach has come upon an important discovery about uneven Montessori implementation through observation and Honest Talk. Now begins the work of calibrating across classrooms by creating strong systems. The two lead guides with systems share what they are using and offer to support the rest of the team in adopting these practices. The work will continue in the one-on-one meetings, and the coach will support the advent and full implementation of the systems across all the classrooms. In addition, the practice of holding children in from recess will end as the team understands this is working outside the Montessori method. Instead, those learners who haven't been able to complete their work will have prioritized weekly student conferences with goal setting, scaffolding, and extra support to allow for success.

There is much more to unpack in this scenario, but this sketch is meant to illustrate the ways a Montessori coach does the work of advocating for and ensuring strong Montessori implementation across the whole school without telling people what to do. Instead, using the method itself and the components of the whole-school Montessori method, the coach guides the adults to greater understanding through reflection and discussion. This results in an improved experience for children, which translates to the capacity for more growth and natural development.

TRANSFORMATION OF THE MONTESSORI EDUCATOR

A related component of the coach's work is the transformation of the Montessori educator, which is something Montessori wrote and spoke about frequently over the years. In her book *The Child in the Family* she writes:[8]

> Observing these children – healthy, tranquil, innocent, sensitive, full of love and joy, always ready to help others – I have been forced to reflect upon the amount of human energy wasted because of an ancient error and great sin that disseminated injustice to the very roots of mankind. It is the adult who produces in the child his

incapacities, his confusion, his rebellion; it is the adult who shatters the character of the child and deprives it of its vital impulses. And more than that, it is the adult who affects to correct the errors, the psychological deviation, the lapses of character that he himself has produced in the child. So we find ourselves in a labyrinth without an exit, in the presence of a failure without hope. Until the adults consciously face their errors and correct them, they will find themselves in a forest of insoluble labyrinths. And children, becoming in their turn adults, will be victims of the same error, which they will transmit from generation to generation.

Montessori is asking us to see that at the heart of many issues in education is the unexamined beliefs and actions of the adult. She observes that without affecting change to the mind-set of the adult there will only be a repeated cycle that will not lead us to live a life fulfilling our potential. To fully support this, the regular cycle of classroom observations, followed by individual meetings with lead guides, allows the coach to work with classroom adults to begin to see hidden beliefs, lack of knowledge, implicit bias, or undeveloped skills that impact children and arrest progress. Through this process, everyone is now working together to explore their unmanifested potential.

In addition, it can help unravel elements in the classroom that aren't working well. If the first thing to investigate when there is an issue is the environment, Montessori tells us that the next consideration is ourselves. We next explore what it is the adult may be doing or not doing to contribute to the concern.

A story that illuminates this part of the work is that of a teacher who is struggling to get Big Work going in her lower elementary classroom. Big Work is the child's own work borne out of their own curiosity and interest often sparked by the Great Lessons, which are big concept lessons taught as part of Montessori Cosmic Education. It is an opportunity for following their questions, exploring material, and finding answers or perhaps more questions. It can result in anything from a papier-mâché solar system to scale to marks in the school hallway illustrating the length of the various dinosaurs, a fundamental needs chart of clothing for the Egyptians, a collection of poetry, or the longest division problem ever created made on 100 sheets of graph paper taped together. By its very nature, Big Work is messy, untamed, and out of the box; it can manifest as an unstructured space in the classroom. It has a contagious energy to it that prompts others to find and follow their own passions.

In past one-on-one meetings with the coach, this teacher had shared that though the Great Lessons are being given, there appears to be no further exploration. When asked what she's observed, the teacher confesses that she hasn't yet been able to observe. There is no classroom assistant, so the teacher is alone as the only adult in the classroom, which causes her to feel uneasy about observing. Despite repeated commitment, she continues on without observing. The coach then establishes that the teacher will join the coach's weekly observation and they will do a side-by-side observation of the class. This plan is reassuring to the teacher, and they do this for several weeks, debriefing after each observation. This support results in two revelations for the classroom teacher.

The first realization came as a result of the practice of observation itself. The teacher understood that she *could* observe the classroom without deleterious effects. And, in fact, this essential practice helped her to see things she would have otherwise missed that altered her course in lessons, making them more targeted and more effective. The second realization came as a result of the debrief conversation in the one-on-one meeting with the coach. Slowly they had unpacked the obstacles to further exploration following the Great Lessons – that it could "get out of hand," that it was disorderly, that the children weren't able to properly clean up. The coach continued to ask questions such as, "And then what might happen?" until the teacher came to realize that at the end of the day there were no real negative results of Big Work on her class. From there she was able to see her own aversion to mess. She shared with the coach that her first words as a child were "wipe it," which she used when she had anything on her hands or face or when she saw something unclean. This was a very old, deeply rooted aspect of herself that through dialogue she came to understand as creating an obstacle for her children's learning. With support of the coach, she devised lessons around cleaning up to support the children in taking responsibility for messes made, and this allowed her to slowly add more materials for the children to use independently, such as papier-mâché, paint, and supplies for science experiments.

Work to support the transformation of the Montessori educator can be deeply personal, as in this scenario, yet the focus is on the impact on children and their learning. It's important to distinguish Montessori coaching from therapy or life coaching since all of these will bring a person into direct relationship with themselves. Transformation of the Montessori adult cannot happen separate from the work to "consciously face their errors and correct them," and at times this may lead to the source of old habits or old ways of thinking. However, the time in Montessori coaching is focused on what is getting in the way that is having a direct impact on their learners, to be sure behavior doesn't continue that ". . . shatters the character of the child and deprives it of its vital impulses."[9] Where therapy is focused solely on the adult, Montessori coaching is focused on the impact on children. What do we need to change to provide the very best experience for children? Their transformation then is in service of the child.

SUMMARY

These three areas of the Montessori coach's work – supporting the implementation of the whole-school Montessori method, advocating for and ensuring a strong implementation of the Montessori program, and supporting the transformation of the Montessori educator – all happen within the larger context of the mission of the school. In specific and discrete ways, the trained Montessori coach cultivates the community explored more in chapters in Part Two. Their role at the school centers around developing and guiding the community for the school to provide the strongest Montessori implementation. Without someone holding this intentionally, the focus can easily slide to meeting external demands that serve the school in the short term yet leave it unable to deliver holistic outcomes. The Montessori coach holds the whole school as a Montessori environment, consistently asking how to move the community closer to its goals.

The coach also assists the adults in a regular experience of reflection and Honest Talk, which we will explore in Part Three. Based on the trust built over time the coach is able to engage in honest talk, allowing adults to see new aspects of themselves and the work. The ultimate goal therefore is that through developed relationships adults become more aware and attuned to the work of serving children through the Montessori method.

As Montessori tells us in *The Discovery of the Child,* "The teacher must undertake a twofold study: she must have a good knowledge of the work she is expected to do and of the function of the material, that is, of the means of a child's development. It is difficult to prepare such a teacher theoretically. She must fashion herself, she must learn how to observe, how to be calm, patient, and humble, how to restrain her own impulses, and how to carry out her eminently practical tasks with the required delicacy. She too has greater need of a gymnasium for her soul than of a book for her intellect."[10] Montessori coaching then creates a gymnasium for the soul, a place for individual adults to stretch, build new muscles, and grow.

Finally, the coach supports Strong Systems, which we will explore in Part Four. These systems are important to allow work to be done most effectively and with the highest level of independence and the greatest equity. The coach supports the implementation of systems in individual classrooms (e.g., how children have snack or manage their time) to those shared across level teams (e.g., what children do when they arrive late or how lessons are recorded) and the systems that support the whole school (e.g., school-wide grace and courtesy norms or the dismissal process).

As a core element of the whole-school Montessori method, all of this occurs with the goal of human flourishing. If people are part of strong communities where they feel seen and valued and able to grow, then they will stay. When they stay, they create the backbone of a resilient school that can weather, withstand, and recover from whatever difficult conditions arise.

NOTES

1. Parker Palmer. *The Courage to Teach*. Jossey-Bass, 10th Anniversary edition (August 17, 2007), p. 10.
2. Birgitte Malm. "Constructing Professional Identities: Montessori Teachers' Voices and Visions." *Scandinavian Journal of Educational Research*. January 2007. Mid Sweden University, Sundsvall, Sweden
3. Olivia Christensen. "Montessori Identity in Dialogue: A Selected Review of Literature on Teacher Identity." St. Catherine University https://files.eric.ed.gov/fulltext/EJ1234685.pdf
4. Christensen, "Montessori Identity."
5. Malm, "Constructing Professional Identities."
6. See https://montessori-action.org/one-school for more information about training a Montessori coach.
7. See the section on observation in Chapter 6.
8. Maria Montessori. *The Child in the Family*. Trans. Nancy Rockmore Cirillo. Chicago: Henry Regnery Company, 1970, p. 120.
9. Montessori, *Child in the Family*.
10. Maria Montessori. *The Discovery of the Child*. New York: Clio Press Ltd. 1986, p. 151.

PART II

One School

When a piece of cloth is to be woven, the warp is prepared first. All the threads lie close together, but parallel to each other. This is like the society by cohesion. They are all fixed at one point but they do not inter-mingle. The second stage is when the shuttle attaches all the threads together. This is like the work of the leader who connects all the people together. Yet it is necessary to have the warp, the society by cohesion, as a basis – or we could not weave a strong piece of cloth.

—Dr. Montessori, *1946 London Lectures*

Of the three components of the whole school Montessori method, *One School* is the lithosphere. It is the land beneath our feet that grounds us and unifies us, allowing us to be connected and to move forward. If we are able to bring this component with us as a landing place, our schools will grow rooted in the land-scape of education. "If we are to walk, we must have ground to walk on; after we have learnt to walk, we may learn to jump, dance, etc., but we will still need the ground."[1]

From teaching in the classroom for just over a dozen years I was recruited by the principal of the first public Montessori school in my state to come on as a coach and mentor for the teachers there. The school was one of five district magnet schools given funds to develop a theme, and this school's "theme" was Montessori. Previously, it was the school children went to if they were unen-rolled in any other school by the deadline, leading to a higher number of stu-dents in foster care or with incarcerated or absent parents. The school closed in

June as a traditional K–5 school and opened in August as a Montessori school to students aged 3 years and older with children's house, lower elementary, and upper elementary classrooms. The district teachers were given the option to stay on and spend three years in Montessori training, with the additional offer of a free master's of education. Any open positions created by teachers who did not want to stay were filled by other district teachers transferring from other schools. At the time of opening the teachers had completed their first summer and had six weeks of Montessori training.

When the children arrived in the fall, they were surprised to discover multiage classrooms with manipulative materials and a whole new way of being. One 10-year-old told her teacher that she was in the wrong classroom – first grade was down the hall. When the teacher asked her what she meant, the girl replied, "You're too nice to be a fifth-grade teacher."

And so it began: the reenculturation of a whole school with 500 children and 40 adults, almost none of whom had a vision of what a Montessori school looked, sounded, and felt like. As one of the two adults who understood the goal – and the only one who had a lived experience of being part of strong Montessori schools – it was evident that one of our first tasks was to unite as one school and develop a cohesion and connection that would see us through the critical first years.

The principal had a knack for this and immediately had the music teacher working on a school song that everyone learned and sang at every gathering. The song revolved around the simple community agreements: respect yourself, respect each other, and respect the materials. This one small act brought the community together through music and served to develop a simple shared understanding of what kind of school this had become. Singing together words that repeated the new values of the school served to bond the children and adults. It lived on as a welcome song, bringing new people into the community and letting them know what they were a part of and what the shared norms were for being together. In spite of the difficulties that arose in those first years, when the whole community was singing the school song we were transported to the aspirational view and the joy in the journey of getting there.

One School means holding the commitment to the unity of the school without divisions or factions. It means making decisions that support the school as a cohesive entity, using calibration and organization to hold it together.

INTERDEPENDENCE

Schools are complex ecosystems of interdependent, mutually beneficial parts, and part of the work is reviewing the areas of possible division. Where there are divisions, there is no longer interdependence, and when the parts fracture, they are no longer mutually beneficial.

Montessori schools can have unique divisions. The land beneath us can become divided, like the lithosphere itself. "The most well-known feature associated with Earth's lithosphere is tectonic activity. Tectonic activity describes the interaction of the huge slabs of lithosphere called tectonic plates. . . . Most tectonic activity takes place at the boundaries of these plates, where they may collide, tear apart, or slide against each other."[2] How then do we hold this awareness in a way that allows us to manage the natural shifts while remaining intact? A beginning is to understand where the tensions may be to anticipate collisions, prevent tearing or splitting, and hold the interdependent whole together.

Areas of awareness for tensions include:

- Montessori trained adults versus untrained adults
- Primary versus elementary
- Teachers versus administration
- School versus families
- Classroom lead teachers versus assistants
- Montessori teachers versus special education teachers
- Experienced educators versus novice educators

Beneath these more evident divisions is also the potential for fissures stemming from systemic racism, sexism, homophobia, and other prejudices inherited from our culture. This would lead to further divisions based on ingrained stratifications carried into school from the wider world.

The One School approach means holding a view of the whole and everyone's unique contribution to reaching the mission. This can be done using the five areas of One School.

AREAS OF ONE SCHOOL

At the start of addressing the work of becoming one school it's important to get a baseline of where your community is starting. There are five areas to consider:

- Unity
- Awareness
- Power
- Structure
- Autonomy

Unity addresses the more obvious aforementioned divisions. Where are the fault lines in your school, and what are the subtle ways you may be supporting these rather than bridging them? Is every voice valued whether they are Montessori trained or not? Whether it is a young, designated aide supporting one child or a seasoned lead teacher, are their perspectives respected?

Awareness addresses the more latent divisions that may be living unconsciously in our community until we decide to be conscious of them. This means getting comfortable with race, gender, class, partner preference, sexual identity, and religious affiliation as standard topics of conversation. It means bringing this awareness to every meeting, every memo, and every interaction and welcoming guidance or correction when we lack awareness. Implicit bias is something everyone carries, and without awareness it is deciding the terms of how our school will function and who will feel included. Working together we are able to unite in supporting each other's growing awareness. This could be everything from hiring only white teachers and Black assistants to having only men in administration and women in the classroom to having enrollment forms that ask for "mother's name" and "father's name," assuming all families are structured that way. From the macro to the micro, we must bring a new awareness that will drive inclusivity.

Power is a category closely linked to awareness, for if it is the old paradigm that establishes power and control then our school will have the same limitations as modern culture. As Audre Lorde wrote in her essay, "The Master's Tools Will Never Dismantle the Master's House," "Difference must be not merely tolerated, but seen as a fund of necessary polarities between which our creativity can spark like a dialectic. Only then does the necessity for interdependency become unthreatening. Only within that interdependency of difference strengths, acknowledged and equal, can the power to seek new ways of being in the world generate, as well as the courage and sustenance to act where there are no charters."[3] What then are the new tools that will empower every member of the community to show up to this work? How will everyone's strengths be acknowledged and held as equal as a way toward a robust interdependent community?

If our task as a public Montessori program is to bring about genuine transformation – to empower all children to grow up and make a change in the world – then we must model these possibilities in our schools. If children see that only the custodian and the assistants are brown and Black and the principal and all the lead teachers are white, then that is sending a stronger message than the words we will say. Likewise, if all the positions of power are male, that also sends a message. Who is the dominant group in your school right now, and what might be done to balance that? How is power leveraged, and is it inclusive or are all the important decisions made by the dominant group?

Structure is an important aspect of One School in that it prevents side conversations, gossip, and fissures resulting from conflict. Conflict will happen – this is a certainty. Having a known structure in place allows people to follow the proper channels to resolve an issue before it grows. If everyone in the community is comfortable with the process, then there will be support for people to use it. In addition, conflicts will be managed in a confidential and dignified manner that allows everyone to focus on the work of supporting all learners rather than getting derailed by side conversations.

Autonomy is the final aspect and an important one for a Montessori school where independence is highly valued. Are there pieces in place that allow everyone – families, staff, and children – to be at their highest level of functional independence? Do we respect everyone's ability to do for themselves? An element of this is transparency. Have we taken the time to orient every new staff member, every new family, and every older child who joins our community? It is through the human tendency for orientation that we are able to become contributing members, so having a built-in way for new people to learn the workings of the school will lead to a sense of calibration and organization.

Figure PII.1 shows a continuum that looks at the five aspects – unity, awareness, power, structure, and autonomy – at various levels of implementation. This tool can help move schools from being exclusive workplaces to becoming fully inclusive through awareness and setting a course for intentional change. At an opening staff meeting, individuals or teams can reflect on where the

One School Continuum

	Exclusive	Passive	Symbolic Unity	Identity in Flux	Fully Inclusive (no say/do gap)
Unity	• Intentionally and publicly divides groups - Use of us/them language - Exclusive meetings	• Allows for divisions without correction - Divisive language goes uncorrected	• Talks about unity without follow-through - Cross level team meetings discussed	• Steps taken to bring groups together with systems to foster inclusivity and emerging Language of Reverence	• Holds a vision of a fully integrated community and actively integrates groups in the day's work using Language of Reverence
Awareness	• Doesn't engage with issues of diversity and social justice • Race goes undiscussed • Fear of revealing diverse backgrounds	• Engages issues of diversity and social justice only on dominant group's terms and in their comfort zone • Race is discussed superficially • Diverse backgrounds are shared with some	• Symbolically engages issues of diversity and social justice • Race and equity are "topics" • Diversity of backgrounds are known but not acknowledged	• Engaging in conversations around inclusion and social justice • Race is an acceptable aspect of identity and the school commits to the race and equity work • Diversity of backgrounds are acknowledged	• Inclusion and social justice are a regular part of everyday conversation • Race is a comfortable aspect of identity and the race and equity work within the school is evident • Everyone feels welcome and celebrated
Power	• Maintains a dominant group's privilege and power, offering limited and disparate access to decision-making	• Maintains limitations on access to dominant group's privilege, power and decision-making	• Expanding view of power and decision-making without real change	• Implements structures, policies, and practices for inclusive power sharing and decision-making	• The life of the school holds full participation and shared power with shared decision-making structures and all members of the community having a voice
Structure	• General confusion regarding where to take concerns, questions, or ideas	• Concerns are shared without respect for boundaries, variation in answers to the same question, ideas not sought out	• Structures are in place for voicing concerns, getting answers, and sharing ideas, but not yet followed	• Structures are in place for voicing concerns, getting answers, and sharing ideas, and are most often followed	• Structures are clear and used - people go to the designated person/group with a concern, question, or idea.
Autonomy	• Systems to support independence are entirely absent	• Systems to support independence are emerging	• Systems to support independence are known but not always used	• Systems to support independence are used by a subgroup	• Systems to support independence are understood and used

Areas of awareness for divisions:
- Montessori trained adults vs. untrained adults
- Primary vs. Elementary
- Teachers vs. Administration
- School vs. Families
- Classroom lead teachers vs. Assistants
- Montessori teachers vs. Special education teachers

Figure PII.1 One School Continuum.

school is in each of these categories. The results can support leadership in setting goals to move the school toward a more inclusive One School environment for everyone.

When people are included and feel like they are part of something important, this leads them to want to stay. People staying and building a strong Montessori school is critical; committed staff and committed families make the school solid, durable, and stable. This gets passed on through generations of people who both work at and attend the school, and the result is a resilient Montessori school.

To reach the fully inclusive stage, there are two components of building One School culture: (1) calibration, or how we work together; and (2) organization, or how we structure the school to include everyone.

Working toward One School we will use the lens of Montessori's human tendencies and the Montessori triad to ground us in Montessori while also using the One School continuum as our indicator of progress.

NOTES

1. Maria Montessori. The 1946 London Lectures.
2. National Geographic Resource Library Encyclopedic Entry, "Lithosphere." https://www.nationalgeographic.org/encyclopedia/lithosphere/
3. Audre Lorde. "The Master's Tools Will Never Dismantle the Master's House." 1984. *Sister Outsider: Essays and Speeches.* Ed. Berkeley, CA: Crossing Press, 110–114. 2007. Print.

Chapter 5
Calibrate

Solidarity among human beings is very beautiful, arising from antiquity and projecting itself as it does into the future, binding the past to the present and the present to the future, for all eternity.
—Maria Montessori, "Human Solidarity in Time and Space"

Calibration is at the heart of the One School approach. It supports all school stakeholders in feeling in tune with the mission and therefore able to give their all to the work. Most often the term *calibration* refers to complex machines that need to be attuned to work properly. However, if we are adopting a holistic point of view – taking the long view, seeing the big picture, and honoring the interrelatedness of the school – then calibration will be an important iterative practice to keep the system healthy and growing. Calibration allows the school to grow strong through our shared commitment to remain connected as a whole in the work. This is a different approach from simply being collaborative. Collaboration without calibration can actually cause divisions among teams and across a whole program.

In this chapter we will call on Dr. Montessori's awareness of human tendencies and explore how our own awareness of them strengthens the calibration across classrooms, level teams, and the whole school. Valuing calibration means meeting the community's needs for unity, autonomy, and structure. It is living into the vision of one aligned community through (a) holding weekly meetings; (b) providing role clarity; and (c) articulating a clear and fair appraisal process aligned with the roles and relevant to the work in Montessori.

To calibrate means to check, determine by comparison, or adjust, and these three practices done regularly will allow for the ecosystem of the school to check for alignment, determine by comparison of views, and adjust to realign in an ongoing manner.

ECCO

Montessori's observation of the following four human tendencies brings forward universal predispositions that span age, race, and culture, and if we attend to them we are able build resilience together as a school community:

- **E**xplore: Everyone in the school must feel agency to be curious and seek to understand.
- **C**ommunicate: Everyone in the school must be on the same page every day across the whole school year.
- **C**reate Order: Everyone in the school must understand and practice shared agreements.
- **O**rient: Everyone in the school must understand their role in fulfilling the school's mission.

Keeping these human tendencies (ECCO) in mind will help when considering the needs of your specific community and identifying the fissures or breakdowns. Here we apply these human tendencies to the One School strategy of weekly meetings using an example from an urban elementary school to see how they illuminate the purpose and outcomes.

At the school, students were having recess on grass owned by the city, and the principal was asked to move the activity into the school's blacktop parking lot. The transition wasn't going well, so the principal's instinct was to shut it down. The coach observed that the assistants who were monitoring the recess all had different ideas of what was permissible. The coach recognized that though they had started the year calibrated about recess, this change in location had disrupted that shared understanding.

Explore

Meetings provide time for the human tendency of exploration. Topics are explored through reflection and discussion. When meetings drive toward fixing before understanding, then time, energy, and trust can get lost. Likewise, meetings that have no clear purpose dull the tendency to explore. Instead, engaging everyone in the process of thinking about something together allows for multiple viewpoints to arise and natural solutions to emerge from the very people who will likely implement them.

In our example, the coach held a meeting with the assistants and introduced the topic of recess. Through discussion, the team saw they had different rules and expectations. From there they generated a list of agreements that they took back and reviewed with their respective classrooms. Recess wasn't perfect and had a ways to go, but within two days of the meeting the principal was pleasantly surprised to find it was dramatically better. They had accomplished this through *exploration*.

Communicate

Many public school meetings revolve around one-way communication where a school leader is talking and everyone else is listening and expected to do what was presented. To build a One School culture, this approach must be retired and replaced by a meeting model that allows for everyone to have a voice in the conversation. Again, the school leader will have information to communicate with the staff, and that can happen in snapshots[1] or emails. Meetings are now focused on one or two topics that are discussed by the meeting participants as a means of understanding multiple perspectives, valuing everyone's input, and creating investment in the various aspects of the school.

In the meeting in our example, attendees ranged widely in terms of age and experience, which meant they each had different ideas about what constituted *safety* at a recess held in a parking lot. In taking time to communicate, those with less experience were able to listen to their more experienced peers share stories about past issues that had motivated them to set certain limits. During this time, those who were older also had the opportunity to listen to their younger peers describe a game they knew how to play and wanted to teach to the children. This two-way communication created an opportunity to find a middle ground.

Create Order

Humans need order to function, and their tendency toward creating it is met when teams get on the same page. If everyone leaves a meeting with more mental clarity about one topic, that satisfies a greater need than leaving with a jumble of information. To create order, meetings must also have order – that is, starting and ending on time with a clear agenda and a follow-up process to ensure action. No one wants to lose minutes of their life in a meeting that holds a circular conversation with no outcome or action. Honoring order also means leading an effective meeting.

In our example, everyone left the meeting motivated to refine, communicate, and uphold shared expectations for recess, which created order on three levels: (1) internal order within each attendee; (2) order among the team members; and (3) order across classrooms for all the elementary children. The result was a more orderly – and in turn more fun – recess experience for everyone.

Orient

When we travel to a new place, our need to be oriented is most apparent Where will I sleep? Where will I eat? Where is the restroom? Orientation helps us to meet our basic human needs and therefore signals safety. When we are oriented, we feel more grounded and more able to concentrate on higher-order thinking tasks. Meetings then should serve the purpose of reorienting everyone toward the mission of the school: the children. How does every topic we spend time on redirect us all to the heart of our work and why we are here? This is established in the direct aim of each meeting communicated through a clear agenda. Even something as tedious as inventory can be more purely motivated if we are focused on how it will allow us to equitably equip classrooms so that all learners have access to the curriculum.

In our example, the orientation at the meeting happened when launching the exploration: "Some of you have mentioned the children don't seem to be having a good time at recess anymore. Why do you think that is?" The topic is oriented toward the shared understanding of how recess serves children and the shared observation that it wasn't working anymore. Dr. Montessori reminds us, "The child is, therefore, a universal spiritual force and a source of love and lofty sentiments; he is the true means to attain unity among the human beings of the world."[2]

WEEKLY MEETINGS

Calibration is an investment of time spent together. When we take the time to engage with one another, we have the opportunity to connect and align. In the life of a school, this largely occurs through regular meetings. These are not ordinary meetings that run through task lists easily shared in an email: Anything that can be communicated in an email belongs in an email. Rather, as Priya Parker, in her book *The Art of Gathering,* suggests, to be a meaningful use of time there should be a bold, sharp purpose that sets the intention for the meeting with a generous authority and an invisible, thoughtful structure.[3]

Therefore, consider each time you gather people in your school: What do you want them to know and be able to do when they leave the meeting? Going into the meeting with a direct aim (bold, sharp purpose) gives it the spine-straightening feeling that this work matters. Having a meeting facilitator (generous authority) means that the meeting won't go off the rails but will stay focused on the direct aim with clear results. Finally, meetings that allow people to connect with the basic human tendencies (bringing thoughtful structure) during the course of the meeting means everyone is fully engaged in the work of the school. When done well, these meetings energize and galvanize the community to continue to move the work forward. These are the types of meetings that create One School.

Bringing ECCO to each of the weekly meetings then allows for these human tendencies to be respected and activated in the work of the school. There are five essential weekly meetings held across the school:

1. individual lead teachers;

2. level teams and lesson study;

3. leadership;

4. student support and child study; and

5. assistants, or classroom and level teams.

First, an essential note about scheduling: These are all of the meetings for the whole school, but each person is likely in two or three of them at different times across the week. With the shared leadership structure in the whole-school Montessori method, some of these are led by the principal and some by the Montessori coach. Table 5.1 shows a sample week schedule for a classroom teacher.

Table 5.1 Sample Teacher Meeting Schedule

Time	Monday	Tuesday	Wednesday	Thursday	Friday
Mid-day (prep)	Weekly classroom team mtg.w/ Assistant			Individual Coaching mtg.	
After school			Level team/ Student support mtg		

Agenda & Meeting Notes			
	Date:	Time:	Attendees:
	Topics to Discuss:		
Time	**Topics**		
	-		
	-		
	-		
	-		
	Resources to share:	Next Meeting:	

Follow Up:

Action Item	Person Responsible	Deadline

Figure 5.1 Sample Agenda and Meeting Notes Tool.

For these meetings to be productive and focused on ECCO, there needs to be both a process and a tool. This process may vary from meeting to meeting, yet having a universal meeting tool used by every team is calibration (Figure 5.1).

These meetings then become a cycle of work that allows each individual to attune with the group and thus for the work to become more interrelated and stronger. It also becomes an aspect of the community value of autonomy since not every meeting will be facilitated by the principal of the school. Once a process and tool are established, in most cases the team will be able to move forward with the work facilitated by the Montessori coach or a team lead. At these meetings, the mission and vision of the school are held at the center of the time, yet practical matters can also be managed and addressed in an ongoing, reliable way where everyone is included and there are very few surprises.

For example, if the topic of the family meeting is fostering independence, a change in the arrival process deserves some conversation. Half the time in the meeting is still spent discussing the Montessori method and the means to foster independence (the mission of the school). Then, grounded in that perspective, the conversation shifts to the new arrival procedure (practical matter). This allows for stronger thinking and a greater receptivity based on the method.

Surprises – common in public education – can throw us off track, so it's important to dedicate time to discussing and managing the work while not neglecting to move the work forward. Building the agenda of every meeting around the philosophy of the school reinforces identity and provides calibration necessary to keep a school humming.

Agreements that come out of the conversation are converted into follow-up items – what people will do after the meeting – that can be tracked at the bottom of the meeting notes tool. This preserves everyone's good ideas and ensures they aren't lost in the shuffle of a busy school day. The follow-up items are used to open up the next week's meeting. If something hasn't been attended to, then either the designated person recommits to it or asks for help to complete it. This regular practice creates a school culture of shared responsibility and following through on commitments resulting in a structure that supports shared power in the One School continuum.

The abbreviation ECCO helps us remember that the message of the meetings is to be experienced after the meeting ends. It should echo, reverberating for everyone who was in the meeting, and also reach those who weren't able to attend. The shared meeting notes tool assists with the reverberation as it holds a record of what was discussed and what actions will be taken in the coming week.

Essential Weekly Meetings

Individual Lead Teacher Meetings

Following the coach's weekly observation in the classroom there is a one-on-one meeting with every lead guide. A copy of the observation tool used by the coach has been shared with the guide already, and they may discuss this or move into a reflective or directive coaching conversation (see Chapter 7). The One School element of these honest conversations is that they happen for teachers at every level, every week. They naturally include the elements of ECCO as they are structured around reflective practice.

The Montessori coach facilitates the meetings somewhere that allows for open conversations and at a time of day when the lead teacher is able to fully engage in a process of reflection, brainstorming, and at times pushing beyond their comfort zone. A meeting in the classroom at the start of the day with children wandering in will not support these aims, whereas a meeting in a quiet space with the door closed and a cup of tea sets the stage for a deeper, more productive conversation.

The coach uses a unique meeting notes form (see Chapter 7), which allows the lead guide to select a weekly accomplishment they commit to with the support of the coach.

Level Teams

Level team meetings provide an opportunity to move the work forward together. Where individual coaching meetings may open insight into areas of personal growth, team meetings foster collective growth. Traditionally, level meetings are filled with organizing dates and times for upcoming events such as testing or picture day – all items that can be communicated in a memo. For these meetings to ECCO, they should be oriented toward the essential work of the team. For lead teachers this must be the Montessori curriculum and its implementation through the use of Montessori materials. This is how teams keep their focus on what really matters – by regularly exploring, reflecting on, and communicating about lessons. The coach uses information from weekly observations to understand what material needs discussion:

- *Calibration across the team*: if teachers are presenting the same material very differently
- *Rejuvenation*: if a material is lying dormant (e.g., thermic bottles, decimal checkerboard)
- *Clarity*: if children are often misusing a material (e.g., red rods as swords)

The coach invites a member of the team who has a good grasp of the selected material to present at the start of the meeting. There is then structured time to allow for reflections on the presentation, exploration of the material, and for the team to create order by coming up with agreements about their future use of the material. This is the calibration that allows equity – if everyone understands the most beneficial way for the material to be presented then all the children will receive the same strong lesson.

This meeting is facilitated by the Montessori coach or level lead with notes kept that allow any missing team members to review the material covered and be a part of any changes in practice that come out of the meeting.

Leadership

Leadership meetings may happen more frequently among the administrative team, yet a formal weekly meeting with a clear agenda, notes, and a place for follow-up supports the team in maintaining momentum in spite of the regular interruptions of daily life at the school. It allows all members of the team to slow down and come together for exploration, communication, order, and orientation for the weeks ahead. Important members of this team might include the principal, director of operations, family engagement coordinator, Montessori coach, dean of students (or child study lead or nautilus lead), and the office manager.

Including the office manager at this meeting is important, yet it may be difficult for them to find time to spare outside the high demands of the front office. The meeting often then gets scheduled around what is best for this person: perhaps after everyone is settled into their morning work cycle or after school. As the main outward-facing member of the team, the office manager's participation in this meeting brings new insights that may impact decisions the leadership team is making, and it's best for that to happen during the planning and not after the fact. In addition, because this person also typically disseminates all information for the school, they must have up-to-date and accurate details to share. So being present to changes made in these meetings allows for that to happen effortlessly.

This meeting is either facilitated by the principal or occurs with rotating facilitation where each member takes the lead once a month. Shared facilitation allows for each member of the team to be in the leadership role, growing their skills and refining the art of facilitation. It also allows everyone to share the burden of preparing the agenda, sending out the notes after the meeting, and ensuring follow-up items happen between meetings.

Student Support and Child Study

There are two types of meetings in this category: (1) student support team meetings, for those who offer support to learners; and (2) child study, meetings for organizing student support.

Often in public schools the interventionists or special educators are seen as ancillary to the classroom rather than important contributors to it. The people who fill these positions are often not Montessori trained, so this perception creates an automatic fracture in the community. Having weekly meetings with those who offer student support allows them to experience being part of a larger team working together to serve the key children in the building. The experience of exploring topics together – especially Montessori topics – will allow for alignment between the constructivist framework of the method and the behaviorist framework some new team members may bring from other settings. Enormous strength can be harnessed by working within the healthy tension of multiple approaches to the same issue. Exploring together and communicating openly about beliefs, best practices, and alignment with the Montessori method will begin to create order within a mixed group of practitioners, and this coherence will ultimately benefit children, which is who we are all oriented toward.

The student support team meeting is facilitated by the child study lead or the nautilus lead and supports transitioning children from child study into special education. It can be a time to ensure that child study action plans and all individualized education plans are being implemented and all children are receiving the support and services in their plans.

Child study is a Montessori approach to identifying and supporting struggling students, some who may go on to be evaluated and qualify for an individualized education plan. These are weekly meetings held with level teams to create the conditions for all children to be successful in the classroom and is discussed in greater detail in Chapter 9.

Assistants

Assistants, as the other adults in the classroom, hold a big role in any Montessori school. The children, especially at the earlier ages, are greatly impacted by the adults as a part of their learning environment and follow what is modeled. This creates a necessity for ongoing learning and coaching as assistants join the community, yet often they are offered the fewest opportunities to meet or the least amount of professional development. This – combined with the reality across public schools that the role is often filled by members of the global majority while many lead teachers are white – creates an unnecessary stratification. Regular meetings can mitigate this as they offer ongoing coaching and professional development communicating that this role is important and valued. The school's investment in the meetings (by providing time for them) not only messages that the role is esteemed but also acts as a pipeline for lead teachers. Through the ongoing learning that happens in these meetings, assistants may become more interested in Montessori training, which with cultivation can result in more trained adults in the school.

There are two regular meetings for assistants: (1) weekly classroom team meetings; and (2) regular level team meetings.

The partnership between the lead teacher and the assistant is a crucial part of a functioning Montessori classroom, and it can make or break the experience for the children and families. Having a weekly meeting to connect creates the conditions for a solid relationship to build over time. In addition, within the busy life of a classroom there may be time to have short exchanges, but teams need more than this to explore, reflect, and create order together; having a designated time to meet supports this work.

Like all One School meetings, this time is not spent on the details. Many teams have a shared journal where they can record the tidbits of information and communicate to keep the classroom functioning. Instead, this meeting has a Montessori component and a practical component. The trained teacher takes time each week to cover an element of the Montessori method in the context of their shared work together. An example of this might be engagement. The lead brings the assistant into a conversation about what engagement looks like in the classroom and how to protect it: adjusting when the adults are interrupting the children to ask them to do something else (e.g., put something away, take their turn at snack). This conversation may arise out of the teacher's observation that the well-meaning assistant is interrupting engaged children rather than waiting until they are no longer engaged. This is the type of important conversation that wouldn't happen in the same way if attempted during class time with the additional need to attend to the children. Having a set time each week to refine the shared practice strengthens the classroom implementation of the method.

The second part of the meeting might be devoted to practical matters such as reviewing child study action plans,[4] reading assessment results to coordinate how to support all learners, or planning forward together. This is equally important for both moving the work ahead and communicating the essential role of the assistant in this shared work.

As with all the aforementioned meetings, keeping notes is an important part of these meetings and is done by the team with the lead teacher facilitating the meeting. Often these notes are housed in a shared space so the Montessori coach can access them in support of the team.

Regular level team meetings are for professional development and discussion. They also have a Montessori component, moving adults learning forward about both the method (e.g., What is isolation of difficulty?) and the materials (e.g., What does the stamp game teach?) as well as a practical component. Since assistants are present for some of the trickiest parts of the school day – arrival, lunch, recess, transitions, dismissal – it's important to have a regular calibration point. The practical component of the meeting, such as the recess question from before, therefore seeks to explore common issues observed across the school, such as: Have you noticed children seem to be having more difficulty moving quietly through the hallways? What do we need to do to prepare for the upcoming assembly? Discussion time with assistants is important for refinement as well as a big part of the whole school's preparation-over-correction approach to upcoming events for everything from assessment cycles to picture day to family conferences.

These meetings are led by the Montessori coach or level lead, though other school members may attend to facilitate targeted discussions. This might be the nautilus lead opening the topic of conflict resolution in the classrooms or the physical education teacher thinking through moving PE classes outside for the spring starting in two weeks. Assistants are contributors to new procedures and routines and may also be the transmitters of information back to the classroom community. The example for ECCO was from an assistants' meeting, so they have been saved for last. Hopefully this will leave a lasting impression of their importance in the school and how essential it is that they are included in a cycle of regular meetings.

NEW WORLD CONSIDERATIONS

As the world became digitally focused during a global pandemic, the fabric that kept communities together was tested. Those schools with a solid One School foundation simply kept up the established meeting rhythm virtually and were able to weather the transition together. All meetings continued, and the principal or coach created links for the meetings and let the community know where to meet during the established meeting times. Schools without regular touchpoints drifted, impacting what information children received during those initial weeks of distance learning.

Having an established location for shared notes allowed communities to build agenda topics together in advance of the virtual meetings since they were no longer able to mention ideas when passing in the hall or in the staff room. These documents, often organized in shared Google drives with shared folders for teams, allowed for the meetings to continue without interruption and for every member of the team to see and contribute to the topics for discussion.

ROLE CLARITY

Another element of functioning as One School is role clarity connected to a transparent appraisal process. These are linked to both Honest Talk and Strong Systems yet fall here under One School: Without each person knowing and understanding both their role and how to fulfill it well, it will be difficult to calibrate to focus the energy and power of the community on the shared mission.

Role clarity begins at the point of being hired and is covered in the onboarding system in Chapter 10. Ensuring that the job description used to advertise the position matches the work the person will actually do is an ongoing task necessary in busy schools. Montessori schools are adaptive by nature, often wonderfully creative in shifting roles to meet the needs of the community or the children. Usually this is done with the agreement of the people shifting to meet the need, but still their job description needs to be redrafted to capture their work. This ensures that if they left the school there would be clarity about what tasks would need to be fulfilled by their successor. In this way, there is a seamless transition for adults moving in and out of every role in the school, which increases the likelihood that all the jobs will be done to keep the interdependent system thriving.

Figure 5.2 shows an example of a tool that created new role clarity when schools shifted into distance learning and Montessori teachers moved into similar yet different roles. For there to be a One School understanding of what everyone was expected to do, leaders created clarity through distributing new roles and responsibilities documentation for all school-based adults, including those on the leadership team. Everyone's job shifted and changed as a result of the pandemic, and calibrating the new expectations supported the community in carrying on with the work of serving children.

Roles and Responsibilities

Classroom Lead Teacher		
Supported by: Montessori Coach Appraised by: Principal	Directly supports: Assistant teacher	Key relationships: Children and Families; Teachers; Leadership team members
Key Responsibilities		
Guiding	**Teaming**	**Growing**
☐ Prepares children and families for success in Virtual Learning with shared procedures and G&C ☐ Creates and keep a schedule of virtual instruction lessons to reach every child at least 4x/week ☐ Plans and present virtual lessons according to shared curriculum ☐ Records lesson plans, presentations, and observations in a shared platform ☐ Gives diagnostic lessons to identify children's skills in math, literacy, and writing in the first 3 weeks ☐ Evaluates children's academic progress by reviewing data from platforms and assessments ☐ Plans additional skill-based lessons based on evaluation of children's progress ☐ Identifies Key children in need of further support ☐ Collaborates with families to implement Action Plans for children in Child Study ☐ Communicates with every family at least weekly	☐ Holds team check-in with assistant teacher at least weekly ☐ Creates written notes of meetings, accessible by Coach ☐ Participates in co-teacher meetings, team, and school-wide planning and professional development ☐ Collaborates with team to implement shared curriculum ☐ Leads classroom family communication and meetings ☐ Participates in Child Study & Curriculum Talk meetings ☐ Holds virtual conferences with families according to the school schedule ☐ Responds to colleagues and families within 24 hours M-F ☐ Co-plans with special educators to align instruction and support children's growth	☐ Reflects with Coach in regularly scheduled meetings at least weekly ☐ Sets goals for improving practice weekly ☐ Co-creates annual professional growth goals with the school principal ☐ Gives and receives written evaluation feedback at least once yearly ☐ Participates in completing surveys ☐ Sends surveys to families and analyze data to identify at least one change to your practice ☐ Pursues opportunities for professional growth annually ☐ Offers coaching/PD to others on your team

Figure 5.2 Sample Roles and Responsibilities.

Classroom Assistant Teacher		
Supported by: Montessori Coach Evaluated by: Principal	Directly supports: Class-room children and Lead teacher	Key relationships: Children and Families; Teachers; Leadership team members
Key Responsibilities		
Supporting	**Teaming**	**Growing**
☐ Participates in virtual class learning (ie: holds a reg-ularly scheduled virtual "work cycle") ☐ Plans and present small group or individual virtual lessons as requested by lead ☐ Follows and supports Grace and Courtesy routines of the classroom ☐ Supports children who need intervention with additional lessons as needed ☐ Supports with technology as needed ☐ Documents lessons and observations in the shared platform as applicable ☐ Assists with the creation and distribution of materials for learning at home	☐ Participates in team check-in with the lead teacher at least weekly ☐ Keeps written notes of meetings, accessible by Coach ☐ Participates in team meetings, school-wide planning, and profes-sional development ☐ Collaborates with team to implement shared curriculum ☐ Participates in class-room family communi-cation and meetings as requested by the lead guide ☐ Participates in Child Study and Curriculum Talk meetings as applicable ☐ Responds to col-leagues and families within 24 hours M-F	☐ Reflects with Coach in regularly scheduled meetings at least monthly ☐ Sets goals for improving practice weekly ☐ Co-creates annual professional growth goals with the school principal, coach, or lead guide ☐ Gives and receives written evaluation feedback at least once yearly ☐ Participates in completing surveys ☐ Pursues opportu-nities for professional growth annually ☐ Offers coaching/PD to others on your team

Professional Standards for Virtual School - ALL STAFF

☐ Arrives at meetings consistently on time
☐ Keeps a shared and posted schedule of lessons/meetings (google calendar or similar)
☐ Returns from breaks on time
☐ Participates in Zoom: video on, uses chat or voice to contribute
☐ Dresses in a manner consistent with school dress code
☐ Maintains a video environment background that is professional and minimizes distractions
☐ Participates positively in the virtual classroom environment
☐ Responds to emails, calls, or texts within 24 hours during the week
☐ In written and live, virtual communication, uses language that could be seen or overheard by children
☐ Seeks first to understand
☐ Prioritizes health and well-being of children and community
☐ Talks to, not about, people
☐ Follows Covid safety protocols about in-person interactions as applicable

Figure 5.2 (Continued)

Role clarity is also important at the leadership level to provide a coherent message to the community. When a team works together, unconscious splitting can occur in which a staff member gets different answers to the same question from different members of the team. To prevent this, offering the community role clarity for leadership positions allows everyone a shared understanding of who to go to for which questions.

An example of this is when a teacher approached the principal with a request about a student. The principal asked a few questions and then agreed to the teacher's request to move them up on the child study docket. She did this without consulting the child study lead or the Montessori coach to be helpful and responsive to the teacher. Meanwhile, the teacher had already approached the child study lead and had a similar conversation with an outcome that felt less satisfactory to the classroom teacher. The principal, by agreeing to her request without checking with the other members of the leadership team, accidentally created a division. As she realized this, the principal, put into practice keeping her door open to teachers while always asking "Have you talked to _____ about this?" That one question automatically looped people back to the point of origin for the conversation.

Similarly, at a different school, a Montessori coach was asked a question about lunch menus and having been in a meeting earlier in the month where this was discussed was pleased to be able to offer that information to the teacher. Unfortunately, it was old information, and the operations manager was distressed to hear what the teacher was now sharing with others, including families. Following apologies, the team created buckets of work illustrating role clarity. They shared these with staff and let them know who to go to with what questions. Then each member of the leadership team studiously practiced rerouting staff members to the appropriate person rather than answering every question they were asked. Within a short period of time, the school-based adults adjusted and went directly to the person who needed to answer the question. This narrowed the amount of miscommunication, created a more efficient experience for everyone, and therefore increased the team's ability to function smoothly.

APPRAISALS

Connected to role clarity, the appraisal tools used to offer feedback in the various roles need to be reviewed to ensure they are directly connected to the job descriptions and target the work people are actually doing. Otherwise the appraisal process becomes less useful and therefore less effective in promoting growth for the whole community.

Appraisal tools in public Montessori schools in particular must be carefully chosen as they will direct the growth and development of both the person and the program. If, for example, the school has adopted the district performance review document as the appraisal tool for classroom teachers and that tool is geared toward traditional classrooms with indicators such as "posts instructional outcomes" or "designs coherent formative assessments," then these will be the targets teachers will begin to focus on. Very quickly a Montessori program can lose its essential elements as teachers shift practice to improve their performance review.

Instead, selecting or creating an appraisal tool that works with the coaching model and aligns teacher growth with coaching will move practice in the direction of strong Montessori implementation. The tool itself, the indicators, and the scale are important, and so, too, is the practice of appraisal. Evaluation is an intimidating process that brings to mind being judged rather than seen. Appraisal on the other hand is less of a loaded term that involves looking at the situation together and determining areas of strength and areas for growth. Having an inclusive appraisal process supports the One School goals.

The whole-school Montessori method for appraisal involves a clearly thought-out, well-communicated, equitable, and inclusive process. As Figure 5.3 maps out, it begins with clarity around roles and responsibilities and leads to full staff involvement in the process.

Each person in the community uses the appraisal tool to offer a self-appraisal, therefore increasing their agency in the upcoming conversation. This also allows for intrinsic motivation toward change rather than simply a top-down approach where the evaluator is positioned as more important or more powerful than the person being appraised. By including them in the process, and even centering them in it, it allows them to have more freedom and responsibility in developing their own growth plan. These small adjustments move the community toward stronger One School practices. Looking back at the One School continuum, we can see that this builds both power and autonomy as it is a policy that supports full power sharing and decision-making as well as fostering independence.

Appraisal Process

For Leaders: How the appraisal process works

Step	1	2	3	4	5	6
What	Clarity	Preparation for reflection	Self appraisals	Meetings and goal-setting	Cycle step-back	Repeat at end of year
When	Beginning of year	Four weeks into school year	Six weeks into school year	Six-seven weeks into school year	Eight weeks into school year	Start 12 weeks before last day of school
How	Give descriptions of roles and responsibilities to all staff. Make space for questions and discussions.	Send all staff the appraisal docs that are aligned to roles & responsibilities and dates for completion of self-appraisals. School Leader calendars meetings for two weeks out.	Each staff completes their own version of their respective document. School Leader completes a version of the respective document for each staff member.	School Leader will have reviewed average score and assigned one as well based on their observations. Discuss areas of agreement, strengths, and improvement Set a goal for the coming year.	Whole-staff PD on trends and debrief	To close year and set goals for coming year; ID staffing changes

Figure 5.3 Appraisal Process.

How the appraisal process works

You have received a description of your role and responsibilities at the start of the school year. That is about *what* you do. The following appraisal documents, aligned with those roles and responsibilities, are about *how* you do it.

The appraisal process has four steps:

6. Rate yourself on a scale of 0–4 for the following items in your role description. Complete a written reflection in the narrative section on the second page.

7. Send this document, with your rating and written comments, to [school leader] by _____.

8. [School leader] will review your average score and assign one as well based on their observations of your work.

9. [School leader] and you will discuss areas of agreement, strengths, and improvement, setting a goal for the coming year.

SCALE

0 Not present or not observed	1 Able to do with help	2 Know and can do some of this	3 Know and can do all of this without help	4 Know and can do this as a model for the community

The human tendencies of ECCO are also honored in this process as everyone is allowed to explore their role, communicate about fulfillment of the role, and create order through goal setting that orients them toward their next steps in the work.

NEW WORLD CONSIDERATIONS

As mentioned already, one of the outstanding issues during the pandemic's forced shift to virtual instruction was lack of role clarity. Because it began in crisis mode, there was no understanding of roles and responsibilities, and an imbalance developed. To rebalance, and since the school-based adults were no longer doing the job they were hired to do, it was necessary for schools to create and distribute new job descriptions and appraisal tools. This essential One School move allowed the community to reset around the new world conditions.

Clearly stating the expectations for each position in the school and clarifying what aspects would be part of the spring appraisal allowed for the focus to return to the work with the children. In particular, the role of classroom assistants and interventionists needed to be clearly communicated to ensure equitable distribution of the workload across the school, preventing resentments from arising between staff members.

In addition, new school-wide professional standards needed to be created to establish grace and courtesy norms and to provide One School guidance for how everyone would be together under the new conditions (Table 5.2).

Table 5.2 Professional Standards for Virtual School

Score	Standard
	☐ Arrives to meetings consistently on time
	☐ Keeps a shared and posted schedule of lessons/meetings (google calendar or similar)
	☐ Returns from breaks on time
	☐ Participates in Zoom: video on, uses chat or voice to contribute
	☐ Dresses in a manner consistent with school dress code
	☐ Maintains a video environment background that is professional and minimizes distractions
	☐ Participates positively in the virtual classroom environment
	☐ Responds to emails, calls, or texts within 24 hours during the week
	☐ In written and live, virtual communication, uses Language of Reverence that could be seen or overheard by children
	☐ Seeks first to understand
	☐ Prioritizes health and well-being of children and community
	☐ Talks to, not about, people
	☐ Follows Covid safety protocols about in-person interactions as applicable
Total	/13 = _____ Average

New World considerations for role clarity and the appraisal process means clearly articulating how the community will proceed virtually (roles and responsibilities) and what the new expectations are for each role (appraisals) while continuing to hold the same One School process of reflection, self-appraisal, meeting, and goal setting. Once these documents are created, then the process can continue virtually following the same time frame.

NOTES

1. See Chapter 8 for more on communication tools.
2. "Citizen of the World: Key Montessori Readings," *San Remo Lectures 1949*, p. 104.
3. Priya Parker. The Art of Gathering: How We Meet and Why It Matters. Penguin Books Ltd, 2019.
4. See Chapter 9 for more on child study action plans.

Chapter 6
Organize

Freedom without organization of work would be useless. The child left free without means of work would go to waste, just as a new-born baby, if left free without nourishment, would die of starvation. The organization of the work, therefore, is the cornerstone of this new structure of goodness [in education], but even that organization would be in vain without the liberty to make use of it.

—Maria Montessori, *Dr. Montessori's Own Handbook:*
A Short Guide to Her Ideas and Materials

To flourish as One School, there needs to be robust organization running behind the scenes. Where calibration is the heart of One School, organization is the skeleton. The way a school is organized can support or hinder calibration. To organize, meaning to arrange into a structured order, as a school community is thus satisfying a human tendency and providing coherence and a shared view of the work.

A first step in this process of getting organized might be to create a big-picture road map of the work that happens over a school year to share with your team. This is a thoughtful consideration of the various parts that make up the whole and acts as a systems map to keep track of and thus be able to support the work across the school year. When laying it out, as shown in Figure 6.1, it will be evident to everyone when the crunch times are and when there is a bit more bandwidth. This will help direct new events to a time when they would be most likely to be attended and enjoyed or even allow the team to turn down some opportunities in recognition of the possibility for overload. The job of a One School leader is to keep track of the whole system to ensure it's not stretched beyond maximum capacity.

Having a whole-school yearlong school calendar also allows you to think about the organizing structures that support each area and to strengthen them as needed. This might be the awareness that there is a lot of work in the Assessment category and no one designated to do this work, which could explain why the whole leadership team feels frazzled for chunks of time across the year. Enlisting a skilled interventionist to hold this responsibility might then provide relief to the whole system as others are then more able to focus on their areas.

While there are many bones in the organizing structures of your school, the whole-school Montessori method focuses on:

- *Observation*: Creating a culture of observers who develop the arc of learning for the children
- *Professional development:* Creating an arc of learning for the whole school
- *Family engagement*: Creating an arc of learning for families

Before looking at each one of these, let's understand their place in our larger One School structure. Figure 6.2 shows the Montessori triad: the environment, the adult, and the child.

This is a guiding image in Montessori and a lens that supports strong implementation of the method. Used here, it is a reminder of the considerations in implementation of our One School tools: that the prepared environment and the prepared adult act in service of the whole child.

Whole School Montessori Method

Yearlong School Calendar

	Assessment Test Coordinator	Appraisals Administration	Professional Development Coach	Classroom Guides	Family Education Coach	Transitions Coach	Enrollment Administration	Community Events Family Engagement	Heads UP! Leadership	Attendance Administration
August	State test Data Review		Staff retreat Distribute PD calendar For the year, staff handbook & review all protocols	Prepare environment Create plan for the year		Distribute Transition Touchstone lists	Send home family handbook	Create staff birthday list	Ready Compact & Reading Logs Home!	Distribute Attendance Policy to families & Staff
September	All: Reading Inventory Primary: Administer Peabody Elementary: MAP	Objective setting by 9/15 Montessori reflection and personal goal setting	Begin 1st & 3rd staff meetings Monthly ½ day PD	Diagnostic assessments review	Whole school Montessori	Planning late transitions	New Family orientation	School picnic		Begin data collection on tardy and absent students
October	Montessori Data team	First set of Appraisals for NT begin 10/15	Monthly ½ day PD	Family surveys Prepare Progress Reports	Supporting Independence	Final class placement decisions for all late transitions	Admissions Open House Tues/Thurs Observations	International Dinner	Halloween	Attendance review by 10/15
November	Reading Assessment District Benchmark	Completed by 11/30 Review and reflection following family conferences	Monthly ½ day PD	Family Conferences Fall assessments Data Teams	Montessori Philosophy	Discuss potential 4th year for students at conferences	Admissions Open House: Tues/Thurs Observations	Gratitude Celebration	Garden Day Diwali	
December	Data Review		Monthly ½ day PD & Holiday celebration		Winter celebration		Admissions Open House Tues/Thurs Observations	Holiday event	Christmas, Hanukkah, Kwanzaa	Attendance review by 12/15
January	Reading Assessment District Benchmark	Review of Montessori reflection and personal goals by 1/15 Second set of Evaluations begin For NT 1/5 Completed by 1/30	Monthly ½ day PD	Optional Family Conferences	Guest Lecture; Preliminary list for transition	Primary guides observe in LE	Admissions Open House Tues/Thurs Observations	MLK		

	Assessment Test Coordinator	Appraisals Administration	Professional Development Coach	Classroom Guides	Family Education Coach	Transitions Coach	Enrollment Administration	Community Events Family Engagement	Heads UP! Leadership	Attendance Administration
February	Data Review	Third set of Evaluations for NT begin 2/1 Completed by 2/15	Monthly ½ day PD		Freedom & Responsibility	Begin class placement process	Tues/Thurs Observations	Black History Month	Valentines, Black History	Attendance review by 2/15
March	State testing	Progress/Modification Conference for TT done by 3/15	Monthly ½ day PD	Spring assessments Data Team	Assessment talk	Tentative class lists Finalize 4th year for students with families	LOTTERY Tues/Thurs Prospective family visits	Pasta Potluck	Administrative Day	
April	Summer School Assessments	Review and reflection following Family conferences	Monthly ½ day PD		Transition talk Primary to Elementary- Invite families to observe Elementary	EI guides to observe Transition visits	Tues/Thurs Prospective Family visits Lottery deadline 4/15	Outdoor Celebration	Garden Day	Attendance review by 4/10 (may impact GFY)
May	Reading Assessment MAP District Benchmark	Year End Appraisal/ Modification Conference for TT by 5/30	Monthly ½ day PD Survey staff about PD	Prepare Progress Reports Family Conferences	Summer with your Montessori Child	Placement Letters go out to families	New Family orientation, dinner	Garden event	Mother's Day	
June	Data Review	Final review and evaluation of Montessori reflection and personal goals	Final PD- Staff Retreat Planning meetings for next year's calendar	Inventory Clean Make materials Order Replacements	Year-end celebration	Simultaneous Visiting Day	Summer reading program	Field Day	Father's Day	
July	District trainings		Create PD calendar for the year			Transparent Classroom roster updates				Review Atten. policy

Figure 6.1 Whole-School Montessori Method Yearlong School Calendar.

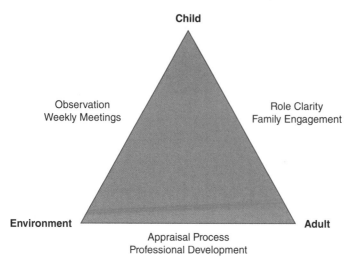

Child

Observation
Weekly Meetings

Role Clarity
Family Engagement

Environment

Adult

Appraisal Process
Professional Development

Figure 6.2 Montessori Triad.

OBSERVATION: THE PREPARED ENVIRONMENT

Observation, as a central organizing principle of the method, is a vehicle to organize our One School approach. Without a shared regular practice of how to engage in observation, communities tend to be split with some knowing how to do it and doing it, some knowing how to do it but not doing it, and others not knowing how to do it at all. To be truly unified, we must all share in this central Montessori practice. What follows is a brief overview, meant to be an introduction, a taste to launch your school's observation journey.

In *The Advanced Montessori Method,* Maria Montessori asks us to put ourselves in immediate relation with the truth through observation:

> The vision of the teacher should be at once precise like that of the scientist, and spiritual like that of the saint. The preparation for science and the preparation for sanctity should form a new soul, for the attitude of the teacher should be at once positive, scientific and spiritual. Positive and scientific, because she has an exact task to perform, and it is necessary that she should put herself into immediate relation with the truth by means of rigorous observation. . . . Spiritual, because it is to man that his powers of observation are to be applied, and because the characteristics of the creature who is to be his particular subject of observation are spiritual.

Molly O'Shaughnessy echoes this in her article "The Observation Scientist":[1] "As Montessori educators we must develop the art of observation and become observations artists—both spiritually and scientifically. The two must work in concert to fully serve the child."

The question is where do people develop these skills? Observation is emphasized in every teacher preparation course for both lead guides and assistants, in Montessori coaches preparation, and in many Montessori leadership courses. It sits squarely at the center of our practice, yet it is not widely practiced on a reliable basis. We know we need to do it, yet in many schools and classrooms it is not prioritized and therefore doesn't happen consistently. Without practice there is no hope of becoming "observations artists," where we are regularly collecting data to inform our work with children. As a result, we are only partially implementing the method, using moves informed by the observations Montessori made 100 years ago but not on our own observations of what is before us now – leaving us outside of an "immediate relation with the truth."

Traveling between public programs across the country and engaging in conversations about observation with practitioners filling every role in the school allowed for some insights regarding obstacles to observation:

- Time: Everything else seems more urgent.
- View: The view people observe from tends to be a negative one.
- Skill: People don't know how to do it.

These impact people's ability and willingness to engage in the cycle of observation necessary to fully implement the method.

Time

The number one reason people offer for not observing is time. There are two parts to this: (1) the belief that there is not enough time; and (2) that observation is not the best use of the time. If the pace is such that everything else seems more urgent, then the deprioritization of this central element often begins subconsciously. It was also shared that teachers aren't comfortable if the administrator of the school comes by and they are sitting there "doing nothing" – especially if all the children are not yet productively engaged. Therefore they don't observe and thus miss the opportunity to gain information and insight into how to more productively engage all their learners. This connects to a school culture where the school leaders observe only for evaluation purposes – a productive task that is required. If school leaders value and prioritize observation, then they are in classrooms weekly, sitting in the observation chair, using the shared observation tool, learning about the school they serve.

View

The second insight regarding obstacles to observation is aversion based on a negative view. As people invested in outcomes, there can be a tendency to note only the discrepancy between what we want to see and what we are seeing – what we want the program to look like and what it looks like in the moment of observation. Rather than noting what is working and building on it, practitioners feel deflated to see the areas that are not working well yet. This often propels them to want to immediately correct what they are seeing, thus blurring the boundaries between observation and active involvement as classroom teachers continue to try to manage things from the observation chair.[2] This adds confusion for the children about the function of the observation chair and opens it up for them to continue to seek help from adults sitting there, which in turn impacts the ability of the adult to truly observe.

These obstacles are particularly true for new classrooms or new schools when there is so much to do and there has not yet been an opportunity for children to settle into work. As a result of not observing during this critical time, much is missed, and it can actually take longer for the program to settle. Without the perspective and insights gained through regular seated observation, it is difficult to chart a course that will lead most expediently through the natural initial choppy days and raises blinders to creating a meaningful arc of learning for the children.

Skill

The final insight rises from both observation and conversation: People don't observe regularly because they don't know how. To observe is not simple. It is a complex task requiring skills built over time through use. The One School approach to observation clarifies the expectation that everyone in the community becomes a skilled observer and offers guidance, time, and tools to support regular observations. As Montessori reminds us in her London Course:[3]

> It would seem that to know how to observe was very simple, and needed no explanation. Perhaps you think it would be sufficient to be in a classroom in a school, and to look and see what happens. But to observe is not as simple as that. Any methodical observation which one wishes to make requires preparation. Observation is one of those things of which we frequently speak, and of which we form an inexact or false idea. It should be sufficient to consider what occurs in all the sciences which depend on observation. The observers in the various sciences must have a special preparation.

To offer the community that preparation, there must be professional development on observation. This begins as part of their orientation[4] and continues through coaching and professional development with colleagues. Having a unified understanding, shared language, and a common tool will support the community in the daily practice.

SCANNING

An important shared starting place is that scanning the room does not fulfill the goal of observation. Though it does have a role in serving the classroom, it is distinctly different from a seated observation.

Scanning: Brief glimpses of the classroom to mentally record the moment-to-moment activities of the class. Done after presentations and while circulating.

Direct Aim

- To get a sense of what is going on in the room: What is the tenor?
- To know where to go and who needs redirection or assistance: Who seems to need support to reengage?
- To track the social dynamics and variations: Are there conflicts arising? Which children are connecting?

Indirect Aim To stay in touch emotionally and spiritually

This is important information to have and a necessary practice, yet it is not authentic observation. The information gained through a seated observation adds exponentially to this beginning, for without further study there can be misinterpretation or misunderstanding based on pieces picked up through scanning.

Seated Observation

A seated observation is where adults are able to step outside of their role to watch closely what is happening before them. There is a designated chair in each classroom as the prepared environment for observation. It is situated to allow the observer to take in the whole classroom simply by turning their head and thus creating as little disturbance as possible. The goal is for the observer to fade and eventually become invisible so that the children may continue working as though the observer was not there.

Observing: Sitting in a chair 3–20 minutes at least three times daily to physically record using an observation tool.

Direct Aims

- To gauge learner engagement: How many children are deeply engaged?
- To notice trends: Do children have work out they are not engaged with?

- To determine grace and courtesy lessons needed: Is there a lot of interrupting?

- To evaluate your lessons: Do the learners know the intended use of the material, and are they learning as a result?

- To note characteristics and tendencies: Are learners showing an interest in order? Is there any sign of a desire to repeat?

- To assess students' academic ability: Are they able to successfully complete tasks with a low margin of error?

- To keep track of student progress and to plan future instruction: What material or lesson are they ready for now?

- To gain insight into the children and come to know them more fully: How are they interacting with each other – shyly, kindly, loudly, collaboratively?

- To understand and evaluate the environment's role: Is there an area where children are tripping or bumping? Is there an open runway encouraging races?

Indirect Aim: To take yourself out of the activity, to center and regain perspective.

Often Montessori practitioners default to the use of only scanning as their observation method, which leaves them without critical information needed for supporting prime conditions for learning for all children. The idea of the seated observation is to focus on something and ask questions about what is being observed.

Objectivity comes into play when we are observing, to reserve judgment if we don't see what we are looking for, to not fall into negativity, but instead think about what we will do next. Observation sparks action. If a tendency is not active – for example, a primary child is not repeating or an elementary child is not engaged – first we look at the environment (What needs to change to offer more ideal conditions?), and then we look at ourselves (What do I need to do next?), allowing us to emerge from observation with a greater sense of purpose and direction.

Observation then is an integral part of being child centered. We do not start with only what we want to teach, which is the curriculum. Our starting point is also the child's needs. It is only through observation that we can offer the child activities that meet their developmental needs. Thus, we use observation to find and follow the children's spontaneous acts. We actually see the child in the process of developing. We see the child make important discoveries and connections between different areas of knowledge. We also see the child integrate knowledge. Without observation, we will not be able to offer right child, right time, right material – matching each child to a specific material at just the right time to capture their interest and move their learning along.

We use observation to gain insights into the nature of the individual child. Developmental stages are universal, but each child is unique. We want to observe life unfolding so we can understand more clearly how to support and guide the children we serve. Ensuring that all members of the community hold this understanding will support a shared sense of responsibility to observe. Whether the person is an interventionist, a physical education teacher, or an assistant principal, their ability to do their job well will be enhanced by time spent observing. Then everyone will come to understand more clearly how they can support and guide the children and the adults who serve them.

One way to ensure observation is to provide time for people to do it. For classroom adults this means condoning it as an important use of their time during school hours with children. This way people will not feel caught "doing nothing" but rather seen as carrying out one of the school's shared goals. It also means modeling it by doing it. One principal, in her first year at a public Montessori school, realized it was the end of November and she hadn't observed classrooms yet except to evaluate. She set a goal to observe daily in December and invited the full staff to join her in the challenge. This opened up the conversation about observation and how to prioritize it across the whole school. Joining in the spirit of it, one of the teachers then created a column in the daily sign-out log for people to check if they had completed their daily observation. The unity that resulted was something a new district principal may have otherwise spent much longer to develop, yet centering her time around the important practice for the teachers spoke volumes about her commitment to the method.

Tools

Offering people training and time to observe is completed by offering them shared tools for observation:

- Whole-class engagement
- Individual child
- The environment

Linking these to the Montessori triad, the environment observation tool supports the work of the environment to meet the needs of its learners, the whole-class engagement observation tool supports the work of the adult through reflection and coaching, and the individual child observation tool supports serving the whole child through nautilus and child study.[5]

Figure 6.3 shows an example of a shared tool[6] to observe for whole-class engagement.

Observing Work Engagement: Primary

This observation rubric helps the observer develop a detailed understanding of the level of engagement in a Primary classroom. It can be used as a tool for self-assessment, in coaching, or group reflection.

School/Classroom:

Visit focus: _____ # of children: _____ Date: _____

Work Engagement of Children

Observe for two minutes or until you count each student once. Tally each category observed, making one tally mark per student.

At the beginning of the visit Time:	ENGAGING IN WORK	USING WORK AS A PROP	IN BETWEEN WORK	RECEIVING HELP	WANDERING/ INTERFERING	DISRUPTING
	engaging in age-appropriate and concentrated work with peers or in presentation	not engaging with material or passively allowing peers to complete without attending	in process of selecting, setting up, observing others, or putting away work	consulting with or receiving direction from a teacher in class	moving aimlessly or conversing without focus	dangerous, demeaning, destructive-prevents others from concentrating
tally marks						
totals						

Work with Montessori Materials Observed

*Indicate material being used as prop

PRACTICAL LIFE	SENSORIAL	MATHEMATICS	LANGUAGE	OTHER

Work Engagement of Children (Repeat)

At the end of the visit Time:	ENGAGING IN WORK	USING WORK AS A PROP	IN BETWEEN WORK	RECEIVING HELP	WANDERING/ INTERFERING	DISRUPTING
	engaging in age-appropriate and concentrated work with peers or in presentation	not engaging with material or passively allowing peers to complete without attending	in process of selecting, setting up, observing others, or putting away work	consulting with or receiving direction from a teacher in class	moving aimlessly or conversing without focus	dangerous, demeaning, destructive-prevents others from concentrating
tally marks						
totals						

Revised 3/2019

NATIONAL CENTER FOR MONTESSORI IN THE PUBLIC SECTOR

© 2019 • NCMPS.ORG

Figure 6.3 Sample Shared Observation Tool.

The *Observing Work Engagement* tool originated in Springfield Public Schools as an alternative to the district walk-through observation tool, which was a series of tallies aligned with the conventional classrooms in the city. The leadership in the two public Montessori schools developed this observation tool to count what counts, which for the Montessori classrooms was engagement and use of Montessori materials. This tool was further developed in Hartford Public Schools and through work at the National Center for Montessori in the Public Sector, where it was shared with schools across the country through the Montessori coaches training. It is now being used in Montessori programs around the world to provide a shared observation tool for school communities.

This tool offers insights and opens reflective conversations around what's going on in the classroom. At the top, observers note what children are doing at the start of the time and then repeat that again as they complete the observation. These tally marks can then become data offering classroom adults information around learner engagement: how many children are fully engaged in the material before them? If multiple observations show a high number of children waiting for or receiving help from a classroom adult, that might spark questions around fostering independence or creating systems to support autonomy or the need to reintroduce procedures and routines. The questions will be specific to the classroom where the observation took place, such as the plane of development, experience of the classroom adults, and nature of the class community. The point is that the observation tool helps to surface questions that will prompt changes within the environment to further support a more optimal learning environment. Here the tool supports the goal of observation as "scientific, because she has an exact task to perform, and it is necessary that she should put herself into immediate relation with the truth."[7]

To rejuvenate the practice of observation, offering the community shared tools will concretize the work. It matters less which specific tools you use and more that you have tools that are used across the whole school. Shared tools allow both seasoned practitioners and newcomers to have a common approach to observation and will allow for a growing calibrated use of the tool leading to generation of shared data in support of all learners.

Beyond tools for classroom adults are observation tools that serve a particular function for the community. As your school grows into the practice of observation and the use of it to guide the program, the need for more shared tools will likely emerge. Here are a few used by many schools to support their implementation of the whole-school Montessori method.

- *Visitor observation:* Distributed from the main office and used by all outside visitors to the classroom. This tool offers guidelines for observation, orients them to the Montessori prepared environment, and focuses their attention on what to look for during their time.

- *Interview lesson observation:* Used by the interview team during the onboarding process to make notes on one lesson given by an applicant.[8]

- *Transition family observation:* Families who would like to observe the new environment their child will be entering in the coming year use this tool to focus their time and note their questions to review with the Montessori coach.[9]

- *Peer observation:* This tool provides a focus on learning rather than judging asking the observer to document reflections on specific questions.[10] It's used as part of a process organized by the Montessori coach with a follow-up conversation to debrief, centered not on the observer's critique of the other classroom but rather on the gained insights about their own classroom and practice.

Whole-School Observation

In addition to classroom observations of children, observation is also used as a way of ensuring the whole school is a Montessori environment prepared for those who work within it. This means attention to the physical organization and preparation that will lead to the desired order and beauty as well as the spiritual preparation that will lead to the desired outcomes of One School: unity, awareness, power, structure, autonomy. This can happen through scanning: What are all those boxes doing there? Why are children's coats falling across the hallway floor? It can also happen through intentional seated (or in many cases standing aside) observation of the various transitions and meetings within a school day: How are people passing through the hallways? What is the experience at recess? Arrival? Dismissal? Staff meetings? Individualized education plan meetings? Is everyone on the same page, working from the same understanding toward the same desired goals?

For the One School component, observation becomes the source of creating the prepared environment of the whole school. Therefore, ensuring everyone is growing and developing skills and doing it regularly is a central aspect of implementation.

PROFESSIONAL DEVELOPMENT: THE PREPARED ADULT

Creating a Montessori environment for both children and adults also means honoring the ongoing learning within the adult community in the school. This needs to be as intentional and well-executed as the learning for the children in a Montessori school. We go into working with children following a sequence of lessons, aware of both the direct and indirect aims of each one. We offer a three-period lesson where we present the information, offer practice with the new information, and return to review prior learning before adding the next piece. We recognize that learners will bring different prior knowledge to that first lesson and that there will be a range of comfort and skill within the learning. We offer a variety of ways a learner might practice the new learning while building in a control of error to support them. We anticipate areas of struggle and use isolation of difficulty to approach these – making time and space for learners to acquire extra practice in these areas before adding the next piece of learning.

Imagine the sense of community that would arise if we applied all of this to the learning that is organized for the adults.

This can be done through a cycle of learning that begins with an assessment of what learning is needed by the community. There is likely a wide range of topics from the art of observation to trauma-informed practices to literacy to antibias, antiracist (ABAR) and culturally responsive pedagogy (CRP) work to curriculum alignment to learning differences . . . the list is endless. The question is, what does your community need the most? Schools that attempt to cover it all in the same year find they have traded going wide for going deep. Because they are covering so many topics they are not able to employ the Montessori method in the way information is shared and digested, and the year ends with the professional development having minimal impact on practice. Establishing priorities for a three-year cycle of development allows for a slower, more intentional, and more impactful experience for the community, which as a result means the learning is more likely to be applied. And that is ultimately the whole point of professional development: to create change in practice so that children may have a richer experience of learning. Once the priorities for the year are established, the next step is to develop a yearlong calendar mapping out what will be learned across the whole year.

One school that implemented this practice began it after they discovered that children's literacy skills were falling in lower elementary. They first set out to understand the assessment results. Through data analysis, team meeting discussions, and observation they first recognized that there was a variation across levels in teachers' understanding of how to give the school's reading assessment. This variation meant higher scores for children leaving primary and a subsequent drop in lower elementary children's scores upon arrival in lower elementary. Further conversation with the primary team revealed that their deep connection with the children influenced their scoring of the assessments: "I know she knows that, even if she couldn't get it that one time." The receiving lower elementary teachers, who had not developed a relationship with the children yet, were scoring simply based on what the child demonstrated during the assessment. This provided greater understanding of the discrepancy. In addition, through further investigation, they recognized an unevenness in teachers' comfort and skill teaching literacy.

With this emerging understanding of the drop in student scores, they recognized that they needed a yearlong focus on literacy to address the issue as a school community. From there, they were then able to create a yearlong professional development plan that focused on literacy. Beginning on an August professional development day, they all learned together how to administer the individual reading assessment and how to use the score as a tool to provide direct instruction to meet the individual needs of the learner. The session was led by a highly competent specialist who understood both the complexity of the assessment and the human inclinations that contribute to misaligned scores. The goal was for the community, across levels and roles, to be able to assess a single reader and arrive at the same reading level.

This was followed by regular sessions that began with everyone together and then divided into level teams to strengthen the understanding of, and ability to implement, the literacy curriculum with all learners. There were special sessions across the year to address remedial work, accommodations, and extensions using Montessori materials.

The year ended with an energized staff, aligned and engaged in ongoing discussions, material making, and lesson innovation. There was also improved data on the reading assessment for the majority of learners with a more seamless transition from primary into lower elementary.

Here we see the power of calibration as a result of organization. A structured professional development plan, such as the one shown in Figure 6.4, was carefully organized and well implemented, allowing the whole school of adults and children to move forward in their learning.

Sample Professional Development Overview

Month	Leads	Assistants	Leadership	Families
August	Introduction of PD structures: Literacy Assessment Training Individual Development Plan goals			Back to School Night
September	System of Justness			Four Planes of Development
	Literacy Instruction	The Assistant's Role: Grace and Courtesy	Systems Reflection Data Review	
October	Q1 Data Team Meetings	The Assistant's Role: Oral Language	Appraisal schedule	Montessori at Home
	Montessori Literacy Materials Focus			Family Literacy Night
November	Linking Literacy Instruction to Montessori Materials		Culture Audit and Learning Environment Review	Gratitude Gathering
December	Step Back: Mission/Vision Surveys			Family Conferences Family Satisfaction Surveys
January	Full Day In-Service: *Q2 Data Team Meetings- focus on literacy Observation and Recordkeeping*			Dr. King Day of Service
February	Literacy Remedial Work and Accomodations		Leadership Roles Review	Family Math Night
March	Q3 Data Team Meetings			Transition Talk
April	Preparing Transitioning learners	The Assistant's Role: Transitions and Observations	Culture Audit and Learning Environment Review	Family Food Fest
May	Class Placement Meetings		End of Year Appraisals	End of Year Celebration Family Conferences
	Q4 Data Team Meetings, Year End Reflections, Inventory and Closing Up			Family Feedback Survey

Figure 6.4 Sample Professional Development Calendar.

As your school completes year one of the whole-school Montessori method it will be important to begin a regular cycle of reflection. One place this will happen is around professional learning. At the end of the year, a professional development survey (Figure 6.5) is distributed that holds all the sessions from that year. Participants are asked to rank them, with #1 representing the most valuable session and the highest number representing the session of least value.

Professional Development Survey

Please rank the following in order of value:

_____ **Montessori Philosophy**

_____ **Montessori materials**

_____ **Literacy**

_____ **Curriculum alignment**

_____ **Special Needs students**

_____ **Great Lessons**

_____ **Transparent Classroom**

_____ **Observation**

_____ **Practical Life extensions**

_____ **Supports for struggling students**

Which session had the greatest impact on your practice? Why? _____

_____

_____

What do you want to learn about in the coming year? _____

_____

_____

What topics would you be willing to present in the coming year? _____

_____

Name:_____ **Role:**_____

Figure 6.5 Sample Professional Development Year-End Survey.

The last question opens the door for a team approach to professional learning and creates the opportunity to cultivate other voices to share their professional knowledge with the wider community. Ultimately this leads to a self-sustaining system that feeds itself where everyone is growing together – coaching and being coached. In the example of the yearlong focus on literacy, a teacher with specialized training on English language learning and experience in that area presented a session. The strategies and materials she shared led to innovating Montessori materials and more sophisticated presentations across all classrooms. It also cued the community to remember that everyone's past learning and experience are valuable and amplified when shared with others. Classroom adults were able to go directly to that teacher if they were unsure about a concept, material, or lesson, which further strengthened the experience of One School.

The leadership team collects and analyzes the results of the professional development survey to see what had an impact on the community (Figure 6.6). This data then becomes one piece of information for the team to use in building the next cycle of learning for adults.

The survey is looked at along with assessment data from that school year and the year-end reflection[11] results from staff. Using all three data points, there emerges the necessary theme for the coming year's professional development. The survey asks directly what the community would like to learn about in the coming year, the assessment data shows where children are struggling and opens the topic of how the adults might be better prepared in that area, and the year-end reflection surfaces school-wide concerns that might also be addressed through the coming year's professional development. In this way leadership is able to provide meaningful learning experiences for the school-based adults, which create an arc of learning that follows through from introduction to practice to mastery.

In addition, the professional development survey results reveal what people found useful, allowing the leadership team to reflect on why some sessions were more successful than others and how to create stronger sessions going forward. Strengthening the learning experience for the unique community being served brings us back to Chapter 2 and the discussion of constructivist thinking. Rather than seeing the adults as empty vessels to be filled with knowledge, professional development is an opportunity to celebrate and use all the knowledge brought from various backgrounds and past experiences. It is an opportunity to interact with the environment to build experiences that lead to deeper insight and learning.

Professional Development Survey Results

Highest ranked PD:

Topic	Total	%	Majority
Montessori Philosophy	18	58%	All
Special Needs	14	45%	Primary, LE
Literacy	12	39%	Lead Teachers
Support for Struggling Students	11	35%	All
Montessori Materials	11	35%	Assistants, Interventionists, Special Educators

Suggestions:

- Special Needs topics: Autism Spectrum Disorders, ADHD, Down Syndrome, ABA
- Reading support: More Guided Reading, Remedial Montessori, Transition skills
- Technology topics: More Transparent Classroom, Excel, Google Docs
- Other topics: Sensorial, observation work curves

Greatest impact:

Topic	Comments
Guided Reading	"Great instruction, which transferred easily into the classroom." "I love this program and it has been easy and fun to implement." "It was in-depth and something we needed to implement."
Montessori Materials	"Practicing with colleagues was super and gave us all an idea of what results to aim for when we work with students." "It helped me to better understand how to use these materials in the classroom."
Support for Struggling Students	"I learned something new to try with my students" "Gave me language to use and steps to follow." "It was informative and useful."

Figure 6.6 Sample Professional Development Year-End Survey Results.

NEW WORLD CONSIDERATIONS

During the shift to all things virtual in a global pandemic, schools that had established a rhythm of professional development – with time allotted and a clear schedule communicated to the community – were able to continue this without interruption by simply converting to a virtual format. What many schools did, however, is to shift the topic of their PD time to focus on the new challenges arising from the change in modality. Since there was already allotted time, teams were able to work together to arrive at their New World Learning plan.

Going forward there will need to be time built into the yearly professional development calendar to reflect on, brainstorm, and adjust the plan toward continuous improvement of identified undeveloped skills. New opportunities for professional development focused on technology will be important to incorporate for the community so that everyone is moving toward optimal use of the tools they may need to reach children.

FAMILY ENGAGEMENT: SERVING THE WHOLE CHILD

An important element of One School is our understanding of families as part of that. As mentioned in Chapter 3, using the word *family* creates an inclusive framework for whoever supports the child rather than a limiting one through use of the term *parent*. Families are part of the ecosystem in which the school exists and need to be held as partners in the education of the children. There are many ways we extend this vision. First, it's essential to understand that families are the child's first educator and therefore an important member of the team. Second, we connect with families through regular family conferences and a family–teacher organization, or similar organization used in your community, that works on unified projects. And third, we are responsible for engaging families around understanding this unique method of education.

Not every family selects a Montessori school for its method and mission, and therefore to live out a One School philosophy we must organize to ensure everyone is brought into the philosophy that unites the school. The aspects of interdependence; school-wide grace and courtesy; and a clear, shared mission can be held by families only if there is sufficient orientation and ongoing opportunities for learning. Crafting a family engagement yearlong calendar will support this process as it communicates the value of lifelong learning to the whole community. It is also an opportunity for ongoing touch points with families that focus less on their individual child and more on the environment in which their child is spending their days.

Reaching out to ensure equitable access to these opportunities is the first step when creating your calendar. Learning when people are available, both day of the week and time of the day, will guide your scheduling, making an effort to vary the touchpoints – morning, afternoon, and evening – to reach everyone.

This prevents family engagement from being owned by one particular portion of the community, especially if there are intentional, personal invitations being given to break down barriers and empower the caregivers for every child in the school. Information is nourishment, yet without organization it can't reach everyone. When it does, however, it allows further agency for families to engage in the ongoing education of their child.

Montessori Family Engagement Calendar for Fall 2020

Date	Topic	Content
8/24 3pm.	Montessori at Home	Overview of how to prepare your home environment developmentally for your child. Concepts: Isolation of difficulty, repetition, control of movement, engagement/concentration.
8/31 8:15 am.	Managing Distance Learning	Review and clarifications about elements of the school's Distance Learning plan. Plenty of time for questions from families.
9/14 7pm.	Fostering Independence	Presentation of independence as a critical element of the Montessori method and the importance of maintaining this at home. Specific examples of how to foster independence during DL.
9/21 3pm.	Working with your emerging reader	Presentation on the skills of learning to read and an example (done by someone with a child at home?) of what reading with your child looks like.
9/28 8:15 am.	Concrete to Abstract	Presentation on the Sensorial/Geometry/Math curriculum as based on this idea. Ideas of how to support some hands-on elements during DL.
10/5 7pm.	Supporting the emotional life of your child during the pandemic	Presentation through the lens of the Planes of Development with examples of what families may be seeing/experiencing during the pandemic and how to respond.
10/19 3pm.	The role of technology	Clear understanding of technology and its role in Montessori education. This could be an opportunity to offer guidance around screen time during this time.
10/26 8:15 am.	Spoken Language	Sharing of oral language games and activities as well as the importance of building spoken language as a foundation for literacy.
11/2 7pm.	Freedom and Responsibility	Exploring the inter-relationship between these two concepts and the importance of balance. Discuss how that relates to expectations during DL
11/16 3pm.	Montessori Math	Unlocking the mystery and magic of the hands-on materials and why it is important not to jump to abstraction.

Figure 6.7 Sample Family Engagement Calendar.

As with the professional development calendar created for school-based adults, the family engagement calendar (Figure 6.7) is also created in advance of the school year based on survey data from families, input from classroom adults, and the need for regular topics such as planes of development and seamless transitions.

Opening the families up to more information and insight around the Montessori approach will not only strengthen their understanding of their child's school experience but also allow them to apply these principles and practices at home. The children in the school will then have a more unified experience of home and school, allowing them to fully engage in their natural development. Thus, through serving families we are serving the whole child.

NEW WORLD CONSIDERATIONS

With learning shifting to the home environment during 2020, there was a need for stronger, more frequent contact and support for families. The sample family engagement calendar shown in Figure 6.7 was created for schools starting the year off virtually. It offered guidance for families as they adjusted to the prolonged experience of children learning from home with topics such as preparing the home environment and fostering independence.

Practitioners discovered that moving from monthly meetings in person to weekly meetings virtually created a stronger sense of the school community, enlarging the One School experience and widening families' understanding of the Montessori method. Now it was no longer theoretical or about the power of learning through isolation of difficulty, but had moved into the shared arena between families and educators as families began to understand why children need to repeat. Through these regular touchpoints, families were able not only to understand abstractly what the program was offering but also to learn some practical skills and strategies to use with their learners at home.

ONE SCHOOL SUMMARY

One School calibration is built around our understanding of the human tendencies and the idea that we share needs and tendencies across the whole school. When these are met, there is a sense of satisfaction that is also shared across the whole school. Calibration means we are all attuned and working together for that shared satisfaction.

One School organization leverages the sturdiness of the Montessori triad. The triangle is the most stable geometric shape; using the lens of environment–adult–child offers us that same stability. Organization of the whole-school Montessori method focuses on these three elements together, allowing us to build a most stable school, an enduring one in which everyone's learning is considered.

The idea of One School is to create institutional clarity so that the school system can learn from itself in a self-sustaining manner, interdependent rather than dependent on any one person.

Calibration Checklist
- ☑ Weekly Meetings Process and Tools
- ☑ Role and Responsibility Clarity
- ☑ Appraisal Process and Tools

Organization Checklist
- ☑ Whole-School Montessori Method Yearlong School Calendar
- ☑ Observation Process and Tools
- ☑ Professional Development Process and Tools
- ☑ Family Engagement Process and Tools

Simple One School Move:

GREETING EVERY STAFF MEMBER AT THE START OF THE DAY.

This can be done a number of ways:

- – Standing in the main office, or where everyone signs in, with a cup of tea and a morning greeting as each person arrives.
- – Traveling to each classroom to say "Good morning! Do you need anything to start the day?" This is not only a regular checkpoint adults come to rely on so they don't have to track you down when there's a need, but it also lets you know that all the classrooms are covered and ready to receive children.
- – Have a morning gathering 5 minutes before the children arrive. All staff meet in a central location for a morning greeting, quick daily announcements, appreciations.

NOTES

1. Molly O'Shaughnessy. "The Observation Scientist," *NAMTA Journal* Vol. 41, No. 3 Summer 2016.
2. Wendy Calise offered this keynote address on the topic at Montessori Aotearoa New Zealand Annual Conference in 2011: The Eight Stages of Observation.
3. Maria Montessori. "Observation and Development from Dr. Montessori's 1946 London Training Course," *NAMTA Journal* Vol. 41, No. 3 Summer 2016.
4. See Chapter 10 on orienting new community members.
5. See Chapter 9.
6. This tool is now part of the National Center for Montessori in the public sector's *Assessment Playbook*. 2019. www.ncmps.org. The playbook includes versions for all three levels: primary, elementary, and adolescent.
7. Maria Montessori. *Advanced Montessori Method,* vol.1. India: Kalakshetra Publications. 1988, p. 113.
8. The full onboarding system is covered in Chapter 10.
9. The full seamless transitions system is covered in Chapter 9.
10. See a sample tool in the resources found at www.resilient-montessori.com.
11. More on this in Chapter 8.

PART III

Honest Talk

For such a delicate mission great art is required to suggest the right
moment and to limit intervention, lest one should disturb or lead astray
rather than help the soul which is coming to life and which will live by
virtue of its own efforts.

—The Discovery of the Child

If One School is the land beneath our feet, Honest Talk is the water surrounding
us. It is tidal, mutable, essential for life. Therefore understanding how to activate real, open conversations in your school is the subject of this next section.

All of the trust that has been built through the moves of creating a One
School culture has established a foundation that will allow for personal and
professional growth through Honest Talk. To cohere as One School, however,
there must be a prepared environment for open, clear conversations and to
understand the great art of the right moment. This allows all members of the
community to come forward as their full selves.

JOHARI WINDOW

To think about this more deeply, it's helpful to use the tool shown in
Figure PIII.1, developed in 1955 by American psychologists Joseph Luft and
Harry Ingham. The Johari window – named by combining its creators' first
names – is a way for people to better understand and cultivate their relationship with themselves and others. We can use their visual to help us understand
how honest conversation supports teaming.

Figure PIII.1 Communication Theory Graphic of Johari Window Model.

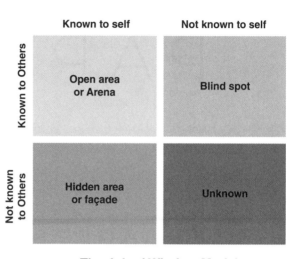

The Johari Window Model

As you see from the image, what we know about ourselves and what we share with others creates the *open area*, or the place of greatest teaming. This makes sense: the more we learn about ourselves and the more we are willing to reveal to others, the stronger we are in our shared work. An example of intentionally widening this area of greatest teaming would be for someone to choose to share that they struggle with writing English, which is not their first language, thus allowing the coach or a peer to offer support reading family communication in advance of it going out to the wider community. In one school where this was the case, a peer teacher went on to support their colleague to pass the state licensing exam. Building a culture that allows for honest talk means people aren't hiding parts they don't feel strong in or good about but are instead sharing those to continue to grow and to create a stronger experience for children and families.

The *hidden area* represents all that we do not say or share with our colleagues. If we work in a school that compels us to keep things hidden from others, then teaming is diminished. Often the school climate doesn't allow for people to openly acknowledge their lack of understanding or skill that could lead to asking for and receiving coaching. This hiding, whether it's that we don't know how to use the recordkeeping system or we no longer remember how to present a Montessori material, weakens our service to children and families. If, on the other hand, we are able to openly discuss pieces we don't know or are still learning, bringing them into the open area, then we grow stronger in our work.

Coaching is an essential component of building honest talk in your school through its natural intersection with exploring the hidden area. The Montessori coach, in weekly one-on-one reflection meetings, supports teachers in an open dialogue. The Montessori coach approaches the conversation not as an expert with all the answers but instead with a curiosity sparking questions, revealing the thinking of the teacher. This allows space for the teacher to see their next step and to be working within their own zone of proximal development to grow as a practitioner.

Without the opportunity to open up and reveal oneself, the hidden area can be a dangerous participant in divisions. When there are insiders and outsiders and information is withheld, this has an impact on the ability to live into one school, and it also has an impact on people's willingness to engage in honest talk. School leaders can do much to lead by example in this area.

There was a school leader who began his position having had a long career in school leadership without any experience in Montessori. His first move was to bring that into the open area by asking the coach for weekly coaching sessions in Montessori. He made these public for the whole staff after school, and any-one who wished was invited to join and participate in his education. These vol-untary 45-minute sessions had an immediate impact on the school community. At first they were joined by a couple people and then more each week until there was a regular mix of assistants, administrators, and even a couple Mon-tessori teachers, laughing and talking about "control of error" and "normaliza-tion" together. This signaled to everyone that the new leader was comfortable not knowing, that he had a fierce curiosity and an active sense of humor. An outgrowth was a full community understanding of the work being done while in service to the education of the new school leader. Within the first few months of his leadership he had communicated, in word and in deed, his commitment to lifelong learning and honest talk.

This resulted in one of the adolescent teachers walking into his office and declaring something like, "Okay, you said we can have honest talk here so I need you to know that I don't have enough background to be teaching science and would like to learn more." From that conversation, they selected a pro-gram, and the school supported her in completing coursework to offer richer content to her students: win–win.

The blind spot is another element of the Johari window that slows the work in our schools. It represents elements other people can see about us that we cannot see about ourselves. An easy way to think of this is having spinach in your teeth. Are you working with people who will let you know? If we are in a community where these things can be said, then we are able to change and grow at a more rapid rate. If in fact we are unaware that we are using a loud, sharp voice with children and no one in the community is willing to mention this, then the practice continues. If, on the other hand, honest talk is one of the school values, then any person might gently approach to say, "Do you need a break?" or "May I help?" These interruptions will allow for reflection and can be followed up with a coaching conversation at another time to discuss tone, volume, classroom management, relationship building with children, stress, or whatever is at the root of the behavior. In this way we are able to see things about ourselves that may at first be difficult to hear yet will lead us to implement the method with more fidelity. As Montessori tells us in *The Absorbent Mind*,". . . What matters is not so much correction in itself as that each individual should become aware of his own errors. . . . I need to know whether I am doing well or badly, and if – at first – I treated my own mistakes as unimportant, I have now become interested in them."[1] Coaching supports a friendliness with error and a community that is interested in becoming aware of errors rather than threatened and hiding from them.

The blind spot is especially ripe for work around implicit bias. Our unconscious behavior around race needs to be a topic that is openly discussed. Without the school-wide engagement in honest talk, led and modeled by school leaders, discussing issues of race can become unnecessarily complex. When we bring an open mind and an open heart, focused on the mission of the school, then we recognize that our changes are to bring benefit to children and families as much as for our own personal transformation. With this in mind, we recognize the power of everyone in the community to support the very best learning environment through honest talk.

These quadrants are not meant to be equivalent. Instead, through work both to bring the hidden area to light and to courageously push into the blind spot, we create a larger area of teaming that might look more like Figure PIII.2.

Figure PIII.2 Lid of the Montessori Binomial Cube.

This image of a Montessori material, known as the binomial cube, offers us a visual of a larger area of teaming. Rather than Figure PIII.1, where all the quadrants are the same size, how might reflection, coaching, and honest conversations allow for a larger open area in which to do the work? Creating a school culture around inviting people to show up fully (reducing the hidden zone) combined with a commitment to coaching (reducing the blind spot) means the square representing the open area could become the largest part of people's experience.

SUMMARY

Much of this work is thus about building relationships and trust over time. This can be done through a school-wide commitment to coaching and being coached. Therefore, the first part of honest talk is to appreciate the fundamental needs of the Montessori educator and to be able to use reflective coaching and directive coaching to guide conversations in service of those needs. Through this we establish norms and can engage in honest talk regularly as an expected part of how we will be together allowing us to nourish what Montessori referred to as the spiritual preparation of the Montessori educator.

The second aspect of honest talk is the commitment to a shared language of reverence and to high communication. We need to be interconnected in our work to develop and grow as educators, and we also need to be interconnected as a larger community. Having everyone on the same page, hearing and processing information at the same time, validates each person's importance in the larger system. When one portion of the school group is privy to information prior to others, this contributes to factions and threatens our actualization of One School. By creating structures for clear, ongoing honest talk, the community is validated as being inextricably important, making it more likely that people will be able to relax and trust.

NOTE

1. Montessori, M. (1949). *The Absorbent Mind*. India: Kalakshetra Publications p. 257.

Chapter 7
Nourish

If we are to have a better humanity, the grown-ups must be better. They must be less proud, less selfish, and less dictatorial. The adults must look at themselves and say, "Yes, I understand the problem."[1]

—Maria Montessori, 1946 London Lectures

There is a saying that information is power: If you are in the know, you have the power to make clear decisions. Information is also nourishment – it feeds people, allowing them to experience abundance rather than scarcity and activates a sense of security. When building One School, a foundational element is the feeling of security and trust. This chapter will move into the Montessori coaching model that serves that goal.

THE FUNDAMENTAL NEEDS OF THE MONTESSORI EDUCATOR

At the start of the work at Gerena Community School, I was in both a state administrative licensure course and a Montessori administrators course. For certification, I needed to complete a research project, and I chose to focus on the topic of coaching and mentoring new teachers. I sent surveys and did interviews with the teachers from both Zanetti and Gerena to understand the role of the Montessori coach. Not being a researcher, I then had a whole lot of information and no vehicle for understanding it. My family went away for a weekend and left me with it spread across the dining room table. I spent hours watching video-recorded interviews, reading survey results, and listening for common themes. Through that process, I found my method for organizing what people were talking about: their fundamental needs.

As a former Montessori elementary teacher, this framework for Montessori coaches working with classroom adults appeared through a Montessori material called *The Fundamental Needs of Humans.* Everything teachers were saying fit into either a material or a spiritual need, so the fundamental needs of the Montessori educator were born (Figure 7.1).

The graphic in Figure 7.1, which is based on the Montessori material but created as an original interpretation, allows us to keep in mind all the different pieces of the work for classroom adults. Each adult will have gifts and strengths

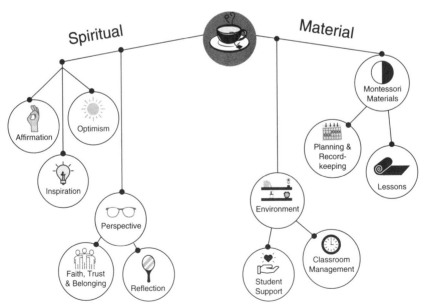

Figure 7.1 Fundamental Needs of the Montessori Educator.

as well as areas of growth. The Montessori coach uses this tool to create an open dialogue with teachers about all of these areas.

REFLECTIVE AND DIRECTIVE COACHING

Understanding the blind spot of Johari's window and recognizing that for all of us there are things we do not yet know and see about ourselves allows us to open into a coaching model that is both reflective and directive. Reflective coaching can be used with adults who are aware of some areas of growth and, when given the space to reflect, can do this work on their own. Directive coaching is appropriate with adults where attention needs to be heightened in certain areas of growth so they can serve the children in the classroom environment. These two approaches are used as needed, though generally directive coaching is used a larger percentage of the time with new teachers or in certain situations explored later in this chapter.

There are three goals for both reflective and directive coaching. These are easy to remember and will provide structure for successful coaching conversations:

- *Connect:* The coaching relationship is built on trust and begins with connection. Without a connection there is no ability to go deeper into the work together. Every coaching conversation opens at a point of connection, allowing the relationship to grow strong and the work to then go deep.

- *Communicate:* Within the coaching conversation there is a dialogue. As a general rule, the coach spends twice as much time listening as they do speaking. This allows the recipient of coaching to think about, talk about, and reflect on areas of practice. The focus of the conversation is their development and thus needs to be owned by them.

- *Collaborate:* Every coaching relationship is a collaboration and should end with the feeling that the person is not alone in the work, with the Montessori coach alongside them for the duration. Whatever risks they are ready to take, the coach is in it with them. Each conversation ends with a recognition of this shared work.

A Montessori coaching tool to frame these conversations is a checklist of the Fundamental Needs of the Montessori Educator shown in Figure 7.2. This can be used as a reminder of the emphasis of these conversations – to keep them from shifting into more therapeutic, less productive topics. At the bottom of each scenario will be the fundamental needs the coach was considering during the conversation.

FUNDAMENTAL NEEDS OF THE MONTESSORI EDUCATOR CHECKLIST

Spiritual	Material
Affirmation ☐ Emotional support and encouragement ☐ Being seen & empowered	**Environment** ☐ Order ☐ Resources ☐ View of the whole
Perspective ☐ Largest view ☐ Growth mindset ☐ Long-term thinking	**Montessori Materials** ☐ Knowledge of how to use them ☐ Understanding of sequence
Reflection ☐ Time for serious thought or consideration ☐ Opportunities to learn from actions	**Planning and Recordkeeping** ☐ Lesson plans & maintaining records ☐ Observation notes ☐ Progress reports & conferences ☐ Student portfolios
Faith, Trust, and Belonging ☐ Belief in the mission ☐ Relying on and predicting that others will do the right thing in times of uncertainty ☐ Equity of voice	**Lessons** ☐ Direct aim clarity ☐ Sequence ☐ Technical skill and grace in presentation ☐ Adaptability
Optimism ☐ Hopefulness and confidence about the future ☐ Ability to reframe to see what is working	**Supporting Key Children** ☐ Flexibility and skill development ☐ Planes of development
Inspiration ☐ Motivation toward greater goal of human flourishing ☐ Capacity to see progress and get energy from it	**Classroom Management** ☐ Preparation over correction ☐ Emotional awareness ☐ Systems

Figure 7.2 Fundamental Needs of the Montessori Educator Checklist.

Reflective Coaching

Reflective coaching in Montessori respects the agency of the adult and is predicated on the idea that we are all seekers and that with reflection we are able to see and understand what is needed to help us take the next steps. The coach is the guide who sits alongside asking questions that enable the adult to think into new areas.

This means that the coach is not the expert. They do not bring their agenda to the conversation: their laundry list of areas for the other person to change, fix, or improve. The Montessori coach, like the Montessori teacher, follows the learner as they unwind their own next steps, leaving their agenda at the door of coaching conversations. The fact that it may not be how the coach would approach the work is irrelevant. That the teacher is asking different questions than the coach would ask, thinking about different elements of the work than the coach is thinking about, is irrelevant. What is relevant is that every adult in the school feels connected to and committed to their own growth and development. They are the owners of this and not the Montessori coach. The Montessori coach, however, does create the time and space for this work, valuing each person's individual growth through the weekly use of time.

Some specific questions asked in a reflective coaching session allow this work to happen and be built on each week.

The Language of Montessori Reflective Coaching Conversations

- Connect: What's working?
- Communicate: What are you noticing? I noticed that too . . .
- Collaborate: What would you like to focus on this week? How can I help?

Connect: The question crafted to open the conversation keeps the emphasis on the positive changes. Strength-based coaching, like Montessori's strength-based learning, relies on building on the gifts of the practitioner to tackle the parts that are not yet going smoothly. In this way people are able to have their own Montessori successes, which we know builds intrinsic motivation. It is notable how difficult it is for many people to answer, "What's working?" Through research on the negativity bias,[1] we understand that without attention to it our default mode is to focus on what isn't working. This problem-oriented approach was once linked to our survival as we were kept alive by being ever-aware of potential trouble. However, in our growth as professionals it may slow us down as it creates conditions of trepidation rather than encouraging experimentation. Therefore the coach opens each session with a question about what is going well. This jumping-off point creates an immediate bond between the speaker and the listener as the speaker is seen and acknowledged for the hard work invested and by the regular opportunity to celebrate the successes.

Communicate: The conversation then moves into the dialogue, which is initiated by "What are you noticing?" This is an intentionally open-ended question that allows the speaker to take the conversation in any direction. It is based on the idea that everyone is using observation as a central tool and giving room for reflection on what is being observed. Again, the coach is listening more than speaking, asking a series of reflection questions to keep the conversation going, such as "Tell me more about that" or "What did you figure out . . ." or "What are the possibilities for what could happen next?" or even "What's your instinct about this?" These types of questions dignify the speaker with the space to unfurl their own thoughts, often coming to their own conclusions. At some point in this part of the conversation the coach will select an area to focus the conversation, offering, "I noticed that too." This forms the connection between the speaker and the listener and also suggests an opportunity to take the conversation deeper. Take this example from a portion of a coaching conversation with a primary teacher in his second year of teaching.

Reflective Coaching Scenario

COACH: What are you noticing?

TEACHER: I've been noticing that dismissal is not going well.

COACH: Tell me about that.

TEACHER: It's very loud and chaotic, and even though it only lasts a short while it's difficult to end the day that way after our more focused time in the classroom.

COACH: I noticed that, too, when I was passing yesterday. Tell me how dismissal begins.

TEACHER: First, I send the 3-year-olds out into the hall to change their shoes because they will take the longest.

COACH: Where are you at that time?

TEACHER: I'm in the classroom with the 4- and 5-year-olds. (Teacher grimaces, realizing a design flaw there.)

COACH: And what happens next?

TEACHER: Next, I send out the 4-year-olds because they will take the second longest to get their shoes changed.

COACH: And where are you then?

TEACHER: (sheepish smile) Still in the classroom! And I can hear it getting out of control in the hall! I should be in the hall?

COACH: What's a possibility for how it could happen instead?

TEACHER: I think I should send my leaders out there first. I'll give them a pep talk about their responsibilities beforehand and let them know they'll be expected to help the 4-year-olds when I send them out next.

COACH: Is there anyone who may have difficulty with that plan?

TEACHER: Maybe Brandon. (pause – thinking) But if I give him a special job he usually does better. (pause – thinking – looks at coach – coach smiles) Maybe a timer? Then he could be in charge of being sure everyone has their shoes changed before the 4-year-olds come out?

COACH: Do you feel good about that plan?

TEACHER: (nods with increasing vigor) I think it could work.

COACH: Would you like me to observe in the hall as you're implementing?

TEACHER: Would you? That would be great.

FUNDAMENTAL NEEDS

Material need: Classroom Management

Spiritual need: Reflection

This conversation was between a Montessori coach and a teacher who had a relationship that had developed over years as the teacher started as an assistant, went through training, and became a lead guide. As a result, there was no backpedaling during the conversation where defenses went up and the standard human default of explaining, defending, or proving was activated. Both people knew he was alone as a single adult in the afternoon and needed to figure out a dismissal plan he could manage. Instead of spending time processing this fact or justifying the approach taken, the conversation was able to move seamlessly into improving the situation.

As listed at the end of the scenario, the coach was holding the teacher's need for support with classroom management and his need for reflection time. As an experienced practitioner, the coach could have given him this plan at the outset of the conversation or when she noticed a rocky dismissal. Instead, by offering reflection time and waiting for the teacher to sort through it himself she allowed for a Montessori 'aha' where the realization happened inside the teacher instead of outside – resulting in even greater self-authorization and intrinsic motivation to take next steps, both important elements of transformative coaching conversations.

In this conversation the connection was fueled by a shared understanding of the issue, a shared belief in the teacher's ability to come up with a solution, and a shared commitment to the implementation of the new plan.

Collaborate: Each coaching conversation ends with a focused plan. This is a short-term accomplishment, or One Little Thing (an OLT) for the week – a small step taken during the time between meetings. In the conversation presented in the previous scenario, the plan was made to rework dismissal. The collaboration lay in the coach's offer to observe based on their shared understanding of both the issue and the plan to resolve it. The coach's observation then allows for a further deepening of the conversation next week as she will know what questions to ask and will have suggestions should the teacher get stuck. If she plans to continue authorizing the teacher, she will share her observations without commentary so the teacher can do the interpretation and come up with the refinement ideas. This might sound something like the following.

Reflective Coaching Scenario

COACH: What's working?

TEACHER: Dismissal is going better!

COACH: Yay! Tell me about it.

TEACHER: The older children really responded to the new responsibility and are taking it very seriously.

COACH: Wonderful. And Brandon?

TEACHER: The timer worked the first day, but then his energy became intense with the other children. They were feeling stressed about time, and this created conflicts so we decided to stop using the timer. Since then Brandon has had a hard time.

COACH: I noticed that, too. What do you think would help?

TEACHER: Honestly I hadn't thought about it until now. I guess I was hoping he would fall into the new routine like everyone else.

COACH: Does that usually happen with Brandon?

TEACHER: (sheepishly) No.

COACH: What do you think would help?

TEACHER: (pause – thinking) I don't actually know.

COACH: I noticed that Brandon values speed. Is that true?

TEACHER: Yes. (chuckling) He's always looking for the fastest way to do something.

COACH: Isn't he the oldest in your class?

TEACHER: Yes, he's 6 already.

COACH: So he's showing some of that second plane of development appreciation for efficiency.

TEACHER: (laughing) That's one way of looking at it!

COACH: Since Brandon is so efficient in getting ready, I wonder what he could do when he's done?

TEACHER: I'm concerned if I give him another job he'll lord it over the other children the way he did the timer.

COACH: Is there something helpful he could do inside the classroom?

TEACHER: So many things! (pause – thinking – looks at coach – coach smiles) The one I think he would enjoy is to bring the trays back to the kitchen. He really likes seeing Ms. D.

COACH: Could you bring Ms. D into your plan?

TEACHER: She is really great with Brandon. (thinking) I bet if I asked her, she could be sure he makes it back upstairs!

FUNDAMENTAL NEEDS

Material need: Classroom Management

Spiritual need: Reflection

Adults should leave reflective coaching sessions feeling energized, focused, and capable of accomplishing what they have set out to do. The emphasis and focus are directly on the impact on children. The Montessori coach then holds the commitments made in the meeting seriously, being sure to follow up and do their part. The idea that people are not alone in the work is made manifest through the follow-up done by the Montessori coach. If these sessions are followed by inaction, people will slowly divest from the process as the coach loses credibility. Being a reliable partner in this work includes showing up for both the reflection conversations and the follow-through.

Let's look at one more reflective coaching scenario that focuses on instruction.

Reflective Coaching Scenario

COACH: What's working?

TEACHER: The new lesson plans are really helping me stay focused.

COACH: Tell me about that.

TEACHER: Well, now that I have them on a clipboard and I'm noting who's there, it reminds me of what I wanted to do next.

COACH: So you're getting to more lessons?

TEACHER: Yes, but I notice that because I'm busier the children are getting better at figuring things out rather than coming to me all the time.

COACH: What else are you noticing?

TEACHER: I notice that even though they're busier they're still not repeating work.

COACH: Say more about that.

TEACHER: So I show them the material and then they go right back to what they were doing before.

COACH: I noticed that today, too, when you were showing Carly the number rods.

TEACHER: Right? When the lesson was over she just left.

COACH: Did your training have a specific way to end the lesson?

TEACHER: What do you mean?

COACH: At the end of a lesson do you say, "Now it's your turn"?

TEACHER: No, I've never heard that.

COACH: One way to support engagement with the material is to build the child's anticipation of having a turn while you are showing them how to use it during your turn.

TEACHER: That seems so obvious now that you say it, but I've always done it with them. (thinking) Maybe then they feel like they've already done it and that's why they don't stay.

COACH: Do you want to try making that change?

FUNDAMENTAL NEEDS

Material need: Lessons

Spiritual need: Inspiration

These conversations are all documented on the meeting notes tool, shown in Figure 7.3.

You can see the tool has a place to write notes about the topics discussed, any long-standing decisions made, and what the teacher has selected as their

Coaching Meeting Notes

Date:	Time:	Attendees:
Topics		
What's working? -		

What are you noticing?
  -
  -		

Other topics discussed:		
Self-care idea: -		
Decisions:	O.L.T.:	

Follow Up:

Action Item	Person Responsible	Deadline

Figure 7.3 Coaching Meeting Notes Tool.

OLT for the week. The bottom part of the tool holds the follow-up items, who will do it, and by when. A copy of these notes is shared directly with the teacher following the meeting.

Directive Coaching

Directive coaching holds the same essential values as reflective coaching; however, the conversation opens with a specific topic to be explored that is directed by the coach rather than the teacher. There are conditions under which this may be needed as a more honest and direct approach to a situation.

There are two types of directive coaching:

- *Proactive:* Conversations that occur over time, leading teachers along through pieces they don't yet know.

- *Responsive:* Conversations that occur as a redirection when something falls outside our method, arises from implicit bias, or is otherwise harmful to the community.

Proactive directive coaching is a straightforward conversation with a new practitioner who needs direction in an area they are not yet aware of, have a skill gap in, or is entirely new to them. Regarding the fundamental needs of the Montessori educator, many material needs can be new and unfamiliar to the new Montessori adult, and it is the coach's task to support them through this new learning. This includes everything from classroom design to recordkeeping to filling out progress reports and holding family conferences. It would not be productive to have a reflective coaching conversation on these topics if the new practitioner has no knowledge or experience to draw from. Instead, the Montessori coach takes the lead in the conversation directing the new person's attention to the relevant topic. These are often relaxed conversations where the classroom adult is relieved and grateful to have the guidance and support.

Responsive directive coaching comes in when there has been an occurrence or an issue and the conversation tends to be more charged. This could be when there is an element of practice that is, or could be, causing harm to children or the larger community. Often it is in the adult's blind spot and they are not aware. This could be a situation around equity, non-Montessori practice, or acting outside the school's values. In these cases, the coach must be willing to raise the issue in the context of the coaching relationship. The community is counting on the courage of the Montessori coach to hold the mission and vision of the school at the forefront and to speak up when boundaries are about to be or have been crossed.

Often, a Montessori coach will seek coaching themselves prior to a responsive directive coaching conversation – talking through the tricky areas and even role-playing the situation to ensure they are clear and steady about both the issue and the needed outcome of the conversation. The whole school's commitment to coaching and being coached is well served here as the coach is also not alone in this work but has a trusted coach to turn to.

Specific questions in a directive coaching session allow these conversations to happen in a direct and honest way.

The Language of Montessori Directive Coaching Conversations

- **Connect:** "I would like to talk to you about . . ."
- **Communicate:** State observation focused on facts. "I noticed that . . ." Name the impact on children, you, or the team. "As a result, children . . ."
- **Collaborate:** "What support do you need with this?"

Connect: The connection between people is fostered by our ability to tackle difficult subjects directly, unwaveringly, and without blame. Opening the conversation with the important topic avoids miscuing the listener (e.g., "How are you doing today?" which might give them the wrong impression about where the conversation is going and lead to later resentment) and lets them know the topic at the outset.

Communicate: Regardless of the listener's response to the opening, the directive coaching conversation moves into the observed facts. It does so without judgmental language or condemnation but rather a frank summary of what was seen and heard. To prevent this from being perceived as a personal attack, it's important to frame it in the context of the mission of the school and the way the topic at hand impacts children, you, or the team. When the person responds, it is important for the coach to listen to understand rather than to respond. Part of raising the topic is wanting to deeply understand the choice the person made to support them in seeing a different way.

Collaborate: There is often a lot of dialogue around the topic before arriving at this final step, and there are times when it happens in the next conversation. Yet ultimately the coach joins the other adult in the action steps toward remedying the situation. The support of the repair is the coach's commitment to each member of the community, and walking alongside them through it will strengthen the relationship and allow the conversation to be a confirmation of that commitment rather than a break in the bond between them.

To understand the difference between the two approaches to a directive coaching conversation, it will be important to delve into actual content. Let's begin by naming the situations under which directive coaching might be called for (Table 7.1).

Table 7.1 Coaching Situations

Proactive Directive Coaching	Responsive Directive Coaching
Teachers just out of training	Equity issues
Teachers new to the school	Acting outside the Montessori method
Adults new to Montessori	Acting outside the school values

Proactive Directive Coaching

This type of directive coaching is for adults who don't know what they don't know. It is hard to reflect on and come up with solutions on your own when you are starting out – either in Montessori or in a new school setting – and are in the unconscious incompetence phase of learning. Then the Montessori coach must take the lead to direct the teacher's attention where it is most needed to serve the children. If the coaching relationship is built and trust has developed, classroom adults are often very grateful for this direction.

Teachers Just Out of Training

In *The Absorbent Mind*, Maria Montessori writes about the new teacher:

> The little hell that has begun to break loose in these children will drag to itself everything within reach, and the teacher, if she remains passive, will be over-whelmed by confusion and an almost unbelievable noise. On finding herself in such a situation – whether it be due to inexperience, or to over rigid (or over simple) principles and ideas – the teacher must remember the powers which lie dormant in these divinely pure and generous little souls. She must help these tiny beings, who are scampering downhill towards a precipice, to turn about and climb again. She must call to them, wake them up by her voice and thought. A vigorous and firm call is the only true act of kindness towards these little minds.

Much as Montessori is directive here, so must we be to support the emergence of solid learning environments for all children. Often the insights, skills, and tools needed to settle a classroom are not covered in Montessori training but rather something teachers are set to discover on their own. Though that will eventually occur, the cost to children, as adults are sorting this out, can be significant. With directive coaching ("a vigorous and firm call"), time is saved and classrooms can settle at a faster rate.

Proactive Directive Coaching Scenario: New Teacher

COACH: I would like to talk about the transition to lunch.

TEACHER: Yes – it's a disaster. The children just go wild, and I don't know what to do!

COACH: Tell me more about that.

TEACHER: As soon as I ring the bell they are all up at once moving before I've even given a direction.

COACH: I noticed that, too. Have you tried any other ways to mark the end of the work cycle?

TEACHER: What do you mean?

COACH: I notice your children have found a nice rhythm in the morning, and they are really falling into work now. Your plan to offer them many lessons has helped, and they seem to understand the cycle of work.

TEACHER: Yes, I think it is getting better.

COACH: I think so, too, so I thought we could talk about how to create a smoother transition into lunch.

TEACHER: Okay – what other ways are there than ringing the bell?

FUNDAMENTAL NEEDS

Material need: Classroom Management

Spiritual need: Inspiration

In this scenario all that was needed was the opening connection statement and the teacher was completely in the conversation. The coach didn't need to share their observations as the teacher offered up her own, nor was it necessary to talk about the impact on the children as the impact on the teacher was already sparking internal motivation to change the situation. The coach used a reflective question – "Have you tried any other ways to mark the end of the work cycle?" – to both learn what had been tried (if anything) and gauge the teacher's awareness of options. This proved fruitful as it made clear two things: the teacher had nothing in her toolbox yet besides the bell, and she wasn't clear that the bell was unnecessarily rousing them from a settled place she had worked hard to get them into. An opening for collaboration was made, and the two were able to create a plan and implement it to positive effect.

One complex element for new teachers is the mastery of many new materials and many new lessons. In their first year of working with children it's an important piece for the Montessori coach to observe and offer directive coaching as needed. Here's a scenario where a new teacher, who is only partway through her training, has just broken through her uncertainty and presented her first material to a group of children in her upper elementary classroom. The coach arrived at the end of the lesson and was able to watch both the close of the instruction and what the children did with the material once the teacher left. The coach and the teacher met in the classroom directly following the observation while the children were at lunch.

Proactive Directive Coaching Scenario: New Teacher

COACH: I would like to talk about the checkerboard lesson.

TEACHER: Did you see? I did it! I showed them a material, and they loved it.

COACH: Yes, they seemed very engaged. Let's get out your album and look at the lesson together.

TEACHER: Did I do something wrong?

COACH: I noticed you were using 10 bars. They aren't used on the checkerboard.

TEACHER: They were in my training.

COACH: That's why I was hoping we could look at your album together.

TEACHER: Okay. (pulls a large, three-ring binder from the closet, full of pages coming out in all directions that haven't been secured on the rings) It's in here somewhere . . .

COACH: Did you have it out to review before you gave the lesson today?

TEACHER: No, I remember it from the summer (pushes the binder toward the coach.)

COACH: (looks through the pages and finally finds the lesson, reads through and understands that the write-up is very difficult to follow.) Let's go to the material. (which is still out on the rug.) The checkerboard came with its own box of bead bars 1–9. Do you see that here (pointing to the write-up) on the materials list? Do you remember unpacking that?

TEACHER: (goes into the closet and after a bit pulls it out) Is this it?

COACH: Yes! The one you have out here is called the decanomial bead bar box. It's used for many lessons but not the checkerboard.

TEACHER: I didn't know that.

COACH: Let's go through it together . . .

FUNDAMENTAL NEEDS

Material need: Montessori Material, Lessons

Spiritual need: Perspective

In this scenario the coach needed to correct a lesson that was given to the children in a way that did not move their learning forward. Though they were enamored with the hands-on material, they had no idea how to use it when the teacher left. Seeing the teacher's album offered the coach insight into the disordered experience of training and the lack of resources the teacher had to move forward to learn the materials on her own. Following this conversation, the coach reached out to the training center for more support, set up weekly practice sessions for the teacher, and collaborated on the development of lesson plans going forward.

Teachers New to the School

Whether teachers are shifting from a private Montessori school into a public Montessori school or from a public Montessori school into your school, these adults will need some proactive directive coaching as part of their ongoing orientation. Many unique elements of the school deserve an intentional conversation to ensure the new member understands and is able to be successful.

Proactive Directive Coaching Scenario: Teacher New to the School

COACH: I would like to talk about the upcoming family conferences.

TEACHER: Oh good, I saw that on the calendar and was wondering about that.

COACH: What did you do at conferences at your old school?

TEACHER: We had 15 minutes with each family back to back. It was pretty crazy, so all I had time to do was show them their child's binder of work and hand them the test results.

COACH: Did you do any goal setting with families?

TEACHER: At the conference? No, there wasn't time for that.

COACH: Okay, so let's look at our school template for how we spend time in conferences.[2]

TEACHER: Wow, this is pretty regimented.

COACH: That's interesting – tell me more.

TEACHER: I mean it looks like you're telling me to follow a script.

COACH: Oh, I see – you're responding to the examples. Rather than a script, this is here to help us all have meaningful conversations with families that support them in understanding two things: how their child is doing and the Montessori method they are learning through.

TEACHER: Isn't that a lot for 15 minutes?

COACH: (smiling) Yes, that's why we have 20 minute conferences here. And even that feels short, which is why we created this tool to help fit it all in. What support do you think you will need with conferences?

TEACHER: What do you mean?

COACH: I'm wondering how I can help as you adjust to this new way?

FUNDAMENTAL NEEDS

Material need: Planning and Recordkeeping

Spiritual need: Perspective, faith, trust, and belonging

Acclimating to the environment of a new school requires flexibility and a willingness to learn new ways of doing things. This may feel disruptive to a new teacher who has likely developed their own way of doing it over time. This can feel entwined with their identity as a practitioner and so requires that the coach offer some perspective about how and why the school's way came about. With that perspective the teacher new to the school might more easily adjust to the new approach. It is the coach's awareness of their need for information around conferences (under the heading planning and recordkeeping) and their need for perspective that allowed for a pro-active directive coaching conversation that will support them in aligning their practice with the rest of the school. There is also an opening for the teacher to feel a sense of faith, trust, and belonging through the proactive conversation preparing them to be part of this new way of engaging with families.

Adults New to Montessori

Along with Montessori trained teachers new to the school, the Montessori coach is aware of the ongoing orientation for all adults new to the school. Much of this is covered in their onboarding orientation and follow-up professional development, yet there may be new adults filling important roles where the coach sees the opportunity for a proactive directive coaching conversation that would support them in adjusting to a Montessori approach.

Proactive Directive Coaching Scenario: Adults New to the School

COACH: I would like to talk about the prepared environment in Montessori and how to do that in the gym.

PE TEACHER: I was thinking about that after our orientation about how the classrooms have such an intentional set up.

COACH: Yes, how might you take what we talked about and apply it in your environment?

PE TEACHER: Yeah, I was thinking about the independence part. I don't usually let them touch anything unless I give it to them, so I don't really want to set up an environment where they can get equipment on their own.

COACH: What do you think would happen if you did?

PE TEACHER: Some of the equipment could be dangerous if they weren't careful.

COACH: What are you thinking of?

PE TEACHER: Well, like the jump ropes could become whips . . .

COACH: They could . . . especially if the children didn't understand how to carry them or use them. The same is true with the knives they use in primary to cut bananas – they could be dangerous if there wasn't step-by-step guidance in how to use them properly.

PE TEACHER: Yeah, I can't believe they use knives in there, and those sharp pins for poking out the continents!

COACH: You're right – the children at this school learn how to be responsible from an early age. Then the environment can support them in their development.

PE TEACHER: I do want my environment to support them in their development. I've just never done it like that before.

COACH: How would it be to take it one step at a time? You could introduce one piece of equipment and show them how to get it, carry it, and use it and practice that for a few sessions to see how it goes.

PE TEACHER: I was going to start with balls. I guess I could set it up where I have them out and teach them all that but then I'm not going to get to the PE standard.

COACH: Perhaps not on that first day, but remember that you have three years for them to reach all the standards.

PE TEACHER: That's true. I'll try it and see.

COACH: What support do you need with this?

PE TEACHER: I could use some nicer bins. I mean, if the gym is going to look as nice as the classrooms and the children will be getting their own equipment, then they should look good.

COACH: That's a great idea. I'll bring it up at the next leadership meeting.

In this conversation the coach is building off the learning the staff member already has about Montessori and applying it to the situation open for discussion. Here's an example of how the parts of the whole school Montessori method talk to each other: this coaching conversation in Honest Talk is mapping onto an orientation process that is part of Strong Systems and is occurring because of One School meetings. The components are intertwined in the same way the parts of the school are interdependent.

Responsive Directive Coaching

Equity

An important time to use responsive directive coaching is around issues of equity. If there is a time when the coach is aware that a school-based adult's unconscious bias is impacting a child or children, it is their responsibility to raise this in a directive coaching conversation. Rather than hoping it will come up, a Montessori coach uses the framework of directive coaching to allow for courageous conversations to occur that will help move the adult's thinking forward and create more just-learning environments for children.

Responsive Directive Coaching Scenario: Equity

COACH: I would like to talk about your nautilus[3] referral data.

TEACHER: What about it?

COACH: We did a data review looking at all the calls for support across classrooms. Then we looked at each individual classroom to see where the support is needed. (pointing to the data sheet) You can see here that the majority of children you are calling for support with are Black boys.

TEACHER: (stunned silence)

COACH: I'm bringing this up because I know it's not your intention to have this group of students missing class time.

TEACHER: No, it's not.

COACH: Are you open to talking more about this?

TEACHER: I guess.

COACH: My intention isn't to make you uncomfortable but instead to open the conversation so we can make changes together.

FUNDAMENTAL NEEDS

Material need: Supporting Key Children

Spiritual need: Reflection

In this scenario there are many possible ways the conversation could go next but there are three strong elements of the opening:

- It was direct.
- There was data to review so this wasn't subjective or personal.
- The coach was aware of and working with, not around, the discomfort.

Empathy is an important quality to bring to these vulnerable conversations: asking what you would want if you were that person and then bringing it into the conversation. Courage does not exist without vulnerability; we need to bring both to directive coaching conversations about race and equity.

Outside the Method

Working in schools with people from varying backgrounds, sometimes adults use techniques outside the Montessori method. This creates another opportunity for the coach to use directive coaching in calling this correct. Straightforward, honest talk helps everyone to understand this is not personal but related to the mission of the school with our focus always on the impact of our choices on children.

Responsive Directive Coaching Scenario: Outside the Method

COACH: I would like to talk about your reading intervention time with Max.

INTERVENTION TEACHER: Why?

> COACH: Yesterday I observed you giving him a pretzel every time he answered a question correctly.
>
> INTERVENTION TEACHER: Yes, it's the only way I can get him to do anything. He's very motivated by food.
>
> COACH: As you know from our Montessori overview, the method doesn't use punishments and rewards.
>
> INTERVENTION TEACHER: It's the only way he'll learn, and it's my job to get him to grade level.
>
> COACH: Have you had the opportunity to observe him in the classroom?
>
> INTERVENTION TEACHER: Sure.
>
> COACH: What do you notice?
>
> INTERVENTION TEACHER: He'll do work for Ms. L. because he likes her.
>
> COACH: So you notice he's productive without a reward?
>
> INTERVENTION TEACHER: Because he likes her.
>
> COACH: Are you saying you think Max doesn't like you?
>
> INTERVENTION TEACHER: (pause – thinking) He only fools around with me.
>
> COACH: You have only known Max a few weeks, and Ms. L. has known him for two years. How about I set up a meeting with the three of us to talk about what Max is interested in and what he enjoys? Ms. L. will likely have some good ideas from when she first started working with Max.
>
> **FUNDAMENTAL NEEDS**
>
> Material need: Supporting Key Children
>
> Spiritual need: Optimism

As you can tell from the scenario, the reading interventionist's past experience is what she is relying on to navigate her work with Max. Partly this is because she doesn't yet have a relationship with Max, and partly it may be because she doesn't yet know any other way. Without a direct conversation she would continue doing what she knows how to do in her effort to support the growth in learning. The Montessori coach interrupts this by creating a space for the teacher to learn more about both Max and a different way of approaching the work.

Another area that calls for a responsive directive coaching is when someone in the community is acting outside of the school values. The coach takes this on to refocus the person on the shared community agreements.

Responsive Directive Coaching Scenario: Acting Outside the School Values

COACH: I would like to talk about your cell phone use.

TEACHER: What about it?

COACH: This morning I noticed you were on your phone both times when I came in the room during the morning work cycle.

TEACHER: What are you – the cell phone police? I had something I needed to take care of.

COACH: I'm bringing it up because it's one of our school agreements to not use cell phones during class time. We've noticed that it has an impact on the class when adults are attending to their phone rather than engaging in the work cycle.

TEACHER: I know that.

COACH: Yes, I noticed you put it away when I came in, so I know you understand the issue.

TEACHER: I do.

COACH: Is there something getting in the way of engaging with the children?

TEACHER: I don't feel very useful here. At my other job the children needed me all the time and I was so busy. At this school there's all this talk about independence and letting them do it for themselves, so I figure I'll let them.

COACH: I see. So you don't feel you know what to do to support learning during the morning work cycle?

TEACHER: I guess not.

COACH: How about if I come to your classroom team meeting tomorrow and we can talk more about this then? There are so many important parts of this work to engage in.

TEACHER: Okay.

COACH: In the meantime, are you willing to keep your phone off?

TEACHER: Yes.

COACH: Great, and if there are times when you don't know what to do, you could observe using the tool on the clipboard at the observation chair.

FUNDAMENTAL NEEDS

Material need: Environment

Spiritual need: Faith, trust, and belonging

Another situation in which directive coaching might be employed is around splitting or the awareness of fractures beginning within the community. The Montessori coach holds the vision of One School and is often the first to notice when divisions begin. A responsive directive coaching conversation with the source of the splitting is often the simplest remedy and a place where the coach can understand what is needed. It also provides more information about what they might have missed in sharing the One School value across the whole community and how to remedy that on a larger scale.

Splitting can begin within anyone, but this scenario is about a parent who would like their child placed in a particular classroom and has been talking to other family members and caregivers about who's the best lower elementary teacher. She has been putting down the other teachers on the team in her zeal about the one teacher she esteems.

Directive Coaching Scenario: Acting Outside the School Values – Splitting

COACH: Hello! I'd like to talk to you about Osvaldo's transition from primary to lower elementary.

PARENT: Yes, I want him in Ms. L.'s class.

COACH: Have you had the opportunity to come to one of our transition talks[4] to hear about how we do class placement?

PARENT: Yes, I know you say you build the community, but I just want him in Ms. L.'s class.

COACH: Tell me more about that.

PARENT: There's nothing more to say. I want him in her class where his sister was.

COACH: So Ashley had a positive experience with Ms. L.?

PARENT: Yes, she loves her, and I trust her.

COACH: You trust Ms. L.?

PARENT: It took three years, but she understands our situation.

COACH: So you're hoping Osvaldo will have Ms. L. because you already know her and trust her.

PARENT: Right.

COACH: Ms. L. is on the team that creates the classes for next year. What if she thinks Osvaldo would do better in a different class?

PARENT: (Pause)

COACH: (Waiting while the parent thinks)

PARENT: Does she?

COACH: We haven't had the meeting yet, but Ms. L. cares about your family. She will want the best placement for Osvaldo where he's with the group of peers that will allow him to grow strong and do his best work.

PARENT: He has more trouble than Ashley.

COACH: Are you concerned about his moving into elementary?

PARENT: (pause, slowly) Maybe a little.

COACH: One of the parts of the work I do at school is to observe all the classrooms and meet with all the teachers. I've had a chance to watch Osvaldo over these past years and seen how much he has grown.

PARENT: That's because of Ms. K.

COACH: Do you trust Ms. K.?

PARENT: Of course. She got him to not cry all the time.

COACH: Ms. K. will be at the class placement meeting, too. She will also be thinking about which classroom will be the best place for Osvaldo.

PARENT: Really?

COACH: Yes, the primary teachers work together with the lower elementary teachers to come up with the best community for each child. In elementary, children care a lot about their social group so we spend time thinking and talking about the best group for each child moving into elementary.

PARENT: I didn't realize that.

COACH: Once the placement has been made the elementary teacher will observe Osvaldo in Ms. K.'s class to see how he is when he's comfortable. Then Osvaldo will go for a visit in his new room to see what it's like. After that, if it doesn't seem like a good match then the team can make a different decision. It's important to all the teachers that the children are happy and comfortable in their new classrooms.

PARENT: I guess I'll wait and see then.

COACH: Why don't we meet again after the class placement meeting and talk about what the teachers decided?

PARENT: Okay.

COACH: Before we end our time, I want to let you know that I am always here if you have questions.

PARENT: Yeah, I should've asked you about it since I know you run those meetings. I just thought you'd say he couldn't be in Ms. L.'s class.

COACH: Why did you think that?

PARENT: Lucia told me the parents don't have any say around here anymore.

COACH: Has that been your experience?

PARENT: (thinking) It's true that we can't carry them into their classroom.

COACH: Is that what Lucia is concerned about?

PARENT: You know she has the twins and she's pretty mad about that.

COACH: Thank you for letting me know. Do you think it would help if the next Family Meeting topic was about that?

In this scenario the coach used both directive and reflective coaching in order to discover what was underneath the initial request that was delivered as more of a demand, from a parent who struggled to engage in community events. By staying silent while the parent was digesting information, rather than adding more and more, the coach was able to stay with the parent rather than alienating her. Once the parent's primary concern was responded to, the coach took the opportunity to understand the underlying split to work toward repairing it on a larger scale.

This is not an exhaustive list of times when directive coaching is called for, but it is a beginning to set the tone for how this may be different from reflective coaching. It serves to create boundaries and to carry forward the One School value. It also prevents matters from going underground, festering, or becoming divisive. It may take a while before these conversations feel comfortable and natural, but over time and with practice they take less preparation and are simply a part of the life of the school. If we can support Honest Talk then difficult conversations become less difficult, less charged, and less personal. When everyone understands the aim is to collaboratively create the best learning environment for children and adults, then change becomes less scary and more a part of the fabric of the school culture.

COACHING CONVERSATION SUMMARY

Both reflective and directive coaching skills will be called on regularly for all members of the school community as the embodiment of Honest Talk. When school leaders engage in coaching they message to the community that being real and vulnerable with each other is valued and saying what's true is welcome. This in itself allows movement on the One School Continuum toward everyone feeling a greater sense of unity and awareness.

Table 7.2 helps make explicit the elements of the two types of coaching conversations. You'll notice that, in spite of the differences, the goal of all coaching conversations is to team with the person in support of their growth. All Honest Talk holds this as a foundational component; people are engaged in honest conversations to help each other grow.

Table 7.2 Elements of Coaching Conversations

	Reflective Coaching Conversation	Directive Coaching Conversation
Opening	Strengths-based question	Honest Talk statement
Questions	Questions to inspire reflection	Questions to understand
Role	Listen twice as much as talk	Direct when blind spots appear
Goal	Team with to carry them through asking what support they need to reach weekly goal	Team with to carry them through asking what support they need to make changes

NEW WORLD CONSIDERATIONS

Coaching, as a central aspect of the whole-school Montessori method, proved to be critical as schools faced unexpected closures that swept the world. Without the face-to-face experience of being together, the possibility of fracturing was large, and it was the Montessori coach who was positioned, through individual and team coaching, to cohere the community through the new virtual venue.

In the post-pandemic new world, the individual coaching meetings became essential and coaches adjusted to offer both reflective and directive coaching in nearly every session. Direction was needed to keep level teams calibrated, and reflection was needed to create time and space to adjust to the new reality Montessori educators found themselves in.

What changed was the observation tool the coach would use and the manner in which the information was shared and meetings were held. Now the observations were of individual lessons rather than whole classrooms, and the focal points for observation became the lesson and the follow-up work options. The indicators for engagement shifted from tally marks based on students' activity to looking at individual children and their ability to tune into the lesson virtually. Rather than documenting Montessori materials in use, now the elements of a strong virtual lesson were observed as a vehicle for supporting all adults in this new way of giving lessons.

Adapting to the new way of engaging with children wasn't left to the teachers alone. The Montessori coach anchored and forwarded the emerging understanding of what best practice was under the new conditions and continued Honest Talk conversations to manage the transition.

NOTES

1. T. A. Ito, J. T. Larsen, N. K. Smith, and J. T. Cacioppo. "Negative Information Weighs More Heavily on the Brain: The Negativity Bias in Evaluative Categorizations." *Journal of Personality and Social Psychology*, Vol. 75, 887–900, 1998.
2. Conference templates can be found at www.resilient-montessori.com.
3. See Chapter 9 for more information about the nautilus approach.
4. See Chapter 10 for more information about seamless transitions.

Chapter 8
Validate

No construction is greater than that which makes humanity . . . [But] what
are the interests of education centred on today? On the child's mistakes!
These small errors hide the true greatness of man. These small errors
hide the giant. We need to change our attitude and see the greatness of
the child's achievements rather than the small and dry leaves of his errors
(errors we have caused).

—Maria Montessori, 1946 London Lectures

In addition to the work with each individual person in
the school, each evolving at their own pace, is the work
with the wider community. The way we are together as
a whole group reflects the way we will be able to bring
whole groups of children together through the power
of living the method. We are high communicators in
the classroom – ensuring everyone understands and
follows the procedures and routines, grace and courtesy
customs, and classroom agreements. These are the what
(procedures and routines) we do, the how (grace and
courtesy) we do it, and the why (classroom agreements

and expectations) we do it at the classroom level. These need to be equally clear in the wider school community of adults – both staff and families.

For each member to experience being a part of the larger whole, they must feel validated and confirmed as an essential member of the community. This chapter looks at ways Honest Talk can support that.

LANGUAGE OF REVERENCE

Montessori reminds us repeatedly that our words are absorbed by the young child and establish the reasoning of the older child, and therefore we are committed to the highest level of respect when talking to or about children. This must be extended to include the adults. In our commitment to Honest Talk we must also commit to using a language of reverence with one another, with families, and with and about children and each other.

Taking care with the way we communicate to and with all stakeholders validates their importance and value within the community. When we are not conscious of this, we can cause great harm. Toni Morrison said in her acceptance speech for the Nobel prize: "Oppressive language does more than represent violence, it is violence; does more than represent the limits of knowledge, it limits knowledge." This is a call for examining our assumptions and collaborating to ensure our messaging is not creating dominance over but rather partnership with.[1]

Schools using the whole-school Montessori method create a language of reverence chart (see Table 8.1) to share widely with everyone in the community. Often the old language comes from words or phrases in the lexicon of the adults that do not convey respect. The community can brainstorm to agree on replacement language.

One school community was uncomfortable with Maria Montessori's term *normalized*, which she used to describe children who have fallen into a grounded, centered way of being in the classroom. After discussion, they decided to replace it with *blooming*. Children were blooming through work or not yet blooming in their classroom. This change supported the Montessori trained and untrained adults in having a shared language with which to discuss

Table 8.1 Language of Reverence Chart

Old language	New language
Parents- implies everyone is a parent	Families- implies everyone is connected
Discipline Policy- people will be disciplined	System of Justness- communicates a just approach
Evaluation Process- invokes judgment	Appraisal Process- invokes assessment
Behavior problem- reduces the child to their behavior and declares it a problem	Key children- implies these children hold keys to our learning
SpEd kids	Children with Individualized Education Plans (IEPs)
English Language Learners	Multilingual learner
Parent work hours	Community Involvement hours

their observations about children. At another school, a Montessori trained teacher who worked with a high number of children with individual education plans could be seen in the hallway with a child having big feelings. Often community members would approach, ready to offer support, which overwhelming to the already activated child. The teacher began using the phrase *committee of one* or holding up one finger to indicate to the passersby that their help was not needed.

These types of shared language create a respectful shorthand that allow communities to navigate a school day in an efficient and connected way. Using reverent language makes the larger philosophy of the school apparent all the time to children, school-based adults, families, and all visitors to the school. Table 8.2 is one school's shared language of reverence chart.

This language is not used to avoid saying what is true but rather to rephrase it in a way that the person being spoken to or about feels more seen. For example, if I were struggling and someone described me as having a tantrum or giving them a hard time, I would feel diminished and put down. Yet if they were to describe me as having big feelings or having a hard time I would feel validated. Honest Talk doesn't mean speaking bluntly in ways that are hurtful but rather finding truthful language that brings the person closer into the conversation.

Table 8.2 Language of Reverence Chart

Old language	New language
Tantrum	Big Feelings
Attention seeking	Connection seeking
Rude	Ineloquent
Defiant	Makes a different choice
Shut down	Seems unavailable
Behind....below grade level	Has lagging skills
Fussing / Whining	Requesting Love
Needy	Has unmet needs
Problem	Opportunity
Manipulating	Using their tools
Bully	Struggling socially
Giving me a hard time	Having a hard time
Melodramatic	Spirited

COMMUNICATION TOOLS

At the root of struggles to develop One School there can be communication issues. There's often not enough (e.g., monthly newsletter that doesn't capture what arises in between) or inconsistent (e.g., a lot of information followed by gaps where confusion grows) or too much in a mode that creates dominance

Table 8.3 School Communication

	For Staff	Responsible Person	For Families	Responsible Person
Daily	Daily morning email	Office Manager	Daily attendance email	Office Manager
Weekly	Snapshot	Coach	Family Update	Family coordinator
Monthly	Meeting	Head of school	Meeting	Coach/ Teachers
Annually	Staff handbook	Head of school	Family Handbook	Family coordinator

rather than access to information (e.g., school leader talking uninterrupted at a weekly hour-long meeting), so getting the right balance is important.

Table 8.3 shows an overview of effective regular communication that, when set up ahead of time, with clear ownership, allows for a rhythm that supports the forward motion of the work within the school.

Though there is a designated responsible person for each of the tasks in the preceding table, this does not mean they are the only one doing the work. Every communication tool requires collaboration on the leadership team to ensure this is done accurately and regularly. For example, the office manager cannot put out the daily morning email until they have heard from the head of school or Montessori coach about the coverage decisions and the operations manager about the food service and transportation changes. However, knowing it is their responsibility, they have it ready and persist in requests for the missing information, which prompts the others on the team, who are likely managing many other things at the start of the day, to follow up and complete their part. Likewise, it is not only the Montessori coach who will contribute to the snapshot, as it needs to contain information from the whole leadership team. However, they fill in the pieces that impact the classrooms (e.g., assessment windows, team meetings, child study[2]) prior to sending it to the rest of the team, and this supports the leadership team in spreading out other demands on the classroom teams. By designating the responsible person to hold, tend, and consistently follow through, it eliminates the confusion that often slows down powerful communication in large organizations. Each person on the leadership team then is facilitating only two of the eight important regular communication components, and through this organizing structure the leadership team is strengthened and the community is served.

In the largest view, these are tools that support the increase of unity, power, structure, and autonomy in our One School plan.[3] Let's explore each of the communication tools to understand the why (purpose), what (outcome), and how (process) of each one.

Daily Communication

Staff

Why: To provide children and families with an orchestrated, seamless experience we need to be coordinated. Having a school-wide daily plan prevents lost time figuring out logistics and misunderstandings and provides for greater safety for the whole community.

What: Every morning, staff receive an email from the main office letting them know who is absent that day and who will be covering those duties. Also included are unexpected logistical changes such as a change in the menu, bus delay, and dismissal procedure.

How: This is a brief, uniformly formatted, and easy-to-read daily communication sent by the office manager prior to the arrival of the children to ensure classroom staff will be able to read it before starting the day with children. Often schools also post this information on a whiteboard in the main office for quick reference throughout the day.

Sample Daily Staff Email Communication

Good Morning and Happy Monday!

Absent today:

Location	Adult	Coverage	Direct ? to . . .
Primary	Ms. Kelly	Mr. Z.	(Montessori coach)
Main office	Mr. Johnson	Ms. Peters	(Operations manager)
PE	Ms. Barb	Ms. Ramirez	(Head of school)

Kitchen: chicken tacos instead of beef

Transportation: ----

Other: Reminder it's picture day!

Families

Why: If families are our partners in the education of the children, then we need to develop strong, trusting relationships built over time. This means we don't let information accumulate and then deliver it when a line has been crossed but rather offer steady communication around areas that are important, and being in school is important. Schools often have different templated communication based on the number of absences, with more information from the family handbook outlining what will happen if the number increases.

What: Every morning, following classroom attendance submission, standard emails are sent out to families of children reported absent. This is also a short, clear message that follows a standard format.

How: This is part of the larger system of attendance, which varies from school to school but is crafted by the leadership team using language of reverence and managed by the front office staff.

Weekly Communication

Staff

Why: By clearly laying out the next week before it begins, teachers are able
to plan around and into what is coming up. It also sets the expectations for
everyone to work with the events as they unfold, allowing the school staff to
take responsibility for the smooth running of the day to day.

What: Every Friday before the end of the school day a snapshot is distributed that holds all the pertinent information for the week ahead – from known
absences of leadership to observers, meetings, and special events.

How: The snapshot (Figure 8.1) is sent out by email, and a physical copy is
put into staff mailboxes to be hung in classrooms for reference

Families

Why: Much like the snapshot for school staff, the family update allows families
to feel connected to the daily happenings at the school. This supports greater communication not only between home and school but also between children and their
caregivers. For example, the family member, having read the family update, might
ask the child if they met the Watkinson students at aftercare today. Or if a child
begins talking about the teenagers in aftercare, family members are not alarmed
because they understand there were expected visitors from the nearby high school.

What: A weekly update goes out to families letting them know what is happening at school that week.

How: It is organized by the family coordinator or other member of the leadership team who holds responsibility for working with families. They base the
family update on the snapshot to support a family version of the week ahead

and provide translation so that all families are able to stay updated. As you can see from Figure 8.2, there is more of a narrative explanation than in the staff version since families have less daily access to ask for clarification.

Your Montessori School Snapshot	
Monday	**January 7**
All day	DRA Window opens today - closes Friday, Feb. 1st
3:00-4:00	Watkinson Student visiting Aftercare Program
5:00-6:00	MKTC Meeting
Tuesday	**January 8 - Happy Birthday Melissa!**
8:00-1:00	Ebony at Principal's Leadership Meeting @ SMSA
Wednesday	**January 9**
12:00	Early Dismissal for Students
12:30	Professional Development for all staff - lunch served
Thursday	**January 10**
12:00-12:30	Elementary Child Study Meeting
3:15-4:00	Primary and Elementary Team Meetings
4:00-5:00	ErdKinder Parent Community Meeting @ Mr. Ligon's Classroom
Friday	**January 11**
10:00-12:00	Jasmine out of the Office
6:00-7:00	MFTC game night - come play! It will be fun.

Announcements/Updates
- **Reminder: School Climate Survey needs to be completed by Wednesday.**
- **Bus Evacuation Day coming next week**
- **Happy Birthday Michelle - Sunday, January 13th!**

"Our care of the child should be governed, not by the desire 'to make him learn things,' but by the endeavor always to keep burning within him that light which is called the intelligence."
Dr. Montessori, *Spontaneous Activity in Education*

Figure 8.1 Sample Weekly Staff Snapshot.

Your Montessori School
Family Update

Monday, January 7

- The individualized reading assessment, which will be discussed again at the Transitions meeting coming up next month, begins this week and lasts for the month. Your child will read to a teacher to evaluate their reading level. The results will be discussed at family conferences.

- Students from nearby Watkinson High School will be visiting the Aftercare Program today. They are considering volunteering with us! If your child is in aftercare they may mention these special visitors.

- There is a Montessori Family/Teacher Committee Meeting tonight from 5-6 pm. All are welcome. There is childcare, and pizza will be served.

Tuesday, January 8

- School Climate Surveys are due today. We want to know what you think, so be sure your voice is heard! Come to the Main Office to use school technology to complete this. Thank you, community, for your support as we seek to improve.

- Final signup for Aftercare for tomorrow's Early Dismissal for all students.

Wednesday, January 9

- There will be Early Dismissal for Students today. Buses leave at noon. Car dismissal 11:45-12:15.

- Our teachers will be engaged in professional development around literacy and how to support all students in beginning their lifelong love of reading.

Thursday, January 10

- Many of you have been interested in extending our school into Middle School. In Montessori, this is called and Erdkinder program. We are hosting an open ErdKinder Community Meeting in Mr. Ligon's classroom from 4-5 pm for all those interested. All are welcome and childcare is available, though Elementary students are encouraged to attend with their families.

- Final signup for tomorrow's game night. If you haven't replied to last week's email you can call the main office to let us know you're coming.

Friday, January 11

- Your Montessori Family/Teacher Committee is holding a family game night in the gymnasium tonight from 5-6 pm. Wear your school T-shirt and let's have some fun together! Please be sure to register by Thursday so we know how many people to expect and can prepare accordingly. Thank you MFTC members!

Announcements/Updates

- Bus Evacuation Day coming next week

- Your Montessori Coach Michelle is having a birthday on Sunday, January 13th. Happy Birthday, Michelle!

"Our care of the child should be governed, not by the desire 'to make him learn things,' but by the endeavor always to keep burning within him that light which is called the intelligence."

Dr. Montessori, *Spontaneous Activity in Education*

Figure 8.2 Family Update.

Monthly Communication

Staff

Why: Many school issues the leadership team manages are unknown by the rest of the staff. This is partly by design as the leadership team insulates the classroom teams for them to stay focused on the children and on unrolling the Montessori curriculum. However, without some way of bringing in the larger community to these wider topics, there can be an unintended fissure. To prevent this, it's important to find a time when the staff is well nurtured and has the bandwidth to digest something not directly related to their day-to-day experience, ask meaningful questions, and offer innovative ideas. This could range from topics such as new district regulations to assessment information and ideas or requests from the wider community – anything that impacts the school. Unlike reading this in a weekly update, which might hold partial, unclear information that may cause unnecessary alarm, the community is able to hear it all together with time to add their voice to the conversation.

What: Schools often create monthly professional development meetings[4] to support the continued growth of the adults serving the school. Though these monthly meetings each have a focus and a direct aim of what people will be able to know and do when they leave the session, it is important to build in some face time to process select, rising events. These are opportunities for the head of school to share a larger context than can occur in the weekly snapshot and offer time for questions or ideas.

How: Offering a lunch together in advance of the professional development session allows for meaningful connection time for staff who rarely see each other. These can occur by having teams sign up to provide potluck items at two monthly sessions a year. This allows time, at the closing 15 minutes of the lunch or at the opening 15 minutes of the professional development session, for the head of school to raise topics.

Families

Why: Family engagement is a large part of developing the strong relationship between home and school that supports the growth of the child. Families, like the school staff, are important stakeholders and need a reliable time and place to hear accurate information from the school in order to prevent the inaccurate dissemination of information by a select few. Having this set time, and building the diversity of voices heard at these meetings, strengthens both the communication and the community.

What: Families need a regular time to discuss ongoing important topics related to their children that are not personal (i.e., their individual child, as at conferences) but rather take a wider perspective of the life of the school. These can range from topics such as assessments and class placement procedures to observations – ongoing aspects of the school that might be new for families.

How: Schools often have ongoing family engagement meetings[5] to support home adults in understanding the unique approach the school takes to education. These sessions can be tailored to allow important topics to be discussed in a context where childcare is provided and families can hear and learn from each other's questions.

Annual Communication

Staff

Why: As part of a full orientation, the staff handbook acts as part of the onboarding process[6] offering new community members a document that contains important information. This is reviewed with them during their orientation by the Montessori coach as a way to personalize and allow for questions and conversation. It is also necessary as a communication tool with existing staff to keep everyone current and informed as changes are made to policy or practice.

What: Each year staff members receive a staff handbook (Figure 8.3) that provides detailed information on a range of topics specific to Montessori and to the individual school.

How: The big lift happens only once as the school is opening and the document is written for the first time. Then every summer the leadership team creates a block of time to review and update the staff handbook. Some schools offer the handbook in a three ring binder so that it can be returned if the staff member is departing or updated with new pages as changes are made. This prevents the need to reprint the entire book every year, which for large schools can be both a costly and time-consuming task. The new pages, as well as updated resources (Figure 8.4), are then distributed and reviewed as the staff is welcomed back in August.

Sample Staff Handbook

Table Of Contents

Welcome To The School

Our Mission

The Whole School Montessori Method

- Core Elements

- Components

Organizational Chart

Role Clarity

Teachers

Instructional Support Staff

Support Staff

Custodians

Administration

Employment

At-will Employment

Change In Policy

Criminal Background Checks

Equal Employment Opportunity

Personnel Files

Accommodation Of Disabilities

Separation From Employment

Employment Classifications

Employee Conduct

Conflict Resolution Procedure and Policy

Discrimination & Harassment

Confidentiality

Conflict Of Interest

Duties Of Employees And Supervisors

Figure 8.3 Sample Staff Handbook Table of Contents.

Sample Staff Handbook Resources
Schedules:

- ☐ Weekly Meetings
- ☐ Specials
- ☐ Lunch
- ☐ Master
- ☐ Coaching
- ☐ Duties
- ☐ Extended Day

Calendars:

- ☐ School academic calendar
- ☐ Staggered entry
- ☐ Assessments
- ☐ Report cards
- ☐ Professional Development
- ☐ Transition Timeline
- ☐ Family Engagement

Staff:

- ☐ Staff list of who is where
- ☐ Map of building and locations
- ☐ Staff phone and address list
- ☐ Parking assignments
- ☐ Payroll schedule

Peace:

- ☐ System of Justness
- ☐ Peace Agreement
- ☐ Nautilus Approach
- ☐ Conflict Resolution Method
- ☐ Peer Mediation
- ☐ Community Harmony Agreement

Forms:

- ☐ Montessori Progress Report
- ☐ Family conference form
- ☐ Family Contact Log

- ☐ Walking permission slip
- ☐ Lesson Study Forms
- ☐ Child Study Forms
- ☐ Data Review Tool
- ☐ Student Portfolio Cover Sheet
- ☐ Taking a business /religious day
- ☐ Taking a professional day
- ☐ Permission to be photographed
- ☐ Consumables order form
- ☐ Incident report
- ☐ Travel Expenses
- ☐ Referral Home Visit
- ☐ Going Out forms
- ☐ Attendance follow-up form
- ☐ Observation Tools
- ☐ Proposal for an assembly

Protocols and Policies:

- ☐ Bad weather policy
- ☐ Attendance
- ☐ Lunch
- ☐ Bathroom
- ☐ Address change
- ☐ Building security
- ☐ Accidents
- ☐ Safety
- ☐ District Uniform Policy
- ☐ Assemblies

Self reflection and Appraisals:

- ☐ Self reflection checklist
- ☐ Coaching tools
- ☐ Appraisal Process
- ☐ Year-End Reflection

Figure 8.4 Sample Staff Handbook Resources.

Families

Why: As we orient families to the community they have chosen to join with their children, we offer them a clear, concise, and translated family handbook (Figure 8.5) with all the information they need. Now they are able to actively participate in their children's education and the life of the school. The handbook provides resources like the family engagement calendar,[7] which specifies dates in advance and increases the likelihood of participation. It also clarifies what the school does and doesn't do, so if there is confusion in the future it can be referenced as shared guidelines.

What: There is an orientation or open house for families where the family handbook is initially distributed with an opportunity to ask questions (Figure 8.5). At this time school-based adults can point out any changes in policies and practices. The document is referenced over the school year as it applies to different topics covered in the monthly or weekly gatherings.

How: Similar to the staff handbook, the initial creation of the document is the most time-consuming. After that, the leadership team modifies and adjusts the material to get ready to redistribute it at the start of the next academic year.

NEW WORLD CONSIDERATIONS

At the start of the global pandemic, clear, frequent communication became necessary as staff, families, and children were managing the schedule for learning during distance learning. Many schools created communication portals or a webpage where adults and children could find the most up-to-date information as well as links to lessons and meetings. The need for regular communication greatly increased to keep everyone on the same page.

The main communication tool that needed to be altered was the daily communication regarding attendance. Now attendance was being calculated differently, with some schools listing multiple ways to satisfy the attendance requirement for the day. For most, a new system arose out of necessity and was further refined at the start of the next school year.

Family Handbook
TABLE OF CONTENTS

Figure 8.5 Sample Family Handbook Table of Contents.

YEAR-END REFLECTION

Reflective practice is a cornerstone of the whole school Montessori method and is made explicit to the community only through repeated opportunities to practice it. As the year comes to a close, and people are winding up the cycle of learning, providing a time to reflect on the year means alignment between what is expressed and what is lived.

The full review of communication tools presented in this chapter positions us well to imagine a community that feels well informed and as a result connected to one another and to the larger mission of the school. This, combined with the Honest Talk emphasis on reflection in the previous chapter, makes way for this next practice: annual end-of-the-year reflections for everyone.

Taking time individually, as well as with teams, allows for the perspective-taking necessary to modify and strengthen all parts of the whole school Montessori method. Without this practice in place, schools run the risk of continuing to do what they are doing even if it isn't working well. With this practice in place, everyone in the community has an active voice in shaping what happens next. It pulls together the five aspects of One School – unity, awareness, power, structure, and autonomy – bringing the school closer to being fully inclusive.

The practice is very straightforward and easy to implement and offers notable results. As the school year draws to a close, the Montessori coach distributes the individual year-end reflection as a template to the whole community. Each person uses the tool to reflect from their own personal experiences on the following:

1. Reflection on what has worked: What went well this year? What do your observations or the data tell you about your successes?

2. Reflection on challenges: What got in your way?

3. Ideas for the coming year: What do you think would improve the situation?

From there, they take some time to think about the school year ahead. What do they want to accomplish? What needs to be in place for them to achieve that? Then, they complete the final sections:

4. Goals for the coming year: What one or two things do you want to focus on?

5. Support needed to attain these goals: What would allow you to reach them?

These are all done digitally and shared with a designated person. Some typical designations are to have all classroom staff send their reflections to the

Montessori coach and all non-classroom staff send them to the principal. This provides an opportunity for school leadership to support the goals set for the coming year and also to see trends across the school. For the Montessori coach, the one-on-one meetings near the final weeks of school are used to review, discuss, and, if necessary, add to these reflections. If a classroom staff member has not found time to fill it out yet, this can be done in the individual meeting with the coach asking the questions and acting as a scribe to capture it on the year-end reflection tool.

Often educators will have fewer items in the first section about what worked in the classroom. The coach is in a position to support additional reflection in this area through the offering of suggestions: "Do you feel your transitions were better this year? What about your cultural lessons?" Once again, this supports a strength-based view of the work rather than a problem-oriented one emerging from the negativity bias.

The other area that may need additions is the last section where each educator reflects on the support they will need to attain the goals they've set for themselves. The coach can brainstorm with them to think about all the resources involved in a fully supported approach to their goal. Figure 8.6 shows a sample year-end reflection template.

Year-End Reflection

Name: Date:

Reflection on what has worked:

Reflection on challenges:

Ideas for the coming year:

Goals for the coming year:

Support needed to attain these goals:

Figure 8.6 Year-End Reflection Template.

An example of the power of the year-end reflection practice occurred at a public Montessori school situated in a community serving a high number of multilanguage learners. In the previous meeting with the Montessori coach, to review the data from the year's observations, the guide saw that he was using the same few language materials over and over. Through reflection he realized this was a result of two factors: the inventory of language materials the school started with that year and the unmade language material he received in his training that he knew was needed by the primary classrooms. On his year-end reflection, he selected the goal of increasing both the number of language materials in the classroom and the variety of materials used to support growing literacy of the learners. When sharing his written reflection at the final reflection meeting with the coach, they were able to brainstorm what supports might be needed to reach those goals. Together they realized the lack of a teacher workroom with equipment to make materials was an obstacle that, if removed, would be a support for the goals. This would allow the primary team to develop more of the teacher-made materials needed in their classrooms. Documenting this on the reflection tool allowed the coach to bring it to a leadership meeting to discuss how they might support the teacher in reaching his goal through fundraising and purchases that would provide him with what he needed.

Year-end reflections also happen at a team level (Figure 8.7). These meetings are facilitated by the Montessori coach and allow groups to reflect together on the school year from a larger context. Where on an individual reflection it would be specific to the person's role or classroom, the team reflection allows everyone to think about school-wide practices that have worked and those that still need work. Often reflections are captured on a long whiteboard or on chart paper with one sheet for each section. The sections include: What's working?

Year-End Team Reflection
Team:_____

What's working?	What needs work?	Ideas

Figure 8.7 Year-End Team Reflection Template.

What needs work? Ideas for the coming year. The reflections are then captured on the tool below as a permanent record of each team's input.

At the beginning of the meeting, guidelines are set that this is a meeting for Honest Talk where everyone is allowed to express their opinion, using language of reverence, without needing to agree. If one person thinks dismissal procedures belongs in the Working category and someone else thinks it belongs in the Needs Work column, then it is included in both. Often through explanation and sharing points of view, someone else on the team spontaneously arrives at an idea that would make dismissal work better for everyone. An example of this is one where the classroom guide feels dismissal went very well and the classroom assistant believes it needs work. For the guide, they dismiss the children from the classroom and then attend to preparation of the environment while the assistant completes the dismissal process. More information about what happens when children leave the classroom helped the guides understand the issue and contribute to the brainstorming of ideas for the coming year that would improve the experience for everyone.

Figure 8.8 is a photograph from one school's year-end reflection with the extended day team. Without intentionally including them in the life of the school,

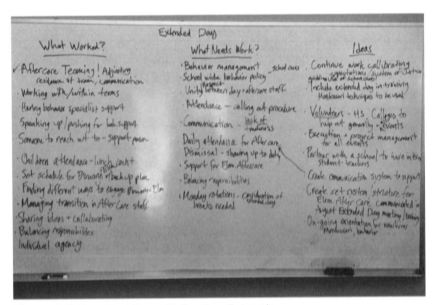

Figure 8.8 Year-End Team Reflection Example.

this team can become ancillary, providing support for the ecosystem of the school without being a part of it. Including them in the year-end reflection process allowed their unique view to be included in the future planning done by the leadership team.

You can see in the ideas section of their reflection some thoughts on creating a stronger One School unity with suggestions such as:

- Include extended day in training, Montessori techniques to be used
- Ongoing orientation for new hires, Montessori, behavior

And some ideas to strengthen Honest Talk:

- Continue work calibrating expectations – system of justness
- Create communication system to support daily attendance for aftercare

As well as thoughts on Strong Systems:

- Execution and project management for all events
- Create a system and structure for elementary aftercare communicated in August at extended day meeting and training

Both the opening guidelines and the facilitation of this practice support a collaborative, empowered experience for the participants. There is an emphasis not on right and wrong or needing to prove a point but rather on how it might be done better.

The final step of this Honest Talk practice is to review and take action. If everyone invests their time reflecting on all the aspects of the school, talking about it openly, and generating ideas to improve the situation then, there needs to be a response from the system to improve the system. This response happens through the leadership team.

Over the summer months school leaders dedicate time to review and analyze the year-end reflections, noting themes or discrepancies across differing perspectives in the school. An example of this is a school that looked at their team results – coding what needs work to look for trends – and found one issue in common across every group they met with, including level teams, special educators, support team members, extended day, and the leadership team itself: communication. The team immediately set to work building off the ideas generated in the meetings to implement new communication systems for the coming year. This included systems as simple as a whiteboard at the front desk showing coverage for the duties of the day to far more complex systems such as the coverage process overall including how decisions are made, how substitute teachers are oriented, and what are the universal expectations for people covering classrooms. They also committed to more regular communication using some of the tools in the previous section.

Creating stronger communication systems and introducing them at the preservice staff meeting not only allowed the whole community to see the results of their invested time but also made for a stronger school year. Since everyone was involved in the initial conversation at the year-end reflection meeting, everyone had a stake in the new systems succeeding and were therefore able to support midcourse corrections or revisions that improved it further. Now the whole team was thinking about improved communication as a shared goal, and, rather than needing to manage top-down mandates that may have felt restrictive or off-point, they were moving from intrinsic motivation, feeling the energy of working in a constructivist organization.

HONEST TALK SUMMARY

As we close the section on Honest Talk, remember that our words create our reality. The narrative we choose greatly informs how the story will unfold, so being intentional with our speech is central to building a resilient school.

Walking into school each day provides an opportunity to further refine respectful language that helps us talk honestly and directly with one another. This is an ongoing process – not one to hurry up to have in place or push to a place of perfection but an organic coming together of the unique members of your school community. With this perspective you will be learning from each other every day, recognizing fundamental needs, strengthening the language of reverence, and living into a vision of the community of reflective practice.

Our One School goals of creating unity, awareness, shared power, structure, and autonomy are built daily through the language we choose, the conversations we have, and the degree to which we've created a community that is able to engage in Honest Talk.

Nourish Checklist

- ☑ Fundamental Needs of Montessori Educator
    - ☑ Chart

- ☑ Checklist
- ☑ Questions of Reflective Coaching
- ☑ Questions of Directive Coaching

Validate Checklist
- ☑ Language of Reverence Chart
- ☑ Communication Tools
  - ☑ Daily Staff Email
  - ☑ Daily Family Email
  - ☑ Staff Snapshot
  - ☑ Family Update
  - ☑ Staff Handbook
  - ☑ Family Handbook
- ☑ Year-End Reflection
  - ☑ Individual
  - ☑ Team

Simple Honest Talk move:

ASK PEOPLE "WHAT HAVE YOU BEEN THINKING ABOUT?"

When you see them in the staff room or checking the mailbox, instead of saying "How are you?" which often provokes a surface response, try asking "What have you been thinking about?" as an alternative that sparks and promotes reflection. This question may allow for greater insight into how a person is doing as they share what's on their mind and highlights the commitment to reflective practice.

Share the answer to this question yourself by offering a reflection at the top of monthly staff meetings. This could be as far reaching as "I have been thinking about global warming" or as specific as "I have been thinking about *control of error*."

NOTES

1. Morrison, Toni (1993) Nobel prize acceptance speech, 13th paragraph.
    https://www.nobelprize.org/prizes/literature/1993/morrison/lecture/
2. See Chapter 9 for more on child study.
3. See Part Two in this book.
4. See Chapter 6 for section on developing a yearlong professional
    development calendar.
5. See Chapter 6 for information on developing a yearlong family
    engagement calendar.
6. See Chapter 10 for a strong system for onboarding.
7. See Chapter 6 for more on the family engagement calendar.

PART IV

Strong Systems

All is strictly interrelated on this planet. And one notes that each science studies only the details of a total knowledge. To speak afterward of the life of man on the surface of the globe is to speak of history. And each detail holds . . . interest by reason of its strict relation to the others. We may compare it with a tapestry: each detail is a piece of embroidery; the whole constitutes a magnificent cloth.

—Dr. Montessori, *From Childhood to Adolescence*

One School is the lithosphere, the land that grounds us. Honest Talk is hydrosphere, the water that holds, moves, and nourishes us. And Strong Systems are the atmosphere – the very air we breathe. The atmosphere is responsible for keeping us alive as it protects us from intensity of the sun by reflecting or absorbing harmful rays. It also offers Earth's inhabitants what they need for respiration, the process by which living organisms obtain energy through breathing. We can think of the strong systems built in Montessori schools as both protecting the unique program from potentially harmful outside influences and supplying the community with energy. When we use shared working systems, we become energized and begin to function at a higher level than when we are gasping for breath.

The role of systems in our school is not to lead but rather to support. Creating systems to support what we do is our goal. This section looks at systems that will support full implementation of the Montessori method in your school. These are strategic moves that leverage One School and Honest Talk, creating unity between the three ideas – systems then bringing the warp of One School and Honest Talk together into "a magnificent cloth."

These systems are not meant to be implemented separate from the other two elements but rather in support of them. When everyone in the community has a vested interest in the mission and vision and feel seen and heard in the conversation, then these systems will flourish. They will support children, families, and school-based adults in their understanding and participation in critical elements of the workings of a school.

A starting place for thinking about Strong Systems is to use the school-wide systems checklist to get a sense of which systems are already in place at your school and which ones are missing. Figure PIV.1 shows the first page of the checklist to give you a sense of the level of detail necessary when thinking about a topic as vast as systems.

School-wide Systems Checklist

√	System	Notes
	Initialized	
	Greeting staff: how are faculty initiated each day?	
	Daily morning gathering	
	Early arrival: Child who arrives prior to start time (__am)	
	Arrival: How do children enter?	
	- Bus	
	- Car	
	- Foot	
	Late arrival: Child who arrives after start time (__am)	
	Breakfast set-up	
	Breakfast clean-up	
	Backpacks and coats	
	Attendance recording	

School-wide Systems Checklist

√	System	Notes
	Dismissal: How do children leave?	
	- Bus	
	- Car	
	- Foot	
	Early Dismissal	
	Specials schedule	
	School schedule	
	Lunch	
	Outside play time: fair weather	
	Outside play time: inclement weather	
	Bathroom	

Figure PIV.1 School-Wide Systems Checklist.

The team can use the checklist to be in a position to fully articulate unclear systems and create missing systems that will further support the smooth functioning of the school. It may prompt a new understanding about an area that hasn't gone particularly well in the past; this may be a result of the lack of a shared system. If, for example, everyone is managing recess during inclement weather in a different way without a shared approach, then this could cause conflicts over use of the gym or discrepancies around what is acceptable indoor behavior. Getting your arms around all the systems needed by Montessori schools will then lay the foundation for these next two chapters.

The theme in Chapter 9 is engage – to occupy or involve a person's interest or attention. These are critical systems that involve the whole community in the shared focus on the child. They are essential to the unique way a Montessori school must function to hold its mission and vision, and they engage everyone in the process. The three systems shared activate the core components – constructivism, equity, and coaching – to support children's continuous growth over the course of the years of their life in the school.

Chapter 10 is about what you will yield or bring to bear through the use of the systems in that section. They are systems that, if implemented and used with fidelity, will have a direct impact on outputs for your school. These systems are meant to produce optimal results in key areas: they promote staff retention, careful attention to student progress and the review of the assessment data to further strengthen the work of the school.

Strong systems are the air we all breathe that keep us functioning optimally. They strengthen everything we do and are the hidden driver of outcomes, enhancing them when they are strong and weakening them when they are absent. These next two chapters are in support of a healthy, clean atmosphere that supports easy respiration for the whole community.

Chapter 9
Engage

Do we believe and constantly insist that cooperation among the peoples of the world is necessary in order to bring about peace? If so, what is needed first of all is collaboration with children. . . . All our efforts will come to nothing until we remedy the great injustice done the child, and remedy it by cooperating with him. If we are among the men of good will who yearn for peace, we must lay the foundation for peace ourselves, by working for the social world of the child.
—Maria Montessori, International Montessori Congress, 1937

Montessori schools are created as places where children feel the safety, freedom, and support to engage in the natural activity, hardwired in us all, to learn. This is the central organizing principle of our work, so considering all aspects of the way a school works from a child's perspective leads us to reenvisioning some standard public school systems. The Strong Systems that support these values include (a) seamless transitions; (b) student portfolios; and (c) system of justness.

Each of these rely on One School and Honest Talk to be fully effective. They will also depend on the Montessori coach to implement them as self-sustaining systems to be repeated by the community each year. As with many things, the first year is the most difficult; it is all new for everyone and can require more time and attention to get started. The clarity among members of the leadership team around the importance of each of these will offset that, and after the first year the traditions will be in place. Often communities are appreciative of these systems as they allow them involvement in proactive elements that support the Montessori program.

SEAMLESS TRANSITIONS

This first system reimagines the entire process of how children experience the move at the end of a three-year cycle from one classroom to a classroom at the next level. In traditional settings this happens every year and is often done by the main office staff or by a computer. By contrast, in Montessori schools children move to a new classroom only every three years, so the transition can be anywhere from unsettling to upsetting if done without a process that allows for preparation and planned steps taken over time. Everyone – children, families, school adults – should see what's coming and be able to walk toward it with a sense of excitement and confidence. Class transitions can then be a celebration of growth and readiness rather than an unknown event that happens to the child rather than with the child.

Table 9.1 is an overview of the full system to support transitions. This approach began in Springfield public Montessori schools, was further refined in Hartford public Montessori schools, and has since been used by many schools across the country. It is a tested, reliable approach to creating balanced classroom communities in a way that involves everyone, allows for multiple vantage points, and considers the needs of key children. In this way optimal learning environments are developed with diverse learners across all classrooms.

Table 9.1 Seamless Transition Overview

Event	Description
Transition Checklist	– Document to determine students' readiness – Acts as communication tool between levels – Provides family communication
Class Placement	A collaborative process for placing students to create balanced classrooms: • Card set up and process • Level overlaps support team insights • Observation and discussion period
Visits	Children visit their new classrooms for informal and scheduled visits.
Family Preparation	– Transition Family Education talk – Family letters – Transition evening – Family observation
Visiting Day	A simultaneous visiting day where all students visit their new class at the same time for one hour.
Portfolio Passing	Student Portfolios are passed from the sending teacher to the receiving teacher with short conversations surrounding Key Children.
Late Transitions	Students begin in previous classroom and transition slowly in fall Decide on a cut off date (Oct. 10th) Create a written plan between level teachers and family

Transition Checklist

To ensure seamless transitions, there must be an agreed upon measure for readiness. Some call these benchmarks, target skills, or skills inventories. Regardless of the name, it is a document that allows adults to have a shared understanding of goals for the completion of a level and is used to gauge each child's readiness for the upcoming transition. It acts as a vehicle for calibration across level classrooms so that children from six different primary classrooms, with six different teachers, likely from different training and backgrounds, share common goals for their oldest children. These are not limited to academic goals but take the whole child into account. Transition checklists[2] (Figure 9.1)

Transition Checklist for Primary

Name of the Child _____   **Date of Birth**_____

Guide _____   **Date completed**_____

SKILL	ABILITY	COMMENTS
Social-Emotional		
Makes independent behavior choices on the basis of an understanding of what is appropriate and acceptable.		
Holds a sense of responsibility towards fostering the well-being of the classroom community.		
Is respectful in interactions with other children.		
Shows an ability and willingness to share.		
Has a solid sense of self-worth (takes on responsibility, proud of contributions).		
Deals well with transitions.		
Embraces new experiences demonstrating confidence in one's skills.		
Collaborates and compromises in group interactions.		
Spontaneously accepts the role of an elder in the community.		
Work Habits		
Chooses appropriate work independently.		
Completes a work cycle independently.		
Shows attention to detail and takes care with a final product.		
Able to focus on projects that can take more than one day to complete.		
Enjoys and accepts new challenges with the ability to persevere in the face of difficulty.		
Cognitive		
Speaks clearly and expresses feelings.		
Listens to and willingly follows directions.		
Participates in the give and take of conversation.		
Writes cursive, simple sentences independently, directly on paper.		
Uses key phonograms in writing and reading.		
Has begun work on phonogram families.		
Knows basic puzzle words (see attached).		
Fluently reads and comprehends simple non-phonetic books.		

Figure 9.1 Sample Transition Checklist.

are used at the end of each cycle, marking the child's shift to a new level, including a list for the final age group your school holds. For example, to be ready for lower elementary these shared goals are monitored throughout their final year in primary using the transition checklist.

In addition, the transition serve as a communication tool with families. Teachers introduce the checklist at the fall conference with the whole year ahead. The winter conference provides an opportunity to share concerns so that families are then teaming up with the classroom adults to support growth in lagging areas. If by spring the child has not made sufficient progress then the conversation does not come as a surprise.

The transition checklists are used in the spring, at each level, to select which children will transition to their next class and this leads into the class placement process.

Spring Focus Lists

As teachers are preparing their oldest children for the upcoming transitions, the Spring Focus lists for each level[3] are helpful to target the use of time over the final days. These lists, created by teams of teachers, call attention to materials that the transitioning children should be working on daily or weekly in preparation for the change to the new level. Some of them (such as dressing frames) are materials that won't be in the next classroom and so offer the child the opportunity to achieve mastery prior to moving on. Other materials will be in the next classroom but need emphasis in order for the child to move into use at the elementary level. The golden bead material is a good example of this as it is in both primary and elementary classrooms, yet the child is to be conversant with it and to have a solid foundation in place value prior to the transition.

These carefully curated lists are not inclusive of every material transitioning learners will use in the spring. Rather they act as a guide for classroom adults to ensure ample time is invested in these important materials and lessons to prepare learners for the coming expectations in the new classroom.

Transition Timeline

To launch this, a transition timeline (as shown in Table 9.2) is distributed to the whole staff with dates for the next five steps of seamless transitions: class placement, visits, family preparation, visiting day, and portfolio passing.

Table 9.2 Sample Transition Timeline

Date	Item
April 1	Hand out materials for class placement
April 10 at 3:30 p.m.	Class placement meetings
April 12–20	Guide observations of potential new students
April 22–May 29	Children visit new classrooms
April 20 at 4 p.m.	Family transition Information meeting
April 29 at 6 p.m.	Transition evening for families
May 3–24	Family observations of next level
May 30 at 10 a.m.	Simultaneous visiting day
June 4 at 3:30 p.m.	Portfolio passing

By understanding this process through the lens of a timeline, both new and returning staff hold a sense of the big picture and are able to keep track of important steps in the process either by putting the dates on their calendar or posting the timeline in their personal space such as the inside of an adult cupboard or in a shared adult space.

Class Placement

In the spring, the information on the transition checklists is used to create balanced classrooms for the coming school year. This is done in three parts: (1) preparation; (2) class placement meetings; and (3) finalization and follow-up.

Preparation for Class Placement

There are two components to preparation: what the Montessori coach does and what the classroom teacher does. The teacher's preparation is dependent on the organization and planning of the coach. The fact that this is a system means that it happens every year, so there are dates, documents, and materials that move the process along.

The Montessori coach prepares a timeline (refer to the sample transition timeline in the Transition Checklist section) based on the school calendar and distributes it two weeks prior to the first date listed. Supplies for the creation of the class placement cards are also distributed to teachers to enable them to do the teacher preparation part. This is a simple plastic bag containing index cards of three colors, dot stickers of four colors, and a placement card sheet (Figure 9.2) of how to prepare the cards. The coach also organizes chart paper titled with each classroom name and places the cards (created in previous years for this process) of children already in the classroom on the chart with an open space on the far left for the incoming children.

Class Placement Cards

DIRECTIONS

Please make a card for each child in your class to bring to the placement meeting on April 10th.

Use a green card for boys and a yellow card for girls and a white card for gender non-specific.

Use the following to indicate race: A=Asian, B=Black, L=Latinx, M=Multiracial, W=White

On the left side place the appropriate colored dots. On the right side, please give scores or rate: H (high), M (medium), or L (low) in each area.

This is what each card should look like:

Student name: Current teacher: D.O.B.:		Race: Previous Teacher: # years:	
○	Green=IEP	Reading level=	
○	Blue=Child Study	Writing level= Math level=	
○	Yellow=ELL	Independence level= Grace & Courtesy=	
○	Red=Behavior or Social concerns		

Figure 9.2 Class Placement Card Sheet.

Teachers prepare a card for each of their transitioning students. Using Montessori color-coding as a way to organize the task, there are colored index cards for gender – one color for boys, another for girls, and a third for non-gender-conforming learners. Commonly used colors include green, yellow, and white.

Teachers use the transition checklist, assessments, and observation data to offer a concise picture of each child knowing that they will also have the opportunity to say more at the meeting. The information on the cards, as well as the dots, allow for a visual scan to ensure future classroom balance.

Class Placement Meetings

Class placement meetings include everyone from the sending level and everyone at the receiving level as well as the Montessori coach, social worker, child study or nautilus lead, dean of students, and any special educators, interventionists, or specialists who can attend. Having people at the meeting who see the children in different settings allows for multiple perspectives as the team seeks to build balanced classrooms that will best serve all the learners.

The meeting opens with the chart paper of current classrooms on the wall. If this were a lower elementary (LE) class placement meeting, then the LE classrooms would be hanging up with the current students shifted to the place they will be in the coming year. This means current first-year students are shifted into the second-year spot and current second-years are shifted into the third-year spot. The current third-year cards are updated, and used for the upper elementary class placement meeting. The primary guides hold the cards they have created for their rising children.

The Montessori coach opens the meeting with reminders:

- There is an agreement to use language of reverence when discussing the children. The dialogue should hold each child and teacher in the highest regard.

- The goal is to match the children to the community that would best serve them and not to a particular teacher. The second plane of development is a time when peer relationships matter more than those with the classroom adults, so bringing that to the foreground is important framing.

- Openness and flexibility are necessary elements of the process. Everyone should be prepared to stretch to find the best placement for each child.

Placement begins with the key children. Each primary guide is asked to order their cards with the key children on top – their most vulnerable learner first. It's important to place the children who need a certain environment at the start of the process and then build the class around them. The sending teacher gives the group a brief summary about the child, beginning with their strengths, discussing their struggles, and then highlighting the type of environment that would best serve them. An elementary teacher then offers their room as a possible location. The team reviews who is already in that classroom looking for potential conflicts (e.g., similar temperaments that might clash) and potential assets (e.g., old friends from last year), and then that child's card is hung in the first-year column on the chart paper for that classroom. If, for example, there is a child on the autism spectrum who often vocalizes unexpectedly, then placing them in a classroom with a child with a significant trauma background and a startle response would not be the strongest placement. Finding the best classroom match for this child then allows for the team to place other key children, who may struggle with that element, into other classes. With this thoughtful approach, key children will be moving into environments that will be more likely to adapt to their natural way of being and learning and therefore will be less likely to be interrupted for any prolonged period.

The Montessori coach, who has observed in all the classrooms and has a sense of the rising children, plays an essential role in the placing of the key children as does the child study or nautilus lead, who has intimate knowledge of the challenges the key children are facing. As facilitator, the coach has the ability to halt a placement that doesn't seem right or to move for a placement not offered by a teacher. The coach will be there for the whole process and will be able to step up to support a reluctant teacher with the transition and can remind everyone that the placements made in that meeting are not final. The process must not be allowed to stall over one key child, and all key children must be placed before the rest of the children are put into classrooms. Often, once the rest of the children are placed, the reluctant, receiving teacher has had time to process the placement and has already begun to adjust. Seeing the balance with all the other children supports a holistic picture of what the next year will look like. This is a critical aspect of the system: every classroom welcomes and supports key children. Everyone receives coaching and has the support of the team through child study, so everyone is building the capacity to work with all children. Without this in place, many schools end up with stark imbalances across a level with select classrooms holding all the key children. This is not healthy for the children or the adults.

This process continues with each of the primary guides describing one key child at a time and looking for an optimal placement. Montessori guides tend to love to talk about the children; therefore, the coach's task here is to tightly facilitate so that sending teachers offer a minimal description with enough detail to allow for a strong placement but concise enough to not impact the pace of the meeting. If there are teachers who have difficulty being succinct, the coach uses some time in a one-on-one coaching meeting to support their rehearsal of the essential talking points.

Once all of the key children have been placed, then the rest of the learners are placed more quickly based on the sending teacher's instinct around keeping strong pairs together or offering them aeration by putting them in separate classrooms. The children are placed in a way that supports racial and gender balance with consideration for temperament, academic abilities, and social needs.

At the bottom of the chart paper for each classroom, the coach keeps track of the girls and boys at each grade as well as total numbers, as seen in Figure 9.3. Also shown in this picture is a card hanging off the side of the chart paper indicating there is unconfirmed yet strong evidence that the learner will not be returning the following year. These children are still placed just in case they return.

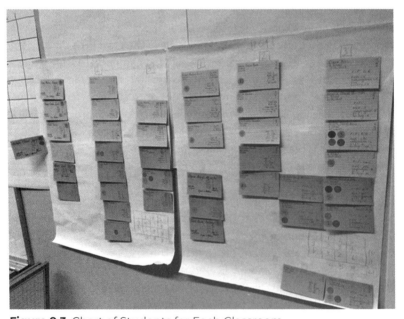

Figure 9.3 Chart of Students for Each Classroom.

Once all the cards are placed, the group reviews the new classrooms. Sending teachers and others tend to move between the classrooms, and receiving teachers stand, reviewing their new class and gathering the thoughts and reflections of others about certain children, pairs, or other general observations. This is often the time when imbalances (e.g., racial or readiness) or conflicts (e.g., a child is in a class with a relative where it would not be optimal) are noticed and alterations are made.

During this phase a designated person types the names into new school year rosters so each teacher will have a potential class list for the coming year at the close of the meeting. They will use this list to organize observations of the incoming children at work in their current classrooms.

When the team feels settled about the new classrooms, the Montessori coach closes the meeting with the following reminders:

- These placements are not set in stone – there is more to the process.
- As a result, these placements are entirely confidential and not to be shared with children or families.
- The next step is for receiving teachers to arrange observations of the children currently placed in their classroom.
- If, following observation, there is concern about a placement, then the sending and receiving teachers meet with the coach to discuss.
- Class placement charts are available for review; however, no cards are moved without the coach.

Following the meeting, the class placement charts are stored in a private, confidential location not used by children or families. This may be as simple as taping another piece of chart paper on top of each classroom of cards. Teachers are invited to visit these for review anytime. Though they have a class list, it does not include all of the information on the cards, which, seen together, provides a clearer picture of the new classroom community.

One aspect to be aware of during this next week of observing and considering the placements is the possibility of splitting. In some communities still working on the goal of One School, there can be side conversations and the instinct for people to move cards unilaterally. This is why only the coach moves cards and why it's important for them to support the observation process and to be involved in Honest Talk conversations about what is best for children. During this time, if someone engages in a conversation that is lacking respect for children or families, the coach should have a responsive directive conversation[4] with them. The system is built around the values of One School and Honest Talk and will not function well without attending to them during this time.

If a teacher is uncertain about a placement, the coach holds a meeting with both the sending and receiving teacher to review the situation. The coach has observed the child in question in advance of the meeting and brings their observations and insights to the conversation. A number of elements can be at play in these conversations, including fear, undeveloped skills of a teacher, or stylistic differences between educators. At the heart of it, however, lies an opportunity to strengthen the school through dialogue. Often these conversations are very productive and result in a stronger transition plan for the child. Perhaps what the elementary guide noticed was a lack of readiness on the part of the child, and through reviewing the transition checklist they decide that a late transition would be the best idea to offer more time to secure necessary skills. Perhaps the primary guide is able to talk about the learner's child study plan, and through review of their child study action plan they decide to create a transition action plan that focuses on elements to support an earlier transition to acclimate and create routines in the new classroom. Regardless of the situation, keeping the focus on what is optimal for the child, while fully supporting the adults in manifesting this, is the ultimate goal of these conversations.

Visits

Following the week of observations and any subsequent conversations, the children begin informal visits to their potential new classroom. These can begin with the child delivering something to the teacher and having a short interaction and build to longer visits along with a peer from their sending classroom. Some schools have a tradition of the transitioning children writing letters to the new teacher to set up a time to visit. This correspondence, arranging the day and time, begins the meaningful relationship that will last three years and cues the child that they have agency in how the relationship will develop.

At the first, longer visit the child has to their new room, they have a host child who is close in age and remembers their transition just a year ago. The host greets the visiting child and orients them to the classroom, pointing out the areas and giving some insight about procedures and routines, such as how to use the bathroom or how to have snack. The child then either works with the host or selects some familiar work of their own to do. In this way the child's first experience in the new environment is guided by their peers and honors the social needs of second- and third-plane learners.

Eventually, over the course of the spring visits, the children are brought into lessons with their new teacher. They are given follow-up work to complete and asked to use the systems that guide the rest of the class. This allows the receiving teacher to assess the child's readiness for the new environment and to get an understanding of where each new learner is academically as well as in the area of work habits and independence.

This is an important, and sometimes revealing, part of the process, so class placement is not considered complete until after this step. Seeing the children in their new environment offers insight (some children want to stay all day in their new classroom while others hesitate to visit at all) and can reveal unexpected complications for the match. Any concerns that arise during this time are also brought directly to the coach for discussion, followed by the coach's observation of the child visiting and a meeting with the sending teacher. Often in the meeting with the sending teacher more information about how to support the child will be shared that may resolve the concern. If not, the conversation continues until it is resolved either through extra support over time as the child grows more comfortable or, if it seems better for the child, a shift to another classroom.

This is why class placement information isn't shared with families until a few weeks into the visits when everyone feels positive about the match. It is especially important in the situation where the coach makes a classroom change based on the lack of capacity of the adult to serve the child and their estimation that even with coaching there will not be sufficient growth soon enough to offer an optimal experience for the child.

In general, however, this system allows for children to visit only one classroom so they can begin the adjustment process immediately – making friends, learning systems, and beginning the relationship with their new community. For a child transitioning from the first plane to the second plane, this is important as it reduces the overwhelm of the experience by focusing on their new environment and new relationships. When children are transitioning within the second plane, from lower elementary to upper elementary, this is important so that their natural tendency of discernment doesn't create a narrative of better–worse about any of the classrooms. For more on this, read the special section later in this chapter about transitioning older students.

Family Preparation

Each family has their own past school experiences, and likely your school is different from what they remember. Like multiage groupings or hands-on material, the three-year class placement is yet another uniqueness of a Montessori school. Offering families multiple opportunities to hear and understand that this is simply how your school works is an essential part of the seamless transition process.

Some families have had the past experience of hand-picking their child's next teacher. Some schools have a request process where families are invited to rank or select the next teacher. This is counter to the seamless transition plan as it is often based simply on perceptions and not on what is best for the child. Sharing the process early and often will begin to untangle this.

The family preparation has four parts:

- Family education transition talk
- Family letters
- Transition evening
- Family observation

Family Education Transition Talk

The family education transition talk is open to the whole community, with special invitations to families whose children will be transitioning that year. Led by the Montessori coach or the principal, the talk gathers families together to hear about the transition process. Having nontransitioning families at the meeting is wonderful as it is indirect preparation for when it will be their child's time and will prevent misconceptions about the process in the meantime.

At this meeting a version of the seamless transition overview (Table 9.1) is offered to families to follow along as the steps are reviewed. Each step is briefly explained without an emphasis on key children but rather focusing on the educational team's attentiveness to the right placement for each child, their expertise, and commitment to the process. Half of the meeting time is reserved for answering questions about the seamless transition system.

The first year of the process, there may be some distress over the change, especially if there used to be a family preference approach to placement. In this case, leadership can offer, just in the changeover year, the option for families to submit a preference – with the understanding that it will be only one factor in the placement decision. Then if the team places the child in a classroom different from what the family requested, the principal (and possibly the coach) meets with the family to discuss the decision and prepare them for the family letter they will receive. Proactive Honest Talk will be important as you shift to a system of seamless transitions.

Family Letters

Once the class placement process is complete and the team agrees with all placements, the main office sends letters out with information about the child's class for the coming year, an invitation to the family to the transition evening, and a short explanation of what this is and why they might want to attend. Here is a sample class placement family letter.

April 15, 2020

Dear _____ [caregiver's name],

At _____ [school name] we understand that your child's school experience plays an important role in their life. With this in mind, we have a carefully created process to make the transition from primary into elementary a great experience for everyone.

We are delighted that _____ [child's name] will be joining the elementary community in _____ [new teacher or classroom name] class next year. There are a series of events across the spring that will help you and your child orient to elementary beginning in ____ [number] weeks on _____ [date].

This transition to the elementary environment marks a new phase in your child's life, which Montessori calls the second plane of development. Over the course of the next few months, you will begin to see new characteristics, patterns of behavior, and needs. On _____ [date], we invite you to join us for a transition evening from _____ [time duration, e.g., 6 to 7:30 p.m.] to learn more from our elementary guides about your emerging second plane child and the process of transition. You will have the opportunity to meet _____ [teacher's name], tour the new classroom, meet other families, and learn more about your child's spring transition.

Please contact our community specialist, _____ [name], to let her know if you will be able to attend this event or if you have any questions. We are committed to your family's successful transition into the elementary community, and we look forward to seeing you on _____ [date].

On Behalf of the Child,
_____ [signature]

These letters have an RSVP element so that in the weeks leading up to the event the person responsible for working with families is able to contact those who haven't responded. The goal is to reach every family of a transitioning child to support getting on the same page about the upcoming transition. This will provide a stronger transition process for the children.

The letter also gives families a person to call if they are having a reaction to or questions about the placement decision. This is a One School move to ensure everyone has a way to be heard. The sample letter directs families to the community specialist. Most of the calls will be questions about the event, but if a family is uncomfortable with the placement then the specialist can let them know that the Montessori coach or principal will follow up with an in-person meeting.

Transition Evening

There are two parts to the transition evening: (1) whole-group introduction to the plane of development; and (2) individual class gatherings.

The evening can begin with a potluck dinner or simply with tea and dessert, but families are greeted with some hospitality that welcomes them to the new level. All the classroom guides from both the sending and receiving levels are present to greet families. Before the program begins, primary guides introduce families to the new elementary guide or elementary guides introduce them to adolescent guides, connecting them to their child's new teacher.

The principal opens the program with a brief welcome that brings the community together around the mission and vision of the school, frames the events of the evening, and turns it over to the receiving-level team. Staying with the example of moving primary children into lower elementary, the lower elementary team then takes the families through some shared components such as characteristics of the second plane of development, cosmic education, support for emerging readers, grace and courtesy at the elementary level, and how to support transitioning children over the summer. These are short talks, each given by a different teacher, with an accompanying handout for the families to follow.

There is both a *know* and a *do* part in each section of the presentation. What do you want families to know about this change from first plane to second plane? And what do you want them to be able to do to support their child in the transition? The same question applies to each of the other sections as well and having elementary teachers discuss and get clear in advance allows for a more streamlined, informative, and helpful evening for everyone. This will prevent teachers from waxing on for 30 minutes about the second plane of development taking most of the time allotted for the whole team and instead provide a framework for the shared time. The first year doing this, teams may want to have an agreement about how time is kept and what shared language is used to stay on schedule. For instance, one team sat in a row of chairs in front of the families in the order they were to speak. When it came to the end of one person's time, the next person would simply stand up and patiently wait for their colleague to finish. This would cue the speaking teacher that their time was up. Another team set a timer that played a friendly sound softly at two minutes before the end of each person's time, so when they heard the jingle they knew it was time to wrap up their section.

From the whole-group presentation, families then adjourn to their child's new classroom. Others who are not classroom teachers have lists of placements so they can direct family members to the right location. In the classroom, one of the adults gives an informal tour of the room, showing the way it is organized relative to the learning environment the child is leaving. In lower elementary this may be pointing out that the classroom now has more areas and sensorial has become geometry or that now activities are not on individual trays because the reasoning mind is at work to determine what will be needed to complete the task.

The group then gathers in preset chairs, and the classroom adults share any specific information distinct to that community and provide time for questions. They also share the spring transition experience, including ongoing classroom visits for the children, family observation opportunities, the simultaneous visiting day prior to the end of the year, and any summer activities.

At the end of the evening the family leaves with a clearer picture of what their child will be moving into in the coming year and the process that will allow for a seamless transition. This opening allows for Honest Talk between adults to support each child and their family.

Family Observation

During the transition evening, families are invited to sign up for an observation slot on a preorganized list of optimal times for observation. The family observation window is open for several weeks, so teachers select enough openings to accommodate new families plus a few extra in case of scheduling conflicts or missed observations.

That list is then given to the Montessori coach, who takes responsibility for greeting and orienting the family when they arrive, establishing the norms for a classroom observation, and distributing the family transition observation tool. The coach then either co-observes or leaves them to observe the active work period of the child's new classroom for 20 minutes. The observation tool offers a helpful focus and provides a place to note their questions.

Following the 20-minute observation, the family meets with the Montessori coach to debrief. Here they have an opportunity to ask any questions that emerged about the structure and flow of the new environment or to have a more personal conversation about their child's transition. This is a 15-minute conversation.

Family Observation Schedule:

Arrival and orientation 5 min.

Observation 20 min.

Debrief with coach 15 min.

Closure and departure 5 min.

Total time 45 min.

This may seem like an enormous investment of time, yet it is one of the parts of the whole school Montessori method that takes time to save time. If you have 50 children to transition from primary to elementary (arguably the trickiest transition as families are newest to the school and trust may not yet be built) then you need to spend a total of 37.5 hours over three weeks, which is about 30% of the coach's time for those three weeks. That would be if everyone signed up and everyone participated and everyone took 45 minutes. What you get from this investment is a clear sense of the family's needs for the coming year to be proactive rather than reactive. As an element of the seamless transition for the child, the seamless transition of the family is critical and needs an investment of time as well.

In these individual debrief meetings with families, the Montessori coach is actively offering Montessori education for the family to understand how the classroom functions, what will be expected of their child, and what is different about this method. Having handouts on executive functioning, reasoning mind, freedom, and responsibility to supplement what they received at the transition evening will support greater understanding of the school their child is attending.

Another aspect of these meetings is the insights the family offers the coach about the child and their family. This cannot be underestimated as an important part of reassuring and settling any potential rising anxiety the family may bring to the change. And it's a practice that supports both the One School and Honest Talk values and communicates them directly to families. This is the action that supports the words.

Experience shows that the families who attend these optional observation sessions are often the ones who, without this process, might be contacting leadership in a more elevated state to communicate their concerns. Having an opportunity to connect early doesn't always prevent this in the end, but it does give the school adults greater insight into what's going on in the family, allowing leadership to brainstorm supports in advance of any issues.

Visiting Day

Hooray – it's visiting day! This is a much anticipated marker of time for all the children in the school. Montessori schools don't have "graduations" for kindergarten students that falsely mark an end to something, as primary is the start of their education rather than a completion of it. Instead, there is a school-wide, hour-long visit for children to move into their new classroom. This means all transitioning primary children visit their lower elementary classroom while all the transitioning lower elementary children visit upper elementary and all transitioning upper elementary children visit the adolescent program. The transitioning adolescent students, or students from wherever the school ends, have a special meeting to work on their graduation speeches. They, too, are gearing up for a transition, also marked and supported by the school community.

During the hour in the new classroom, there is a meeting to honor and admire the group as it will be when school resumes after summer. Then the classroom adults introduce a special project that will begin on that day and be completed on the first day back to school, such as:

- An *art* project where everyone sews a quilt square that is assembled in the fall or paints a tile that is created as a mosaic in the fall.

- An *academic* project such as having teams explore continents and draw flags to represent work that will continue in the fall, write poems that will go into an anthology in the fall, or assigning pairs of students to select a card from the "Who am I?" set and begin a research project that can continue over the summer and resume in the fall.

- A *social* project in which teams use a feeling chart to explore an emotion and create a superhero to support or students draw a self-portrait to begin identity work that will continue in the fall.

Regardless of the project, this is the transitioning child's link to their new classroom. They have begun something to look forward to that places them in and with the new group of peers on a shared project. This has been important for students who are anxious about transitioning; it gives them something to focus on over the summer or to connect to as they gear up for the return.

Across the whole school, this is also an opportunity for the future leaders of the new classroom communities to feel that for the first time. Now the other children are looking to them for guidance, and they are the ones who know what to do.

Observation is essential during this hour. Classroom adults and the Montessori coach note the new, emerging dynamic between the group of learners with attention to leadership, independence, and grace and courtesy. They also have the opportunity to observe key children to gather information that may generate more ideas for how to support them over the summer and in the upcoming transition. Often, unexpected leaders emerge in this first experience in whom these qualities can then be cultivated over the remaining days of school.

Portfolio Passing

The final component of this Strong System connects to a student portfolio system, where classroom guides carefully collect and organize files prepared with a special cover sheet. On a designated day, these are passed with the child from level to level, which allows each new teacher adequate time to get to know the new student and prepare for their arrival in the classroom.

One school created an afterschool hour for teachers to meet to discuss the children as they handed off the portfolios. They called it *portfolio speed dating*, as it was set up in the community gathering space with stations. The teachers had crates with portfolios at their stations. The first part was primary teachers seated at stations passing to lower elementary, who moved from station to station in a loop. Upper elementary teachers were also seated at stations and passed to adolescent teachers, who moved from station to station in another loop. The coach kept a timer with six minutes for each station. When the timer went off, the visiting adults moved to the next station in the loop. Often this wasn't enough time to fully discuss the more complex learners, but it was a starting point that led to follow-up meetings arranged individually between receiving and sending teachers.

The second part of the meeting was lower elementary teachers at stations with upper elementary adults moving from station to station in a loop. The primary teachers then received information about their incoming three-year-olds and the adolescent team reviewed their graduating student records to ensure team readiness to send to the receiving high school.

It was a wild hour, but at the end the classroom adults felt invigorated to have accomplished something they always wanted to do but had never previously found time for: honoring the transition of each learner.

LATE TRANSITIONS

In Montessori, not everyone who is the same biological age is expected to be ready for the same thing at the same time. We do not expect they will all lose their first tooth on the same day, so we do not also expect they will all begin elementary on the same day. Part of every Strong System is its alliance with the method; therefore, a seamless transition system allows for the fact that there may be some children who visit in the spring and never leave and others who aren't ready to visit until the following fall. For those children, we offer a late transition where they begin their visits when school resumes. The same visiting process is followed from the short incidental visit to the longer hosted visit to the regular times to be in the new elementary environment.

Families of children who are not quite ready to move into the new classroom at the beginning of the year are invited to observe in the fall and debrief with the coach to create a plan to support their child's transition. There is no urgency or sense of shame; rather, there is acceptance of the child's progress and confidence in their ability to make the transition with supporting conditions. These are largely children who have been in the child study process and are known to the school as needing extra support.

In most district schools, there is a cutoff date when enrollment is finalized and all children need to be entered into Powerschool (or other enrollment platform) at their current "grade." This also then becomes the deadline for late transitions and for a determination of whether a child is ready (or nearly ready) to attend "first grade" in their new classroom. This doesn't mean that they are spending all day, every day by the district cutoff, but only that the team is confident the transition will be successful and the child is ready for the transition. They will be assessed at that grade level, but more importantly from a whole-child perspective they show characteristics of the next plane and the capacity to move into the new environment without detriment to their sense of self.

TRANSITIONING OLDER STUDENTS

In this short section there are some thoughts about supporting older children in a seamless transition where their sense of self now rests in the social world and how they are perceived by others. Some special considerations include (a) readiness for the upcoming transition and (b) fit with the new community.

To ensure readiness for all children moving from lower elementary into upper elementary or from upper elementary into middle school, that process needs to begin at the start of the year. Weekly conversations with these learners are needed to begin to turn their mind to what is coming up and what they need to do personally to prepare. Are they ready academically? Do they feel they've mastered the skills they will need to be successful at the next level? Are they ready socially to move from the oldest back to the youngest again? Do they feel they have the fortitude to be successful managing this change?

One way to do this is to have a designated person take on the group for the year. This could be the Montessori coach, the nautilus lead, an interventionist, or someone appropriately skilled who does not lead their own classroom. This person then meets with the group weekly. To be consistent let's plot the course for children moving from lower into upper elementary.

The first meetings happen within the individual lower elementary classrooms with only the oldest children in the conversation. The children are given special transition journals, and at the front they begin a list of everything they think they should know and be able to do before they go onto the next level. This list, which begins as the child's own list, can be quite charming and has included everything from knowing how to talk on the telephone to using the decimal checkerboard. They then share these out loud and are encouraged to add their peers' suggestions to their list if they agree with the ideas. Here we are activating their intrinsic motivation while also orienting them to the big transition ahead.

Over the fall the group continues to meet weekly to work on important skills, with follow-up work to be done between the meetings. As a result, a growing body of data about readiness is helpful in conversations with the teacher, the student, and the family. Then comes the considerations around the fit and selecting the just-right community for each learner.

Beginning in January, the groups now meet in the next-level environments. For lower elementary students, they are brought together by class to a different upper elementary environment each week. At the start they still have their set lesson with the facilitator and are not yet integrated or working in the upper elementary classroom. This allows for some subtle orientation to the new rooms as they see who is in each classroom and where supplies are kept, should they need to sharpen their pencil or use a ruler. They then move to weekly visits with mixed groups of lower elementary children to test out the chemistry between learners from different classrooms prior to class placement. Following class placement, and prior to the formal visits, the groups are structured around the intended classes for the upcoming year, and the upper elementary teacher now offers the children lessons. In this way there is far more information about the match should adjustments need to be made. Upper elementary students are savvy and understand that, when visits begin, this marks the start of their transition to their new community, so any changes should be made in advance of these visits.

Upper elementary students generally travel independently to the adolescent environment where they also meet on location with their facilitator, but this lesson may now also include others from the adolescent community who may lead the lesson or facilitate the discussion. The original facilitator begins to fade in importance as the adolescents themselves support the transition of the new students. This could be structured as a literature circle with pairs of adolescents leading the upper elementary student groups from each classroom or connected research to something already going on in the adolescent environment. In one school, the rising upper elementary students joined the adolescents for their days on the farm, supporting the work there, and joining the community through that experience. Regardless of how this is done, the goal is to seamlessly orient the rising students to the next environment that offers experiences over time and allows for observation prior to class placement.

NEW WORLD CONSIDERATIONS

If school is in distance learning mode with children learning virtually from home, then much of this happens through technology. The only component that happens differently is the family observation, which is replaced with individual class gatherings held over the spring for families to raise questions or share concerns. These can be one-time occurrences or ongoing meetings structured as open office hours – however families can best be provided with time to process and prepare for the upcoming transition and supported in their connection to the school. Table 9.3 is an overview of the new world transition components.

SEAMLESS TRANSITION SUMMARY

This system offers:

- A child-centered approach to developing classes
- An open, clear system for how children move from one level to the next
- Guidelines for how to participate in the process
- Inclusion of families through communication and events
- Balanced classroom communities
- A seamless transition for all learners and their families

This system prevents:

- A school year starting with unhappy children and families
- Families of privilege and power selecting classrooms for their children based on the perceived "best" teacher.
- Imbalanced classes developed from internal perceptions of teachers who are gifted with key children, or some teachers' unwillingness to engage with key children.
- Resentments between team members about classroom makeup

To begin slowly, consider adopting the class placement part of the system as a starting place. From there you can build on the other parts over time as the school builds capacity for the full seamless transition system.

Table 9.3 New World Transition Overview

Event	Description
Transition Checklist	– Documents are distributed at the start of the year – Early spring they are completed by lead guides and shared in a virtual team meeting
Class Placement	A collaborative process for placing students to create balanced classrooms: • Card setup happens digitally • Placement meetings happen virtually with use of screen share to view cards & classroom lists • Observation and discussion period happen through use of technology
Visits	Children are invited to community meetings in their new classroom and virtual lessons with their new teacher
Family Preparation	– Transition Family Education talk done virtually – Family letters sent as usual – Transition evening done virtually with breakout rooms for individual class meetings – Family observations are replaced with individual classroom meetings with the coach (and teacher if possible) to discuss concerns/questions
Visiting Day	A simultaneous visiting day where all students visit their new class at the same time for one hour happens virtually with a shared whole group meeting time. This is a shorter time but still holds the shared activity started to be continued at the start of the following year.
Portfolio Passing	Student Portfolios are passed digitally from the sending teacher to the receiving teacher with short conversations surrounding Key Children which happens virtually.
Late Transitions	Gradual transitions are carefully constructed by the coach, level teachers and family to determine a plan that covers all the new world considerations with most children starting at the opening of the year. A cut off date is still determined.
Transitioning Older Students	The weekly meetings happen virtually in a breakout room from their classroom or on a separate link. Physical journals can be distributed as well as orienting the students to the learning platform used at the next level and expected use of that for the weekly assignments.

STUDENT PORTFOLIO

A student portfolio is a collection of documents that tell a story about the learner. When laid out in the final student-led conference at the end of their time at the school, there is physical evidence of their growth and development. Experienced by the learner and their family as a walk down memory lane, student portfolios provide a carefully selected assemblage of artifacts to tell the story.

This story is also used to support the seamless transition system by allowing adults a peek into the work and life of the new students they will be receiving into their classroom in the coming year. When student portfolios are passed at the end of the year, as described already, teachers are then introduced to artifacts that offer a deeper view of the child they are just meeting.

The student portfolio holds a number of documents, but the bulk of it is select work samples. These are collected twice a year (fall and spring) over the three years at each level. Each season one or two choice work samples are reserved from work going home and kept as examples of the child's growth and development. In the early years, this is done by the classroom teacher, who often chooses "firsts" such as the first metal inset, the first time they write their name, or the first puzzle map and ends with the most elaborate metal inset or the most complex story. In elementary and adolescent programs, the students are involved in the selection process during their student conference with their teacher. They aren't asked to choose their "best" work but rather the work they are most proud of completing. This could be a heavily erased cube root problem or, as shown in Figure 9.4, one out of a series of paper books with hand-drawn

Figure 9.4 Example of Student Choices for Portfolio Work.

lines and extra staples binding it that represents their exploration of the time-line of life. Regardless, it is the student's choice. The classroom adult also chooses one piece of work to add to the portfolio and explains to the child or adolescent why it was selected – what elements are impressive, stand out, tell a story of learning. This process in itself is a productive part of the relationship building over years between the classroom adult, the learner, and their growth and development.

Student Portfolio Cover Sheet

Student Name:_____

D.O.B.: _____   **Classroom:**_____

Contents:

- ☐ Student work samples
- ☐ Reading Assessment results
- ☐ MAP or other Assessment results
- ☐ Transition Checklist
- ☐ Family Contact Log/ Conference notes
- ☐ Child Study documents

The student has received:

- ☐ Special Education services
- ☐ ESL services: phase_____
- ☐ Reading Intervention:_____
- ☐ Child Study support
- ☐ Counseling services
- ☐ Speech services
- ☐ OT or PT services

Teacher Name:_____**For grades:**_____

Figure 9.5 Student Portfolio Cover Sheet.

At the end of a three-year cycle there should be about a dozen pieces of work (2 each semester x 2 semesters x 3 years = 12) in the student's portfolio. In addition, the classroom adult sends along other important information about the child to the receiving teacher. These items are checked off on the Portfolio cover sheet (Figure 9.5) and include items such as: assessment results, transition checklists, family contact logs, and conference notes. If the student was in child study, then any documents associated with that process are also included in the portfolio.

The second part of the portfolio cover sheet (Figure 9.5) is a series of checkboxes offering the receiving teacher a sense of the child at a glance. This will support them in asking the right questions (e.g., how long have they been receiving counseling?), seeking additional documents (e.g., a copy of an individualized education plan), anticipating additional meetings (e.g., with a reading interventionist to understand academic needs), or awareness of additional assessments (e.g., for a child for whom English is a second language).

The cover sheet acts as a table of contents for what can be found in the portfolio; for those who use folders, it can be stapled on the front. From a pragmatic standpoint, folders work well as they contain information at one level. As an upper elementary teacher, this meant I had three folders for each child contained in a hanging file folder in my file cabinet: the two I received (from primary and lower elementary) and the one I started for our three years together.

As new children transitioned into my classroom I was able to understand their journey from all the way back to their year of entry. The work samples for primary helped to identify early trends such as those who had fine motor challenges, early interest in planets, or gifts in numeracy. The work samples from lower elementary offered more recent information relevant to their transition such as their skill with cursive writing, ability to express themselves in words, interests, and based on their work sample choices – their values. This information, triangulated with data from assessments and recordkeeping documents of material mastered, allowed for a feeling of preparation to greet the learner where they were and fluidly support the continuation of their learning journey.

SYSTEM OF JUSTNESS

Every school must have a way of ensuring just action when something unexpected happens. This is to address not equality, not even equity, but liberation: to remove systemic barriers that restrict and prevent all children and families from freely accessing a strong Montessori education. Given the referral rates for children of all the global majority in schools in this country, every school leader must have this on their radar. Rather than associating this with justice, as in the criminal justice system, it is framed for you here as a System of Justness – just and fair for all. Justness, defined by the Cambridge dictionary,[5] is "the quality of being fair or morally correct," and that is the goal of this system.

A distinguishing feature of the System of Justness, which is meant to replace a district discipline policy or behavior plan, is that, like Montessori itself, it is constructivist rather than behaviorist. It does not seek to punish or force children to submit to the word of adults. Rather, it is created to respect the formation of self and the natural moral development of the individual while also protecting the needs of the community. In this way it is a system that supports the values of One School: unity, awareness, power, structure, and autonomy. Having systems to support what we do means having a way the school community can learn to live these values rather than simply discussing them.

In this section we will be thinking about key children. These are the children who struggle in school and may need extra support to find their rhythm. As a part of language of reverence we do not call them frequent flyers or behavior problems but rather key children. These are children who hold keys to how to improve our implementation; they are our greatest teachers.

The Montessori System of Justness is divided into three major areas: (1) Montessori implementation; (2) the nautilus approach; and (3) child study.

Figure 9.6 offers a visual overview of the System of Justness and its three parts. As you can see, Montessori implementation rests on the three components of the whole school Montessori method. The nautilus approach, which is at the heart of the system, holds both proactivity and responsiveness, which are essential for the approach to be fully realized. The last part is child study, which is a child-centered way to support all learners who continue to be of concern.

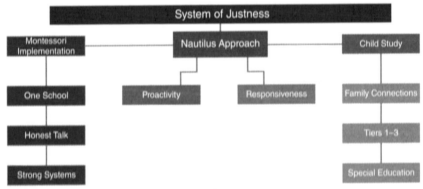

Figure 9.6 System of Justness Overview.

MONTESSORI IMPLEMENTATION

At the core of our method lies the insight that work settles us. When we lose our way, due to big feelings, conflict, or circumstances beyond our control, focusing deeply on something helps us to recenter. Maria Montessori observed this over 100 years ago and wrote about it in her book *The Secret of Childhood*.

> Among the revelations the child has brought us, there is one of fundamental importance, the phenomenon of normalization through work. Thousands and thousands of experiences among children of every race enable us to state that this phenomenon is the most certain datum verified in psychology or education. It is certain that the child's attitude towards work represents a vital instinct; for without work his personality cannot organize itself. . . . Man builds himself through working, working with his hands, but using his hands as the instruments of his ego, the organ of his individual mind and will, which shapes its own existence face to face with its environment.[6]

Therefore, for the System of Justness to exist, there must be classrooms where children are able to deeply engage with work. If children build themselves through work, then every classroom needs to offer full implementation of the Montessori curriculum where children are paired to the right material at the right time to fulfill their natural-born need to learn and to ignite in them the curiosity and motivation to push beyond what they can already do. If Montessori classrooms become dependent on supplemental materials[7] to achieve test scores, then this weakens the very foundation of what is needed by our most vulnerable learners.

In the implementation of the whole school Montessori method where a Montessori coach works weekly with classroom adults to support ongoing growth in their work, then the critical skills named on the material side of the fundamental needs of the Montessori educator[8] are considered and met. These are areas of focus and growth for every practitioner for the strong Montessori implementation to move from aspirational and become realized.

Without this in place, the other components of the System of Justness will not be able to flourish. They will become merely systems that are spinning wheels without traction for the traction is found in the sincere application of the method and the rigorous work of connecting children to meaningful work.

THE NAUTILUS APPROACH

The nautilus approach is built around Montessori's insight of centering through work with a direct aim of bringing children back to engagement in meaningful learning. This is very different from the goal of most discipline systems in public schools where the goal is removal of the problem.

As the nautilus creators explored this idea of bringing the child back to work as opposed to out of the classroom, we began to draw the trajectory we imagined. Through this idea of work at the center and the value of repeatedly bringing the child back to center, we found ourselves drawing a nautilus shell. Many discipline policies use a ladder to show the steps to be followed. That image of a ladder implies moving the child progressively farther away from the place of learning, whereas the nautilus shell (Figure 9.7), structured as a spiral, reminds us that our goal is to move them always back to the place of learning. In a conventional classroom where children are doing workbooks and worksheets they may take this with them when they are removed from the classroom. However, for Montessori schools the learning is situated in the prepared environment, so when children leave the classroom they are leaving the learning.

Figure 9.7 The Nautilus Approach Image.

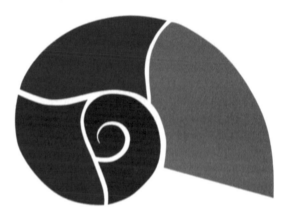

NAUTILUS APPROACH
Montessori Implementation . Proactivity . Responsiveness . Child Study

In Figure 9.7, we are reminded that the nautilus approach rests on the other components (Montessori Implementation, proactivity, responsiveness, and child study) and will not work in isolation without the other parts of the System of Justness in the same way that a car frame will not go anywhere without a motor (Montessori implementation) or wheels (child study).

Also in Figure 9.7, you see that Montessori implementation is at the center of the spiral and where practitioners are focused. Often disruptions can be managed entirely through our Montessori method using grace and courtesy norms, classroom agreements, and strong relationships within the classroom community.

Proactive strategies, learned in the nautilus training,[9] add a next level of support for learners who may need more. Working in a proactive way with our key children allows them to grow skills they are missing in order to feel more comfortable and successful in their classroom environment.

Figure 9.8 RELATE.

One of the proactive strategies is to focus on relationship building. There are many elements of building strong relationships, but as a simple tool to support school-based adults in developing relationships we start with six (Figure 9.8):

- **R**espect: At the heart of the Montessori method is respect for the child. Montessori invites us to treat the child as a social equal. In this way, we do not need to use a special voice, tone, or language to communicate. Rather, using a normal voice and tone with the language of reverence we would use with a respected colleague is our way of building a solid foundation with children.

- **E**ngage: When we engage with individual children, we come to know them as unique beings with their own interests and gifts. Through our awareness of these we are able to develop a stronger relationship with them, feeding what they are thinking about, curious about, and drawn to doing.

- **L**ead: Children need adults to take the lead in the relationship to support their growing decision-making skills. It will not do to "follow the child," as they are making poor decisions that will negatively impact them or the community. Montessori reminds us in *The Absorbent Mind* "to let the child do as he likes when he has not yet developed any powers of control is to betray the idea of freedom."[10] Children ultimately appreciate the care beneath the leadership adults show in setting and holding boundaries. They also appreciate the leadership adults show when they model what they expect to see, tell the truth, apologize, and make a repair.

- **A**cknowledge: It is Marshall Rosenberg who teaches us that acknowledgment is not agreement.[11] This means even if we don't agree with a child's perspective it is still important to acknowledge it. This might mean acknowledging a feeling before it grows so large as to overshadow all else. "It looks like you are frustrated because you believe this was your chair. Is that right?" A sentence such as this will frequently calm a rising situation simply because the child feels seen and understood. To feel part of something we all need acknowledgment, and this can also mean appreciating what a child has done or brings to the community simply by being themself.

- **T**rust: Building trust with children is a direct aim of building relationships and the first four elements support this: respect, engage, lead, and acknowledge. With these trust will be built, yet keeping the trust of children requires that we don't overextend and promise what we cannot deliver. It means no say–do gap and maintaining fair and equitable practices within our classrooms and schools to allow children to relax into learning.

- **E**njoy: It is easy to move away from the joy of the work we have chosen. The cognitive load of teaching can become quite heavy and this often separates us from being fully present in work we love. Bringing back the pleasure in the work has a significant impact on the children we serve. When we enjoy a lesson, a conversation, a day at school, it is contagious. An essential part of building relationships with children is the messages we send that we enjoy them; we enjoy spending time with them, we enjoy our time at school.

This is a summary of one proactive strategy that will support resolving some of the ongoing issues that arise in the dynamic social world of a Montessori classroom. Yet we must remember Montessori's insight shared in the 1946 London Lectures: "The children must be attached to the material; if they are attached to the teacher they cannot be independent."[12] Our ultimate goal in building strong relationships with children is not to gain their esteem or have them adore us but to support their connection to learning. They are in school to luxuriate in the human tendency for exploration that leads to learning, and for key children we sometimes need to take a more prominent role in connecting them to that natural experience.

The nautilus approach uses other proactive strategies (reviewed in the training), but what happens when a situation escalates anyway? In spite of strong Montessori implementation and proactivity, sometimes a child's level of distress is not resolved. The nautilus approach offers all the adults in the building a series of phases – each leading back to the child's engagement in real work – to follow when a child is in distress. This level of calibration means key children receive a consistent, predictable response, which in itself allows for a more rapid return to work. When adults each have their own varied approach to disruption this can be confusing, particularly to key children who represent our most vulnerable learners. In this way, justness is built into the approach as all children can rely on a predictable response that no longer rests on someone "getting in trouble" but instead values reengagement with learning and the feeling of being capable and productive.

The nautilus approach also has paperwork that reflects the Montessori values. The referral report is filled out only if a child does something dangerous, destructive, or demeaning (known as the 3 Ds) or if their distress has risen to the level where others in the learning environment are no longer able to concentrate. The classroom adult fills out one side of the referral, and the nautilus lead fills out the other; the learner fills out a separate page if it is developmentally appropriate. In this way the team is able to process, reflect on, and document times when a child needs to leave the classroom, which leads to a critical part of the nautilus approach – the repair.

For the child to continue growing with a strong sense of self, and self-worth, there must be an opportunity to repair whatever was torn or broken. This may mean a relationship with a friend or the classroom adult that needs to be repaired through an apology or an honest conversation about feelings. It may mean restoring order when a material was left in disarray or papers were scattered. This may mean rebuilding trust with the larger community that was broken when something more seriously dangerous, destructive, or demeaning occurred. Regardless of the incident, part of the just system provides every child the right to a repair, and no child returns to the classroom without following the defined reentry process that allows for that to occur. Consistent reentry practices following a child's time out of the classroom allows the whole community of learners to settle back into learning, knowing there is a respectful process that will restore order.

Every time a child leaves the classroom learning environment and a referral report is filled out, some basic information is recorded in the nautilus tracker. This allows for data collection around who is out of which classroom, for how long, and why. For data collected on the tracker to become usable knowledge, it must be put in accurately and consistently and then analyzed. The nautilus tracker alone won't support change in your community without the commitment to regular reviews – scheduled times to analyze and reflect on the collected data. Since the nautilus tracker is developed in Excel, it allows the lead to sort the data by any domain, such as classroom, race, gender, type of incident, and time of day. Disaggregating the data in this way brings to light trends such as 62% of all children are coming out of one classroom or 90% of all children are boys or 75% of all children are in upper elementary classrooms.

Now that there is information, that can be put in service of the school's mission. Maybe more professional development is needed on proactive strategies or relationship building. Maybe there are overidentifications of subgroups of students or students coming out of a particular classroom or level that calls for stronger coaching to those in need. This process of reviewing the data turns it into information that can then become usable knowledge.[13]

Since Honest Talk is a norm within the school, this can then be discussed through directive coaching in a one-on-one coaching meeting. "I'd like to look at your nautilus data with you today" starts a conversation where the sorted data for a classroom is shared. Montessori adults will inevitably notice the same trends, as the data speaks for itself. If not, the coach must be prepared to point out the trend and ask what their thoughts are on the data. "How do you understand this?" or "Why do you think that is?" might allow the teacher an opportunity to be reflective rather than reactive, ultimately resulting in a partnership toward change.

In one school, the nautilus lead was feeling very positive in the first six weeks of implementation. Following a school-wide professional development session on the approach, the team had worked hard to implement with fidelity and to hold to the phases before calling the nautilus support team. The nautilus lead had done a lot of both embedded and directive coaching with teachers to support any skill gaps in working with upset children. The result was a drop in referrals only six weeks into the school year. This was following the previous year, prior to the implementation of the nautilus approach, where incidents increased across the year, causing many students to spend regular time out of their classroom and thus impacting their academic progress.

As we began sorting the data in different ways, we saw the general drop in referrals. It wasn't until I asked the nautilus lead to sort it by race that we were caught up short. Without awareness of this fact, the school had mirrored national trends in the inequitable referrals of children of the global majority. A quick scan of that data suggested further disaggregation – to look at that same data by gender and then by classroom. When the nautilus lead did this, it was startling to see that most of those referrals were of Black boys coming out of the same classroom: one with two white, female teachers.

When I asked the Nautilus lead, if she knew this, she acknowledged that she knew it in her gut but not in her head. The classroom was led by a newly trained elementary teacher who was very kind and caring. The assistant brought a lot of public school experience and compensated for the new teacher's generous nature by holding firm limits. There seemed to be conditions in this particular classroom under which the Black boys in the class were not being successful.

Though this was not what the nautilus lead was expecting or hoping to find, it allowed her, along with the head of the school, to make lasting changes that continue to impact learners. She began with an honest conversation about the data, followed by directive coaching with the classroom team focused on the concern until the data noted change. She also began school-wide regular anti-bias, antiracist (ABAR) work, bringing the topic of race to the forefront of the conversation and having all teachers engage in the work of exploring equity.

This is a story of where data had the power to create change that will impact learners' access to the Montessori curriculum and to ongoing learning in their classrooms far into the future. It affected many of the same students from the previous year who showed a loss in academic gains due to time out of the classroom. Prior to the implementation of the nautilus approach and without the data collection, the team was not able to pinpoint and remedy the underlying issues.

The data collected through the tracker serves two purposes: equity reviews and child study referrals. Equity reviews are scheduled, monthly times when the team sorts the data various ways to begin looking for discrepancies or trends involving any particular demographic. As described already, this serves to protect every child's access to the curriculum regardless of race, gender, age, special education status, or classroom teacher.

The child study process begins once a learner has three nautilus referral reports. Regular data reviews allow the lead to keep track of which children have had multiple upsets that necessitated leaving the classroom and to ensure they are moving through the child study process. The nautilus lead is the initial contact with families, so if they are not also the child study lead then they are the one to set and lead the first child study family meeting where the family learns about this new level of support available for their child.

The Nautilus Lead

The nautilus lead is the school-based adult that holds the center of gravity for the full realization of the nautilus approach as a whole-school method for responding to children. There are three main areas of focus for the nautilus lead:

1. *Implementation:* They ensure full implementation of the approach across all areas of the school from classrooms to recess to dismissal. Their task is to train, coach, and support all staff members in the use of the phases and the proactive strategies.

2. *Ongoing support:* They are both proactive and responsive in support of children maximizing their time focused on learning. This includes work with children, families, and educators. They create and run social–emotional learning groups that support students in building skills in areas such as self-esteem, emotion regulation, flexibility, executive functioning, and affinity groups.

3. *Data collection:* They collect data to support equitable Montessori implementation and to ensure children receive necessary support through the child study process. They are responsible for the daily reporting, regular review of the data, and responding to information emerging from the data to promote change in policy, practice, or behavior.

NEW WORLD CONSIDERATIONS

When children are learning at a distance and are no longer in school, the nautilus lead continues with their ongoing support and data collection. These two parts act to ensure the most optimal experience for the school's most vulnerable learners.

Ongoing Support

This now had multiple components: support for key children, support for families, and support for staff members. For the children, they continued to hold the social–emotional groups and to engage in regular proactive support of all learners, observing virtual lessons to ensure key children continue to have access to the learning.

The nautilus lead also took a larger role in supporting families through this time, many of whom expressed uncertainty about how to manage learning at home. Some began weekly meetings with topics generated by observation or from the families themselves. These are coffee conversations, informal and meant to open a place for families to ask questions, express concerns, and receive support from others to rise to the occasion. The nautilus lead prepared a 15–20-minute presentation on a topic such as fostering independence, sparking intrinsic motivation, and setting limits and invites the whole community to join in conversation around the topic.

Then, when any school adult was meeting with a struggling family, they could specifically invite them to join the next coffee conversation. This often provided the kind of ongoing support people needed to navigate the times when they were in quarantine and had fewer outlets and less space to process and reflect.

The regular meetings held with classroom teams also continued; however, now there was a slight shift where the nautilus lead was listening for how the staff member was with the new conditions. It opened up new possibilities for providing extra support for key children to relieve some potentially rising pressure on the lead guide.

Data Collection

The data collection shifted to reviewing attendance data. Here new key children emerged based on the capacity of the family during the time of learning at home. Attendance at the social–emotional learning groups was tracked to ensure the children were being reached and had the support they needed. In addition, attendance was taken at the coffee conversation through the chat function to keep track of who was attending. Equity was the lens through which this data was reviewed to ensure it held a balance of families and was not dominated by any particular group. It was also used next to the data around key children to be sure their families were aware of, invited to, and attending the support meetings.

CHILD STUDY

Child study[14] is an approach for offering early, Montessori-oriented support for children and families. It guides children who arrive at school unsure of how to engage in a Montessori learning environment or who, over time, struggle to move forward in their learning either academically, behaviorally, socially, or emotionally. We call this the BASE (Behavior, Academics, Social, Emotional), as is it the lens through which we consider the main question "What's going on with this child?" Which of those areas is creating the greatest challenge and what adjustments could be made to support them in that area?

This Montessori approach to tiered instruction originated in Springfield public schools and was further refined in three Hartford public Montessori schools. The National Center for Montessori in the Public Sector then went on to develop a training so Montessori schools and practitioners could use it in place of a more typical student support system commonly used, such as response to intervention (RTI) or multitiered system of supports (MTSS).

In spite of the fact that it is central to the Montessori method, often in busy schools there isn't an opportunity for adults to collaborate with families or with each other to adjust to the needs of each individual child to support their growth and development. This can lead to increasing frustration and a decline in the relationship between the staff and the child, the staff and the family, or both. Child study offers schools an opportunity to slow down, consider one child's needs at a time, and build skills together through the process.

When a concern is not resolved through the typical alterations a classroom guide might make and multiple conversations have already occurred with the family, a child study family meeting is set to begin the process. Here the child study lead and the lead guide meet with the family to discuss the situation. The meeting notes are taken by the child study lead and if possible are made visible to everyone at the meeting while they are being taken to ensure accuracy and family comfort with the process. The teacher opens the meeting sharing the concern. Then the family, as the people who know the child best, shares information. The teacher talks about what has already been tried to resolve the situation and the team brainstorms what might help. An action plan is made, listing what will happen at school and what will happen at home as well as when the team will reconvene to discuss the progress.

If, after multiple family meetings, the situation is still not resolving then it moves to the level team meeting. Now the child study protocol is followed.

Written as a protocol, it fits into a 45-minute meeting and results in a tailored action plan to support the child moving forward. To begin the process, the classroom teacher presents the child to the team and answers questions. This is followed by a discussion of the main concern to define the problem. As support for identifying this the team looks at unmet needs, lagging skills,[15] and obstacles.

Here it becomes clearer where the difficulty is at the BASE, and a primary concern is identified.

The next step in the process is to articulate a goal that is specific, measurable, achievable, relevant, and timely. In other words, it's a SMART goal.

Examples of SMART Goals:

> Behavior goal: Bella will wait her turn at lunch 80% of the time by September 29.
>
> Academic goal: Bella will know 26 letter sounds by March 5.
>
> Social goal: Bella will play with others at recess by October 8.
>
> Emotional goal: Bella will smile at least 3x during morning meeting by October 29.

The next step is a team brainstorming process that results in three or four actions to support the child in reaching that goal. These ideas should incorporate everything the team already knows about the child with special attention to their interests and their strengths. Building a plan around these two elements increases the chances of success. For example, Bella loves handwork and wants to spend all of her time in practical life doing embroidery, knitting, and sewing. For Bella's action plan she will start a letter quilt. Each letter sound she learns she will add to her quilt.

By activating the specific child study brainstorming process, it allows all members of the team to contribute, bringing their various experiences to imagine supportive actions for this particular child to reach this one goal. The calibration that occurs within level teams to support children who are struggling is a form of professional development as it helps everyone begin to think more creatively about how to prepare a stronger environment for their key children. An example of this is a primary team that created an action plan for a child working on impulsivity. One component of the plan was to carry heavy objects: the book basket to return to the library, jugs of water to the garden, or the recess bin with equipment. This was so successful that often primary teachers could be seen walking with a young child investing great effort in carrying something the teacher would have previously easily carried instead. The smiles of recognition that occurred when passing in the hallway on these occasions represented the shared experience building on the team.

An important component of the action plan to be identified in the team meeting is an indicator of progress to show whether the plan is working (Table 9.4). This challenges teams to make the goal measurable and to find a data collection tool that can be completed daily without an egregious amount of extra time and effort. Finding something that is already part of the classroom routine or designating a set amount of time within the day helps to make this manageable.

Table 9.4 Examples of Indicators of Progress

Goal	Indicator of Progress
Bella will wait her turn at lunch by Sept. 29th	Graph of lunch observation
Bella will know all her letter sounds by Mar. 5th	Letter sound card
Bella will play with others at recess by Oct. 8th	Tally chart of recess observations
Bella will smile at least 3x during morning meeting by Oct. 29th	Smile tally

In this table, three of the indicators of progress depend on a central part of the Montessori method: observation. To keep this manageable, each one is at a specific time that is naturally short in duration. For example, for the first goal a designated person would be selected to fill in whether Bella waited her turn at the start of lunch. Each week the data would be reviewed for how many times out of five days she was able to wait. At the outset this might be zero or one as a baseline. Then the data will show whether the selected interventions were supporting her ability to wait, through an increase in days out of five that she was able to wait at lunch. In this way every impulsive move does not need to be observed for and tallied, and the emphasis of the data collection is on the positive behavior – the desired change. It's a simple daily notation at the start of lunch that gives the team information over time.

From here the child study lead distributes the newly created child study action plan to everyone who will have a role in implementing it or collecting data to evaluate its effectiveness. In four to six weeks the team reconvenes, and the plans in place are reviewed looking at the goal next to the data collected as indicator of progress. If the child has made progress, the plan may be continued or the objective may be increased. If there is little or no progress, then the plan must be modified and strengthened. If the next action plan is also unsuccessful, the team might try changing the goal. Ultimately, though, if there is no progress the child will move to a tier-two action plan, which now holds multiple goals with multiple interventions for each goal. Now there are more people involved in addressing the concerns. If there continues to be a lack of progress, the child may move to tier three and begin intensive interventions as well as move toward the evaluation process for special education.

From this brief description of a complex system[16] you can see that it echoes the MTSS process in that it is focused on the whole child. MTSS is thought to hold within it both the RTI model, known for its focus on academics, and the positive behavior interventions and supports (PBIS), a multitiered framework for behavioral supports. Child study is a Montessori alternative to these models as a method of looking at the whole child and then focusing on one aspect of growth and development. It is designed to support the child's growth rather than hinder it, to allow the emergence of true inner discipline rather than simply conform to a discipline system.

Montessori reminds us in *The Discovery of the Child*, "In our system we obviously have a different concept of discipline. The discipline that we are looking for is active. We do not believe that one is disciplined only when he is artificially made as silent. . . . Such a one is not disciplined but annihilated. We claim that an individual is disciplined when he is the master of himself and when he can, as a consequence, control himself when he must follow a rule of life."[17]

New World Considerations

The child study process was essential for keeping track of key children during distance learning. Child study action plans created during distance learning were done in family meetings with the family weighing in on how the staff could support their child while they are learning at home. Interventionists and classroom assistants continued to offer extra support to these children through additional points of contact throughout the day or the week.

All future plans created by the team were done so with consideration for the possibility of needing to implement it virtually. Current in-school action plans needed to be revised so that they could be implemented at home with virtual support.

One of the unique challenges during distance learning was communication between school-based adults serving key children. During in-person learning it was visually evident when an adult was working on an action plan item often with short check-ins built into the school day. To create more overlap, some schools using child study developed shared Google documents or Google sheets for educators to record their ongoing work with learners.

SYSTEM OF JUSTNESS CONCLUSION

These three elements of the System of Justness – strong Montessori implementation, the nautilus approach, and child study – work together to ensure all learners are given optimal conditions in which to thrive in school. They work somewhat sequentially and are therefore interdependent. If there is not a strong implementation of the Montessori method in the classroom, then children tend to be more off-task and have more conflicts and upsets. This leads to a flood of calls and referral reports, which can overwhelm the nautilus team. Likewise, if there is strong Montessori implementation but no nautilus approach or a weak implementation of the nautilus approach, then this leads to a flood of referrals to child study, which now overwhelms that system.

For systems to be strong, they must be implemented with fidelity. This requires a One School commitment to their execution and the use of Honest Talk to reveal and remedy areas of system breakdown. If the whole school is committed to a System of Justness that responds to all children equitably and has a just process for meeting unmet needs and addressing lagging skills, then children and adults alike are served in a respectful way. This is the ultimate goal of a System of Justness: to respond to the community with utmost respect and reverence as a way to build a stronger society.

NOTES

1. Most public schools set a cut-off date when enrollment is finalized and all children need to be entered into Powerschool (or other enrollment platform) at their current "grade," which impacts assessments (what grade test they will take) as well as promotion. This also then becomes the deadline for late transitions.
2. Visit www.resilient-montessori.com for complete transition checklists for all levels.
3. Visit www.resilient-montessori.com for spring focus lists for all levels.
4. See Chapter 7.
5. *Cambridge Dictionary.* Cambridge: Cambridge University Press. 2021.
6. Maria Montessori. *The Secret of Childhood.* London: Sangam Books Limited. 1978, p. 195.
7. Angeline S. Lillard and Megan J. Heise. "Removing Supplementary Materials from Montessori Classrooms Changed Child Outcomes." *Journal of Montessori Research*, Volume 2, Issue 1, 16–26, Spring 2016.
8. See Chapter 7, "Nourish," for more information on responsive directive coaching conversations.
9. See Public Montessori in Action website for more information on how to bring the nautilus approach to your school. https://montessori-action.org/register/p/nautilus-approach-training.

10. Maria Montessori. *The Absorbent Mind.* New York: Holt, Rinehart and Winston. 1995, p. 204.
11. Marshall B. Rosenberg, *Nonviolent Communication: A Language of Compassion* (1st ed., 3rd printing). Encinitas, CA: Puddledancer Press. 2000. https://www.cnvc.org/.
12. Maria Montessori. *The 1946 London Lectures.* Amsterdam: Montessori-Pierson. 2012, p. 231.
13. https://www.westfallteam.com/data-information-knowledge.
14. See the National Center for Montessori in the Public Sector website (at: https://www.public-montessori.org) for more information on how to bring the child study approach to your school.
15. *Lagging skills* is a term used by Ross Greene in *The Explosive Child: A New Approach for Understanding and Parenting Easily Frustrated, Chronically Inflexible Children.* New York: HarperCollins Publishers. 1998.
16. For more on child study, read Ann Epstein, *Montessori Inclusion, Strategies and Stories of Support for Learners with Exceptionalities.*
17. Maria Montessori. *The Discovery of the Child.* New York: Clio Press Ltd. 1986, p. 51.

Chapter 10
Yield

If the idea of the universe be presented to the child in the right way, it will do more for him than just arouse his interest, for it will create in him admiration and wonder, a feeling loftier than any interest and more satisfying. The child's mind will then no longer wander, but becomes fixed and can work. The knowledge he acquires is organised and systematic; his intelligence becomes whole and complete because of the vision of the whole that has been presented to him, and his interest spreads to all, for all are linked and have their place in the universe on which his mind is centred.

—Maria Montessori, *To Educate the Human Potential*

Jumping off this observation Dr. Montessori made about the elementary child, how might we present the universe of the school to support everyone in experiencing it as organized and systematic and thus linked to the whole? This next section will look at systems that support community members in a whole-to-parts view and focuses on what we may yield – produce or provide – through the implementation of strong systems. We look at three systems that will affect our harvest:

- Onboarding: Impacts staff retention
- Recordkeeping: Impacts student outcomes
- Data analysis: Impacts ability to keep our mission

Yield can also mean being flexible under stress of physical force, and these three systems provide an alternative, flexible approach to standard aspects of school life that can create stress. Much like the systems shared in the last chapter focused on engaging the community, these also require an interdependent team to implement them and carry them out to their fullest potential. Only then will they begin to yield the desired results.

ONBOARDING

How people enter your community is the start of the work. Having a well-thought-out, intentionally constructed, strong system to guide that process offers a foundational experience that will be more easily built upon over time and increase the likelihood of staff retention. By beginning with a personal introduction to One School, Honest Talk, and Strong Systems, each person being interviewed has the ability to decide for themselves if these are values they hold and if this is the kind of school where they would like to work.

Often, people who apply to Montessori public programs come in without a clear sense of what is different about a Montessori school. Thus, the onboarding system needs to offer a clear, personal experience of what a Montessori school is about, one that follows them through the process of being hired and beginning their work. Without orientation, people will default to what they know how to do. A strong onboarding system will allow your school to continue as it was intended without mission creep that may inadvertently occur with the addition of each new person.

The onboarding process has two parts: (1) hiring, or how people are brought on; and (2) orienting, or how people are acclimated.

Hiring

Our relationship with each new member of the community begins with the first point of contact. Whether it is an email or a phone call, the feeling that people have after that first contact is responsible for drawing people to your school. This leads to an important element of the system: the roles and responsibilities. Ensuring the roles are clearly named for each step, so that everyone knows who will do which part, means steps will not inadvertently be missed. Table 10.1 shows an overview of how hiring works from the first point of contact through to an offer of employment.

Table 10.1 Whole-School Montessori Method Onboarding Process

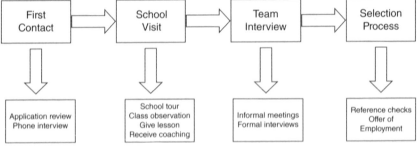

Step 1: First Contact

Application review: The process begins with responses to a job posting or query about a position. These are read by the operations manager with an eye for certain experience based on the open position. Promising candidates are shared with the knowledgeable person within the school who works most closely with those in the position. For example, if it was for an open teaching position, then the Montessori coach would be the natural person to review the applicants, and if it was for a designated aide position then likely it would be the special education coordinator who would review those. For promising candidates, a phone interview is scheduled involving the person or people who reviewed the applicants. All others are sent a warm email letting them know that the school is in the process of filling the vacancy but if for any reason the situation changes, their resume is on file and the school will be in touch with them.

Phone interview: The operations manager sets up the phone interview involving the knowledgeable person or people. The interviewer asks a standard set of questions for each position to keep the call short since this is not the formal interview but rather a way to get a sense of the interviewee and to let them know the team approach the school takes to hiring. If the phone interview goes well, there is a follow-up call with the candidate to outline and arrange for their school visit.

Step 2: School Visit

The school visit is organized from whole to parts, allowing for the human tendency for orientation and order. Applicants are considered guests in the school and receive the grace and courtesy extended to all esteemed visitors. They are given the widest view of the school, followed by a focus on the part connected to the role they would play in the community.

School tour: The candidate is greeted as a visitor, following all the same procedures and routines in the main office and offered an outline of their day with times and locations. The principal or the Montessori coach provide a tour of the whole school, offering mission and goals (One School, Honest Talk, Strong Systems) as well as logistical information regarding layout and location of upcoming parts of their day.

Classroom observation: The candidate always observes in a Montessori classroom even if their position would be outside of the educational setting. Observing allows for an immediate experience of what is unique about the school. Candidates applying for a position within the classroom would observe a classroom at the level of the position they are interviewing for but not necessarily in the room where they would ultimately work. Like any other guest, they are shown to the observer's chair, given the observer's clipboard, and left to observe the classroom in action.

Lesson: Following the observation, the candidate then gives a lesson in that same classroom. This has been prearranged with the classroom adults, and the lesson has been discussed and selected in advance. This happens in an email with the Montessori coach, classroom adults, and candidates.
The lesson is given again in a different classroom following coaching, so this step involves coordinating with two classroom teachers in advance of reaching out to offer the lesson choices. The coach frames this part of the visit and offers the candidate some options of lessons to present, based on the lesson plans of the classroom teachers involved, providing choice as well as ample time for the candidate to prepare.

Between the observation and the lesson, the interview team arrives and settles to observe the lesson. They each have a copy of the interview lesson observation sheet (Figure 10.1), which they use to make notes during the lesson. Once the team is settled, the Montessori coach lets the candidate and the classroom teacher know it is time for them to invite the children and begin in the area of the classroom where the team is set to observe.

Candidates are assessed in five domains: (1) love of children; (2) self-authorization; (3) effective communication; (4) planning and organizational skills; and (5) ability to collaborate and receive coaching. These are noted on the observation sheet along with areas for observations, questions, and discussion points.

Interview Lesson Observation

Candidate:	Date/time:	Lesson:
Lesson Observations:		
Questions:		
Discussion Points:		
Five domains: ☐ Love of children ☐ Self-authorization ☐ Effective communication ☐ Planning and organizational skills ☐ Ability to collaborate/receive coaching		

Figure 10.1 Interview Lesson Observation Sheet.

Coaching: Following the observation of the lesson, the interview team meets briefly to discuss the lesson and the candidate. The team decides on a maximum of three coaching points to be shared in the coaching sessions. These are actionable moves that would increase the effectiveness of their lesson, such as learning and using the children's names during the lesson or setting guidance for how to engage with the material for follow-up. The team passes their observation sheets to the Montessori coach to review before they meet with the applicant.

The candidate then has a one-on-one coaching meeting with the Montessori coach, just as they would if they got the job and worked in the classroom. The coach uses a combination of reflective and directive coaching to guide the conversation and ensure the points raised by the interview team are discussed. This session is in preparation for the candidate to do the lesson again in another classroom, so the goals coming out of the conversation must be clear to the candidate. What follows is a coaching scenario that goes well.

In this coaching session, the candidate is open to the conversation, reflective, and responsive to the coach's questions. The unique circumstances of the interview lesson are openly discussed, and the candidate's thinking about best practice is revealed.

Interview Coaching Scenario

COACH: Thank you so much for presenting that lesson for the team!

CANDIDATE: Yeah, that was intense!

COACH: What do you think worked in that lesson?

CANDIDATE: I was surprised by how receptive the children were. They were really eager to participate and that put me at ease.

COACH: Yes, the opening story you told pulled them right in.

CANDIDATE: I was so nervous I wasn't sure about telling it but once we got into it, and I felt them responding I was glad I did.

COACH: What else did you notice?

CANDIDATE: I noticed that I laid the cards out upside down, and it wasn't until that one boy pointed it out that I realized.

COACH: Yes, I noticed that too, but then you just acknowledged the mistake, turned them around and continued.

CANDIDATE: I didn't know what else to do with everyone watching.

COACH: What would you normally do?

CANDIDATE: The same thing. I just wasn't sure how that would look.

COACH: It looked like you had a friendliness with error and that you respected the opinion of the children.

CANDIDATE: I wasn't sure of their reading level and so was planning to read all the cards, but it worked better having them do it.

COACH: I noticed that you connected with the children during that part where you had them take turns reading, but it seemed like a barrier not knowing their names. Did you feel that?

CANDIDATE: Yes! I should have had them introduce themselves at the start, but I was so nervous I didn't think of it then.

COACH: So that will be a good way to start when you do the next lesson in the other classroom.

CANDIDATE: Definitely.

COACH: I also noticed how eager they were to get a turn to do the work once the lesson was over.

CANDIDATE: Yes, that was a bit messy.

COACH: What did you notice?

CANDIDATE: As I was getting up the two boys began pulling the cards from each other.

COACH: How do you think you might close the lesson next time to avoid that situation?

CANDIDATE: I usually give clear directions about follow-up, but since it wasn't my classroom I wasn't sure how to end it.

COACH: What would you have said if it was your classroom?

CANDIDATE: I would have organized pairs and turns.

COACH: Why don't you try that when you do it again in the other classroom?

CANDIDATE: That's a good idea. Now that I will know their names, it will be easier and more natural.

COACH: Great, so in your upcoming lesson you will remember to begin with introductions, turn the cards to face the children so they can read them, and end with clear directions for what the children will do next. Did I miss anything?

Now let's look at the same scenario where the conversation goes in a different direction.

As you can see, a lot comes out of a coaching session that might not be revealed in a formal interview. In this scenario the teacher's beliefs about children and attitude about race vary greatly from the beliefs of the school, and the coaching session is the part of the interview process that reveals this. It is

Interview Coaching Scenario

COACH: Thank you so much for presenting that lesson for the team!

CANDIDATE: Yeah, that was intense!

COACH: What do you think worked in that lesson?

CANDIDATE: I was surprised by how receptive the children were. They were really eager to participate and that put me at ease.

COACH: Yes, the opening story you told pulled them right in.

CANDIDATE: I was so nervous I wasn't sure about telling it, but once we got into it and I felt them responding I was glad I did.

COACH: What else did you notice?

CANDIDATE: I noticed that they weren't used to sitting in lessons.

COACH: Say more about that.

CANDIDATE: By the time I was reading the second card they were squirming and fidgeting.

COACH: Why do you think that is?

CANDIDATE: They are inner-city kids, so maybe they're not used to real lessons.

COACH: There's a lot in that thought to discuss, but let's stay with your observation that they became restless when you were reading the cards. I noticed that, too. I noticed it happened after Ace asked you to turn the cards around so they could read them. Tell me about your decision not to do that.

CANDIDATE: Well, I wasn't sure of their reading level so I thought I would read them all and that would be easier.

COACH: Did it turn out to be easier?

CANDIDATE: No, because they wouldn't pay attention. And then I didn't know their names so I couldn't bring them back.

COACH: I noticed that, too. Tell me about your decision not to learn their names at the outset of the lesson.

CANDIDATE: They aren't my students, so I didn't see the point in establishing a relationship with them.

COACH: Do you think it would improve your connection in the lesson if you did learn their names?

CANDIDATE: Probably not.

COACH: When you do the next lesson, why don't you try opening with learning the children's names and let's see if that makes a difference.

CANDIDATE: Okay.

COACH: Also, since the children you'll be working with next are also readers, why don't you try having them read the cards? Since you'll know their names you can select readers.

CANDIDATE: I'm not sure that will work.

COACH: Are you willing to give it a try?

CANDIDATE: If that's what you want me to do.

COACH: I also noticed in your last lesson how eager the children were to get a turn to do the work once the lesson was over.

CANDIDATE: Yes, the children got out of control.

COACH: What did you notice?

CANDIDATE: As I was getting up the two Black boys began pulling the cards from each other.

COACH: How do you think you might close the lesson next time to avoid that situation?

CANDIDATE: I don't think there's anything different I could do in that situation.

COACH: What do you usually do at the end of a lesson to support the children?

CANDIDATE: Usually I don't need to do anything. The children know the expectations and just get back to work. They have work to do, and they know I have work to do, too.

COACH: I see. So in your classroom do the children have work journals or work plans?

CANDIDATE: Work plans definitely. There are no children wandering around in my classroom. Every child has a work plan to finish, and they know I'm serious.

COACH: I understand. The children in these elementary classrooms have work journals to work on time management, so they are used to clear direction at the end of a

> lesson. In this case, giving some clear directions for follow-up will help you when you give this lesson again.
>
> CANDIDATE: What would I say?
>
> COACH: What do you want them to do?
>
> CANDIDATE: (pause) Go back to their work.
>
> COACH: You don't want them to use the material you just introduced?
>
> CANDIDATE: I've already read it to them, and we did the matching.
>
> COACH: So the children in your classroom don't have the opportunity to work with the material independently?
>
> CANDIDATE: Not nomenclature.
>
> COACH: Why is that?
>
> CANDIDATE: It takes a lot of work to make, and the children aren't careful enough with it.
>
> COACH: I see. Well, at this school children do use the material for follow-up, so at the end of your next lesson you will need to give them some direction about how to do that.
>
> CANDIDATE: (shifting) Alright.
>
> COACH: Great, so in your upcoming lesson you will remember to begin with introductions, turn the cards to face the children so they can read them, and end with clear directions for what the children will do next. Did I miss anything?

also evident that there's less of an openness to both reflecting and coaching as the candidate has more of a fixed mindset compared with the previous candidate, who brought more of a growth mindset to the conversation.

Following the coaching session the candidate does the same lesson again in a different classroom, with different children, and is observed by only the coach. The same interview lesson observation tool is used with a focus on the named coaching points that were summarized at the end of the coaching session. Ensuring that the candidate understands the new moves that will strengthen the lesson will highlight whether they elect to employ them. Candidates who do not incorporate the improvements are not considered a good match for a school that holds coaching at the center.

Some candidates believe they want to be part of coaching and talk eloquently about their commitment to growth and development of their practice but choose not to adjust their lesson the second time. Having the coaching session as part of the application process allows for the discovery of any say–do gaps that candidates may bring. Because the team interview is a separate step, there is no need to move forward with candidates who will not be a good fit for your school.

Step 3: Team Interview

This final step is reserved for the candidates who have successfully completed the school visit where both the school team and the candidate feel a rightness of fit.

Informal Meeting: The team interview begins with an informal gathering – coffee, fruit, and muffins before the school day begins – or midday, where the candidate meets their peers. This can be limited to the level team or opened to include more of the community. The gathering is attended by the interview team so that the first-time meeting is not in the formal setting of the interview. The candidate is encouraged to ask questions about what it's like to work at the school, and people are free to speak openly about the joys and challenges of working in a public Montessori school. The goal is not to sell the applicant on the school but rather to be real with them so they will feel comfortable being real in return.

Formal Interview: Following the gathering is the formal team interview. This occurs in the conference room or other professional setting. The team has a series of questions on the interview question sheet that are used for every candidate applying for that same position, based on the role in the school. The team has prepared ahead of time who will ask which question. They each have a copy of the questions, and when it is not their turn to ask they take notes about the candidate's response. The person who asked the question maintains eye contact the whole time so that, though intentionally formal, there is a point of connection for the speaker.

In the public sector, where equity is at the forefront of this system, asking uniform questions allows for an equitable experience for candidates. Once those questions have been completed, there's an opportunity for anyone, including the candidate, to ask follow-up questions or probe into a topic raised by one of the other questions. This allows for unique conversations within an established structure to give the team the information they need to make the hiring decision.

Once the candidate has left, the team takes a minute to complete their interview sheet before turning it over to the operations manager or human resources person coordinating the process. The five aforementioned domains on the interview lesson observation sheet are also on the bottom of the interview question sheet, and each team member takes a moment to reflect and make notes regarding the five domains.

The final part of the team interview is the closing meeting. Here the team comes together with all of the documentation (candidate's resume and cover letter, interview lesson observation sheets, and interview question sheets) to review the candidate, talk openly about concerns, and determine whether it would be a strong hiring decision to bring them onto the team. By the end of this short meeting a determination has been made allowing the person coordinating the process to move to the final step.

Step 4: Selection Process

Should the interview team decide not to hire the candidate, the operations manager or person coordinating the process contacts them directly to let them know that they have not been chosen to fill the position but that the team is grateful for their time and, unless they were not a fit at all, will keep their information on file should another position open in the future. This supports the system in holding a pool of qualified candidates who have already been introduced to the culture of the school.

Reference Checks: Should the interview team decide to hire the candidate, then the person coordinating the process completes the reference checks. If something concerning arises in this step, the interview team can be reconvened to discuss. Otherwise, the coordinating person is authorized to make the employment offer, which includes the specifics of salary, benefits, and other details. Hooray!

Offer of Employment: At this time the new hire also receives an updated copy of the school's staff handbook.[1] This is the first step in orienting to their role as a newly hired employee, and it sets in motion the second part of the onboarding process: orienting.

The hiring process is summarized in Table 10.2.

Table 10.2 Hiring Process Summary

Application Screen	Phone Interview	School Visit	Team Interview	Reference Checks	Offer
Resume and cover letter reviewed	Overview of school culture discussed Core values discussed Montessori background and understanding of pedagogy explored	Lesson and coaching Classroom practice and skill level observed Ability to respond to suggestions and to improve practice	Meeting with the team and honest discussion of the role	Assess overall core value fit and gather past data on areas of growth and concern, the latter of which are addressed	Offer given

Orienting

Like the first part of the onboarding process, there are four steps to this second part, which involves getting new employees acquainted and adjusted to the school. Orientation is one of the human tendencies, something we all share, and providing a codified orientation process allows people to begin to relax into their new role. Another Montessori value is preparation over correction. In this context, it means taking the time to discuss roles and responsibilities and school expectations so people will be prepared to do their new job and thus begin successfully.

The orientation process is slightly different for those who arrive Montessori trained, so it is partially divided into two tracks to allow for optimal and not redundant orientation (Table 10.3).

Table 10.3 Whole School Montessori Method Onboarding Process

Role	Step 1- Initial Orientation	Step 2- Montessori Orientation	Step 3 - Role Orientation	Step 4 - Ongoing Orientation
Montessori trained employee	Orientation to the school/ district- the ins and outs of working in this new place	Orientation to Whole School Montessori Method	Orientation to your new role by Montessori Coach	On-going meetings to support you in your new role
New to Montessori employee		Orientation to Montessori Method	Orientation to your new role by the appropriate person	

Step 1: Initial Orientation

The operations manager leads this first meeting with support from the principal and Montessori coach and in the framework of school-wide grace and courtesy norms, which sets expectations and strikes the right tone. In attendance are all school team members, ideally including the office manager, lead custodian, head of the kitchen, dean of students or nautilus lead, and school nurse. First, the operations manager introduces the school team so new hires can begin to recognize their new colleagues. Then the new additions each have an opportunity to introduce themselves, talk about their new role, and share one thing they're excited about in their new position (or something equally general to begin the relationship-building process).

Next, the school team members leave and, led by the operations manager, the group reviews the staff handbook, including topics like cell phone use, meeting participation, hallway etiquette, and communication norms and followed by details that may need further clarification. Making this an inclusive experience where all voices are heard and respected is the beginning of building One School.[2]

Finally, the principal or Montessori coach orient the newcomers to school assessments by giving a brief overview of the data system.[3]

Step 2: Montessori Orientation

In this step the new employees divide into those already trained and those new to Montessori. For those new to the method, the coach offers a Montessori orientation, which provides an introduction to both the person and the method. Common topics during a Montessori orientation presentation include:

- A brief biography of Maria Montessori
- Four planes of development
- Preparation of the adult
- Introduction to observation
- Montessori vocabulary
- Brief introduction to the whole school Montessori method – One School, Honest Talk, Strong Systems

Having a slide deck and handouts for these to use every year, which are then shared with participants, allows new members to process the information in their own time as well as providing a way to communicate this same information to any late hires.

Goals for Montessori Orientation:

Know:
- That Montessori is a person, a method, and a mindset
- That this school follows the whole school Montessori method
- That observation is at the center of the work

Do:
- Identify planes of development
- Model the behavior we expect to see
- Support the Montessori program through ongoing observation

The new members who are already Montessori trained are instead offered an introduction to the whole school Montessori method. Here they are introduced to One School, Honest Talk, Strong Systems as well as the role of coaching in the school. Reflective coaching is explained, and they have an opportunity to role-play a conversation using the three Cs and reflective questions.[4] They are oriented to the shared observation tools used within the school and the meeting notes tool used in one-on-one meetings.

Goals for Montessori Coaching Orientation:

Know:

- That One School, Honest Talk, and Strong Systems frame our work and that you are an important part of that
- That everyone offers and receives coaching here
- That observation is at the center of the work

Do:

- Daily observation and use the shared observation tools
- Participate in one-on-one meetings
- Offer reflective coaching to others

A shared topic for both orientations is the role of observation in a Montessori school. As this is a central part of the method that is very often deprioritized, the orientation offers time to understand how and when to do it. With this shared understanding all members of the community are able to participate as discussed in the One School section.

Step 3: Role Orientation

Schools often forget this part of the orientation process. Even if you are coming from another school where you filled the same position, orientation to how the work will be done in this new setting is an important part of preparation over correction. In this way people can begin as we hope they will continue.

For those who will be filling a role as a classroom teacher, their orientation to the task is done by the Montessori coach in two settings: individually and within the new team. A team meeting prior to the launch of the new school year allows for introductions and the beginning of collaboration between practitioners. The new teacher is often paired up with an experienced neighbor so they can pop in and ask the small questions that arise in spite of the efforts to fully orient them. Rather than being the central knower who answers all questions, one of the tasks of the Montessori coach is to create connections on the level team to facilitate interdependence and the possibility for spontaneous peer coaching. In the team meeting the coach reviews: arrival and dismissal duties, prep times and coverage, weekly team meeting schedule, professional development calendar, recordkeeping systems, assessment schedule, and family conference reports and schedule. Some team planning begins soon after this to organize for the back-to-school open house.

Step 4: On-going Orientation

In one-on-one meetings with the new lead guides, the coach takes them through the elements of their specific classroom role using a number of tools, including the work style survey, procedures and routines planning, classroom daily schedule, class list, and student portfolios. The student portfolio has a cover sheet that gives the new teacher an idea of what is in each file. This is an important orientating tool for the new teacher so they can begin to plan the opening days of school appropriately. Recordkeeping is discussed in greater detail, and if the teacher is not already familiar with the platform in use, then a training is scheduled with their team partner.

The whole onboarding process is shared across roles as outlined in Figure 10.2. This means new people joining the community have met at least five people from the community during the hiring process and many more during the orientation process.

Roles and Responsibilities

Step	Action	Responsible person
Part I, Step 1	First contact	Operations Manager, HR
Part I, Step 2	School visit	Principal, Montessori coach
Part I, Step 3	Team interview	Principal, Montessori coach, Peers
Part I, Step 4	Selection process	Principal, Operations Manager, HR
Part II, Step 1	Handbook/School Orientation	Operations Manager, HR, Office manager
Part II, Step 2	Orientation to Coaching/ Montessori	Montessori coach
Part II, Step 3	Orientation to new role	Montessori coach
Part II, Step 4	On-going meetings	Montessori coach

Figure 10.2 Onboarding Roles and Responsibilities.

They are brought into the work of the school in known stages that allow what Montessori called *pause for absorption* between each part. In this way, newcomers have a measured approach to employment, one that offers them the opportunity to realize it's not a fit and change their mind. It also gives them a sense of the One School component from the start of the relationship, prompting them to be more willing to engage in Honest Talk sooner in their time at the school. This lengthy process supports the hiring of people who share the school's values and commitments who are thus more likely to stay and build their careers at the school. The time invested in the onboarding system then allows for fewer open positions over time and greater stability for the children and families.

NEW WORLD CONSIDERATIONS

Much of the onboarding system proceeded as usual after schools were forced to quarantine in 2020, with most of the adjustments made in the first part of the school visit. This portion happened with the Montessori coach introducing the candidate to one level team member, who included them in their virtual morning meeting and had them observe lessons onscreen. The sample lesson was done in various ways depending on the local technology regulations. If the candidate is currently teaching virtually, then the coach is able to observe a home lesson and have the one-on-one coaching session following that. Both the original and subsequent lesson can be recorded to be reviewed by the rest of the hiring team as the coach reports back on the candidate. This is not ideal but still allows the coach insight into how the candidate responds to coaching.

During the pandemic, orientation was accomplished much more easily with everyone joining the orientations virtually and viewing the slide deck together without the distractions of other elements of the new job, such as the ongoing work of setting up the classroom environment.

RECORDKEEPING

It's important to have a system across the whole school as to how people will keep track of what they do. This encompasses everything from attendance to family participation events and impacts everyone who works at the school. Creating structures for each person around documentation will allow for smooth daily functioning of the school that is not dependent on one person but rather is interdependent.

Whole School Montessori Recordkeeping:

- ☐ Matches roles
- ☐ Fosters independence
- ☐ Provides data sources

With a focus on full Montessori implementation, let's look at the record-keeping done by the Montessori classroom adults.

Classroom recordkeeping:

- ☐ Lessons planned
- ☐ Lessons given and student progress
- ☐ Data and data team action plans
- ☐ Observation notes
- ☐ Child study documents
- ☐ Transition checklists
- ☐ Student portfolios
- ☐ Family contact log
- ☐ Progress reports
- ☐ Family conference notes

This list is not exhaustive but does highlight the two areas of classroom recordkeeping: inward facing and outward facing. Educators keep some records internally to enable them to target their lessons and better serve the children they are with every day. Using all of this information, they are then able to do the next outward part, which is communicating that progress to families. Creating shared systems for each of these allows for mutual support and peer coaching to occur across levels with better school-wide results.

An important aspect of this Strong System is that it is accessible by everyone and frequently visited by the Montessori coach and the principal as a window into the work unfolding in the classrooms. Since the recordkeeping system is shared across the whole school, everyone is able to look at the growing body of data to step back and reflect on individual children as well as whole groups of children.

Inward-facing records:

- ☐ Lessons planned
- ☐ Lessons given and student progress

- ☐ Data and data team action plans
- ☐ Observation notes
- ☐ Child study documents
- ☐ Transition checklists
- ☐ Student portfolios

In reviewing this list, an important item not covered in any other section of the book is recording lessons given and student progress. This task is one of the central challenges for public schools that can impede the delivery of a strong Montessori program. That is because Montessori offers a rich, complex, and intricate curriculum that reaches the whole child. A complicating factor is that Montessori teacher preparation programs provide a variety of versions of the curriculum so that people trained at different centers emerge with diverse views on lessons, lesson names, and their sequence.

To create a shared recordkeeping tool, then, level teams must begin with a shared understanding of the curriculum being followed. A universal approach to tracking assigned lessons and progress will be successful only if this alignment is there to start. Multiple online platforms are available to Montessori schools, and once they're set up and learned they simplify the process for everyone.[7] Selecting one of these is only the beginning. Creating a shared lesson set across each level is a critical step. The work here is at the front end; once this is established for your school then it is in place to be followed. Newly hired educators are oriented to the shared set and, through coaching, are supported in adjusting to it.

Why is this important? Why not let everyone create and use their own lesson set? When each teacher devises their own tailored lesson sets based on their training, the records cannot be passed to a new teacher. This means when a teacher leaves, the school loses information on students in the midst of a three-year cycle. Without this there is no clear picture of a child's progress or ability to seamlessly pick up where they left off, which impacts outcomes. The motivation for this work is the commitment to the children to allow them a meaningful, coherent learning experience across many years.

Let's review the educator's task of recording lessons and student progress using the whole school Montessori recordkeeping checklist to understand why these three aspects shape recordkeeping.

Whole School Montessori Recordkeeping: Lessons Given and Student Progress

☐ Matches Roles

Multiple adults may be working directly with children. This means every-one in this category, from the trained guide to the assistant to the inter-ventionists, and special educators need to use the same document to record their information. It is their role to support the forward motion of learning, and having a shared platform will allow collaboration across those roles. By looking in one place, the team is able to develop a unified view of the child's progress. This helps everyone understand that this work does not belong solely to the Montessori teacher leading the class-room but includes all educators.

☐ Fosters Independence

For everyone to fulfill this task independently, they need orientation and training in the school's process. Sharing clear expectations, through sched-uling professional development time prior to the opening of the school year, will allow for everyone to get on the same page from the start. Ongoing support will be needed for new people using the platform or tool for their first year. Pairing advanced users with new users who are working with the same children will support skill mastery and encourage the teaming around this work. Having a shared lesson set across classrooms fosters this collab-oration as it allows special educators, interventionists, and others to record work and progress independently for children across various classrooms.

☐ Provides Data Sources

Using a shared platform with a shared lesson set will allow for data col-lection and review. If each adult is documenting the student progress in their own way, there will be no data available to support the strength-ening of the Montessori implementation across levels or the whole school. Montessori schools value the lesson progression as a form of assessment, so if the recordkeeping in this area is aligned, school-wide data is available as an outgrowth of the teachers' work.

Selecting tools to be used across One School for educators to keep track of individual student progress within this vast, integrated curriculum is essential. It is one of the most powerful ways to systematize and there-fore align the work of the school-based adults to support reaching each individual child where they are within a multiage structure.

Outward-facing records:

☐ Family contact log

☐ Progress reports

☐ Family conference notes

These are three parts of recordkeeping done by classroom adults that support a strong outward connection to families.

Family contact logs have become particularly important for larger district schools working to develop community within the greater context of their city. They are a simple sheet for each child that acts as a place to record: date, time, which home adult made contact or was contacted, method used (e.g., in person, phone, email), and the result of the contact.

Educators are required to remember vast amounts of details on any given day, and there is only so much brain storage capacity to hold it all. Having family contact logs allows adults to independently store this information outside their brain so that it isn't lost. It also allows them to independently recognize when more contact is needed and to take action. Much like the lesson and student progress data, family contact logs are filled out by all educators in a shared digital location. This creates a place for everyone to see what other conversations have occurred and for educators of the same child to connect with each other to ensure unity. The request to keep this record expresses to all educators the shared value of reaching out to and connecting with the children's families. Family contact logs are also a great data source and support for the child study process as well as the school's ongoing equity work.

Progress reports are the direct link to the recordkeeping teachers are doing to track lessons and student progress and should be aligned to reflect that same view of the curriculum. This will allow an easier transfer at the times when teachers are completing the progress reports for families. Ideally, it is also aligned with the transition checklist so families are able to see points of arrival as children complete a three-year cycle.

Because classrooms hold a large number of children and educators complete progress reports two or three times a year, it's important to keep the reports simple. If the time has been taken to align it properly, then it will provide meaningful information to families without requiring pages of individual narratives. Keeping a small area for comments will allow for personalization without regularly overwhelming teachers. They are completing these reports while also continuing to plan lessons, prepare their classrooms, give lessons, review follow-up, observe, attend meetings, and complete the aforementioned list of recordkeeping. Having a succinct report will also allow appropriate review by the Montessori coach prior to their distribution.

Finally, the **family conference notes** are there to support educators and families to be on the actual same page. They make tangible a conversation had during the course of the child's life at the school and are another marker of progress.

Elementary Family Conference Notes

Child's Name	Date
Guide	Family Member(s)

Topics

- Check-in & Appreciations
- Updates on:
    - Student progress in lessons
    - Follow up work completion
    - Assessment results
- Goal setting for the coming term
- Roll out Reading Logs

Goals for the Student

Follow-up

Figure 10.3 Sample Family Conference Notes.

An example of a simple family conference notes tool is shown in Figure 10.3. Here you can see there is a place to record discussion topics, goals for the learner, and follow-up items that may emerge during the conversation.

The classroom guide prefills the topics to ensure every family receives impor-tant information at the conference. It also allows for a more efficient meeting as they are generally short with a lot to cover. The area for goals comes out of the topics discussed about the learner's progress. It is filled in collaboratively between the school-based adults and the family, honoring both the observa-tions and knowledge of the educator and the insights and wishes of the family. These goals are set at the first conference, checked on midyear, and hopefully celebrated in the closing conference of the year. The last section, titled Follow-Up, is for tasks to support the learner that can be completed following the con-ference. This includes ideas for classroom adults (e.g., make copies of books to send home) and for families (e.g., get a library card).

Let's review the educator's task of completing family conference notes using the whole-school Montessori recordkeeping checklist from earlier in this chap-ter to understand why these three aspects shape recordkeeping.

Whole-School Montessori Recordkeeping: Family Conference Notes

☐ **Matches Roles**

Family conference notes are filled out by the classroom adults in the meet-ing with the family. The Montessori teacher is often conducting the confer-ence while the supporting adult adds to the family conference notes. This clarifies for families that the two adults are a team, yet they should bring their concerns to the Montessori teacher.

☐ **Fosters Independence**

The family conference notes, when completed, are copied and shared with families. This acts as both a record of the conversation and an artifact of the collaboration between the adults at school and at home. This fosters independence for the families to provide additional support to their child at home to help reach goals set together at the conference.

☐ **Provides Data Sources**

Following the conferences, each classroom teacher organizes their family conference notes for the Montessori coach to review. Families with more urgent needs, or with whom the meeting went less well, are placed on top of the stack. This allows the coach to understand arising concerns that will then prompt a discussion at the next individual meeting between the coach and the teacher. It also allows for data across all classrooms regarding any missed conferences so the family coordinator or appropriate staff member can follow up. In addition, the teacher keeps these in the student portfolio, and each previous year's goals can be reviewed prior to setting new ones.

New World Considerations

As schools went remote during the global pandemic, the strength and alignment of the recordkeeping systems were tested, and they became an important communication tool for everyone in the school. A number of schools shifted to digital recordkeeping platforms like Seesaw that involved children and families. There also was an increased need for lessons in areas like grace and courtesy, which made room for the creation and use of new recordkeeping tools like the one shown in Figure 10.4.

New World Grace and Courtesy

How to . . .	done √
Enter a Zoom Lesson - (before, on time, late)	
Be in a lesson	
- clothing - limit distractions: food, pots, toys - sitting upright	
Greet others virtually	
Use the mute button	
Use the chatbox	
Comment on a post	
Be excused from a lesson (bathroom, early dismissal)	
Ask for help	
Take turns during group discussions	
Actively participate	
Interact with your family when in a lesson	

Figure 10.4 Recordkeeping for New World Grace and Courtesy Lessons.

Newly created tools for recordkeeping served to support the educators in identifying the new lessons needed, designing them, and ensuring they were given to all the learners. Having a checklist handy supported everyone in the adjustment of this new way of being together. It also provided the Montessori coach with data to see what was being emphasized and perhaps neglected during this shift in instruction, allowing a way to offer more support in the transition.

DATA REVIEW

The final element we will explore is data. This can be a tricky topic for Montessori educators as it can feel reductive, as though it's obscuring the view of the whole child. Yet data collection has long been a part of the method, and Dr. Montessori's own data collection has resulted in much of what we continue to offer in classrooms today. In addition, in public Montessori programs there will be no avoiding data as an element of existence and an ongoing external expectation that can translate as pressure. Without our own approach to analysis, those external pressures might well drive the program away from its essential elements and land schools in a *middle road* educational model: where Montessori materials exist, diluted by the presence of supplemental materials or traditional methods adopted as a response to falling test scores. These might look like worksheets, workbooks, textbooks, or non–Montessori manipulatives such as tangrams.

Test pressure can impact implementation. One common element of this is the loss of the three-hour uninterrupted work cycle, an essential aspect of the Montessori method that, among other things, allows children to fall into deep concentration, explore learning of interest, and build time management skills. It also allows the adults cycles of present, circulate, and observe, where they are able to give a lesson, circulate around the room to support reengagement, and then sit to observe both the class as a whole and the lesson just given. Without this expanded time, the method is being minimized and is less likely to generate the intended results.

In addition, some schools default to out-and-out test prep using skill and drill tactics to accelerate students' learning. This often serves to confuse the learners. The Montessori method exposes children to concepts concretely first so that there is a strong foundational understanding where learners then transition to abstraction over time with the guidance and support of the materials and the trained adult. Unfortunately, some adults are unclear about how to support this transition to abstraction, so not all children make the transition seamlessly, much in the same way that not all children transition seamlessly into reading. Here's where the school's professional development plan[5] for the year plays an important role: to orient and prepare all teachers to support the transition to abstraction and strong literacy and to spend time getting comfortable with assessment data.

If we do not embrace the current assessment measures and make them our own, we risk ongoing movement away from the strong implementation of the method that will get the results. The middle way – doing both Montessori and traditional – results in doing neither well. It doesn't create the conditions for the Montessori model to flourish, nor does it fully access traditional teaching methods that get results. Ultimately, the school will not thrive, and this appears to be a reflection on the veracity of the Montessori method rather than a failure to fully implement it.

Anticipating this, there is benefit to using a Montessori structure for data analysis that will preserve full implementation. First and foremost is the ongoing principle of preparation over correction. If we set up a strong system to analyze data regularly, then we can orient classroom adults to the school assessments, the cycle of testing, and data review process. Table 10.4 is an overview of the components that are shared with staff so they are aware of the process and their role in implementing it.

Table 10.4 Data System Overview

What	When	Who
Annual assessment calendar distributed	August	Leadership
Calendar of Data Review meetings distributed	August	Principal/Coach
Orientation for new staff[6] held	August	Leadership
Assessments given	Fall/Winter/Spring	Leadership
Data entered	Fall/Winter/Spring	Teachers/Coach
Individual review of results	Fall/Winter/Spring	Principal/Coach/Teachers
Data Review meetings held	Fall/Winter/Spring	Principal/Coach/Teachers
Action Plans implemented	Fall/Winter/Spring after Data Review	Teachers/Coach
Next year PD & Assessment calendars created	Summer	Coach/Teachers

Most public Montessori schools give assessments in the fall, winter, and spring, allowing for three opportunities to review, discuss, and use data to focus instruction to generate stronger results. Called data review meetings, they have both a process and a tool for communities to use.

As seen in Figure 10.5, the process opens when the data is available. It is distributed for review openly to everyone, including classroom assistants, interventionists, and specialists. Anyone who has contact with children is included and brought into the conversation for how to support all students.

Data Review Process

What	When	Who
1. Distribute and individually review the data (e.g., for MAP)	As soon as the data is received by the school (e.g., right after the MAP)	-Distributed by Coach and/or school leadership -Reviewed by everyone
2. Convene Data Review Teams: Use the Data Review tool to guide the process.	A week after receiving the data	-Meet by level teams. -Coach and/or Principal facilitate and keep copies of all plans to support implementation
3. Share out with others to support the in-class Action Plans.	Immediately following the Data Team Meeting	Teachers, school leadership, student support teams
4. Meet weekly to support the implementation of the Action Plans	Until all Action Plans are fully implemented, then review after the next assessment cycle.	Coach, teachers, student support teams

Figure 10.5 Data Review Process.

Following the data review, the principal or Montessori coach convenes a one-hour, level meeting that includes interventionists, special educators, and any other support staff available to attend. Before the meeting, classroom adults have completed the top two portions of the data review tool shown in Figure 10.6. The top portion notes children who have shown progress. These are the successes and aren't necessarily the children who are proficient or advanced but rather those who have shown notable – even surprising – growth. They may be children who are not at grade level yet but show significant improvement. The second part shows children who are below grade level without significant gains or children who have not made growth even if they are considered at or above grade level. For both sections, the classroom adults fill in the third column with ideas to understand either the growth or lack of growth. What's been going on with that child? What particular work have they been engaged or disengaged with over the past season? What observations of the situation offer insight into this growth or lack of growth? This reflection is done by classroom adults in advance of the meeting and can be supported in the one-on-one meetings with the coach.

Data Review Tool

Class: _____   Date: _____

Data source: _____   Team:_____

Successes

Child	Previous/current score	Ideas to understand

Challenges

Child	Score/target	Ideas to understand

Action Plan

Student/s	Score	Plan

Figure 10.6 Data Review Tool.

The team meeting opens with a sharing of successes and notes any particular practice that helps to understand the gains. A primary guide might share a practice of daily oral language lessons given to a small group that seems to have benefited the whole class. A lower elementary guide might share about a game played to dismiss for lunch that emphasized combinations of ten and strengthened children's mental math showing gains in the math data. An upper elementary guide might share about a class weekly writing rhythm that has resulted in children starting novels and writing a chapter each week so that their stamina for, and ability with, open-response questions has improved. An adolescent guide might share about a "justice around the world" project started by two students that has caught the interest of the whole group, inciting a focus on statistics and explaining gains in that area.

This part of the meeting serves the community in a few ways. First, it aligns with the Montessori practice of focusing on strengths. By opening with what's working, the emphasis lies in what supports students. This serves as professional development for everyone as people on the team harvest good ideas they can try in their own classrooms. It also loops in the larger team of adults in the school to learn more about the experience of children they may see outside of the classroom.

The second round of sharing is teachers talking about the challenges – children who are not making progress and what is impacting learning (e.g., attendance, low literacy, trauma). Most of these children should already be on child study action plans, and the ones who are not should be added to the child study docket.

The third part of the meeting is where classroom adults team up with others in the meeting. These groups are organized ahead of time by the Montessori coach to provide extra support for the classroom team in thinking about the challenges and developing action plans. The classroom team with low literacy scores may be paired with the reading interventionist who works at that level, or the classroom with a high number of individualized education plans may be paired with the special educator who works with those children. The extra people are there to share ideas or insights that may help the team to develop strong plans for their struggling students and to support the classroom team in not losing track of time while talking about one child.

The goal of this part of the meeting is to come up with action plans in response to the insights around the children with assessment results that indicate little or no progress. In primary, these may be individual action plans, but for elementary it will be small groups of children who are struggling in a shared area of learning who will come together for something additional each day or each week that will specifically target those lagging skills. Being part of the development of these plans, the additional people often volunteer to support the focus for the next season. For example, the physical education teacher may offer to play a ball game with a small group of children around linear counting or skip counting twice a week or the reading interventionist may have a reader's theater script for a group to practice that will help with their fluency. Being in the data review meetings moves the school community from talk into action. We don't just say we all care about the children's progress; we all show up and contribute to their progress. If every staff member is aware of which children are faltering or need extra guidance and encouragement, then there is a larger net for those children. They will be caught and held by everyone.

Following the meeting, the lead classroom teacher is responsible for completing the data review tool and sharing it with the principal and the coach. From there the Montessori coach creates time in one-on-one meetings with teachers to touch on the action plans each week and to observe the plans in action in the classrooms. In this way any support needed to implement those plans is given early and often to ensure the written plans are being followed and children are receiving what they need to thrive.

New World Considerations

School teams are continuing to assess children and to meet virtually for data review meetings. For the third part of the meeting, classroom teams go into breakout rooms with their extra support people to make action plans for the students who are struggling. Using shared Google documents, the principal and coach can see teams filling in the data review tool and visit breakout rooms where there is less progress on the document.

The coach connects with all teachers – the same way virtually as in person – following the data review meeting to establish start times and necessary support to implement the plans. The plans are then discussed weekly in the virtual one-on-one meetings between the Montessori coach and the teachers.

Observing the implementation of the action plans virtually is not able to happen through the weekly classroom observation and now must be scheduled separately. This simply means adding a column to the data review tool that includes the link to the additional element of the children's day or week and then having the coach join periodically. In this way, the coach is able to observe if the additional support is benefiting the children in the group, moving their skills along, building their confidence, and likely impacting their achievement. And if not, the coach can reconcile the situation early to avoid losing meaningful learning time and ending up without progress in spite of the adult's effort.

STRONG SYSTEMS SUMMARY

As we close the section on Strong Systems, we remember to breathe. Each one of these systems is a complicated yet self-sustaining approach to supporting strong Montessori implementation. They won't all be built in the same year, nor will they be rolled out perfectly. However, with commitment to the whole-school Montessori method – putting into practice the values of One School, Honest Talk, and Strong Systems – the community will benefit from them. These systems can then grow stronger and more nimble each time they are used.

Engage Checklist
- ☑ Seamless Transition Overview
  - ☑ Sample Transition Checklist
  - ☑ Sample Transition Timeline
  - ☑ Class Placement Card Sheet
  - ☑ Sample Class Placement Family Letter
  - ☑ New World Seamless Transition Overview
- ☑ Student Portfolio System
  - ☑ Student Portfolio cover sheet
- ☑ System of Justness
  - ☑ RELATE

Yield Checklist
- ☑ Onboarding Overview
  - ☑ Hiring
  - ☑ Orienting
  - ☑ Onboarding Roles and Responsibilities
- ☑ Recordkeeping
  - ☑ Family Conference Notes
  - ☑ Grace and Courtesy Checklist
- ☑ Data Analysis System
  - ☑ Data Review Process
  - ☑ Data Team Tool

Simple Strong System Move: Custodial Care System

- Create and print out a simple, colored chart of basic Montessori materials the custodian will likely come in contact with during an average day cleaning the floors of the hallways and classrooms (e.g., smallest pink cube, bead bars, golden beads, chain arrows, movable alphabet letters, grammar symbols, word study cards, puzzle map nobs, pin map flags).
- Review this chart with the custodian and staff, explaining the high cost of replacing small parts for children to have access to the complete material. Ask them to please collect these and anything else they may suspect is part of a material in the basket you will provide.
- Place the chart in the custodial work space along with the basket.
- At the outset, monitor the collection more closely to communicate the importance of this new system.
- Share this system with classroom adults, inviting them to check the basket when they notice material missing.
- Bring the basket to monthly staff meetings for classroom adults to collect missing materials.

NOTES

1. See Chapter 8 for contents of the staff handbook.
2. See Figure P2.1.
3. Discussed next in this chapter.
4. See Chapter 7 for more on reflective coaching conversations.
5. See Chapter 6 for more on yearlong professional development.
6. This is included in the onboarding process earlier in this chapter.
7. Transparent Classroom offers a Public Montessori Lesson Set for Primary, Lower Elementary and Upper Elementary. These can be used to calibrate across classrooms and are aligned to the CCSS.

PART V

Take Action

I am certain that all of us together will wish to pursue this new road, each one of us bringing a personal contribution to the cause of the child. Even if the way of considering the problems of education will vary according to different points of view, a transcendent idea will unite us above all things, an idea that perhaps before today was not clear and evident to all. That is, the conviction that, from the beginning of life, great powers exist hidden in the psyche of the child and that it is our task to appropriately assist their full development lest they lose all vigour and completely disappear.

—The San Remo Lecture 1949, Citizen of the World Key
Montessori Readings

Now we have reached the concluding chapters, with the child remaining at the center of the work, holding our aspiration to "appropriately assist their full development" and the development of all the adults, through the work of the whole school Montessori method. This big work is not something to begin all at once or in fits and starts but rather something to plan out and work toward as a school community.

Since your school is a complex ecosystem of interdependent, mutually beneficial parts, for each component there needs to be both a process and a tool: how will we do it and what tool will be used that we can all refer to in understanding and following through to action. This is the Montessori in action part. The structures of building resilient schools, in line with Montessori education, allow both the method and the means.

There are some considerations as you prepare to implement the whole-school Montessori method. The first is resources and how they are allocated. To put these components in place, there may need to be some shifting to support the new structure of your school. Here are some resources to consider:

- The people
- The materials
- The school building
- The use of time

All of these contribute to the ecosystem of your school. To honor and strengthen it, you must consider how the reallocation of resources will happen to manage and support the changes you envision.

THE PEOPLE

The adults and their development is a through line to the work of the whole school Montessori method. As such, it's important to ensure that every person employed by your school is in the right position, spending the right amount of time for their job and continuing to grow overtime. A difficult yet important task at the outset is to evaluate each of the positions in your school and determine if they are essential to the method.

Here are some questions to help you think through how you might shift and change roles to serve the creation of your resilient Montessori school:

- Who are your nonclassroom adults, and how do they serve?
- What are the leadership roles? Is there an assistant principal? A dean of students? How do they serve?

Nonclassroom adults:

Reviewing all the paid positions for staff not in classrooms gives you an idea of where your budget is being used and if those positions are directly supporting the infrastructure you intend to build. This can be an enlightening review with some difficult decisions to make as a result. For example, there is a school with a minimal number of children in special education whose plans call for speech services, yet one of the school's highest paid salaries is for a full-time speech therapist. Reducing this role to a quarter-time position would continue the necessary services for children and also allow the school to hire a child study/nautilus lead. This type of reconfiguration adds no strain on the budget while strengthening the team working to create a resilient, fully implemented Montessori school.

Leadership roles:

Coaching is a core element of this work. If you do not already have a trained Montessori coach, to implement you will need to shift the established roles in your school to accommodate this position. Often an assistant principal or dean of students position can be filled by a Montessori coach who will serve to support the full implementation of the whole-school Montessori method. Regardless of how you rearrange roles, there will need to be a Montessori coach on the leadership team in order to implement the whole school Montessori method.

THE MATERIALS

Annual inventory is a fact of public Montessori programs. It is not a favorite activity, yet it is essential to create equitable classroom environments serving all learners. Every classroom at each level should have the same amount of child-sized furniture (e.g., number of tables, chairs, low tables, shelves) and the same inventory of Montessori materials. Gone are the days when Montessorians emerged from training with their own handmade materials that they carried with them into their classrooms. In public schools, each classroom at a level holds the same material – same timelines and charts and nomenclature – to ensure the curriculum is reaching all children and not dependent on the teacher's decision to bring or make the necessary materials.

Therefore, part of taking action is developing an inventory system[1] that is completed every year in every classroom. Once digitized, this is a straightforward process done by classroom teams at the close of the school year allowing for the equitable replacement of missing or broken materials. This system will prevent the gradual diminishment of the educational program based on unevenly, ill-equipped classrooms.

A carefully curated, well-equipped classroom creates an inviting environment where children and adults feel inspired to learn. This is the basis for strong Montessori implementation, and the whole school Montessori method rests on this foundational allocation of resources.

Storage of materials is another part of the work that needs to be done well. A location in the building for shared resources allows teams to work closely together to monitor used Montessori materials and consumables such as wood polish for primary practical life or vinegar for elementary science experiments. If this space is well organized and has a strong system for use, then level teams can work together to monitor and equitably use resources rather than each individual housing (and potentially stockpiling) material. One school developed an area where primary guides were able to share all practical life materials from pitchers to trays, allowing them to change over their practical life shelves frequently as needed. The elementary team developed kits for the Great Lessons that were signed out of the storage area, moving from one class to another to ensure all classrooms received all five of the lessons. The kits held everything the classroom teacher would need to give the lesson and offer follow-up.

The School Building

Whether your school is public or private, the structure itself is a resource. School buildings or other repurposed spaces being used can be marvelously unique and hold great potential for Montessori programs. The important part is in how that space is used. The layout of your building contributes to the narrative and the felt experience of your community, and the goal is that it communicates One School values. Consider the location of the classrooms relative to one another: Are the levels isolated from each other or integrated? Do children and adults from various levels see each other regularly, or is the adolescent program off in another wing?

Consider the location of leadership: Are the offices of the coach and principal in proximity to the classrooms or in a far-off location separate from the daily rhythm of the learning environments? Are school leaders easily accessible and living each day with their finger on the pulse of the school?

Consider the families: Do they have a space to gather and connect that provides access to information, resources, and Montessori books? Is there meaningful work to engage in such as material making or cutting lamination? Is this space far enough from the classrooms that children's growing autonomy and independence is supported and not undermined by the presence of their family members in school?

Consider the access to outdoors: Is it maximized to support even a small version of the outdoor classroom, privileging the younger children who need closer supervision? Is the outdoor environment a prepared environment for work, study, and play?

Consider your entryway: Is there an obvious main entrance, easily found and accessible? When entering the school, is there an immediate feeling of welcome, beauty, and order? Are there systems in place for greeting visitors and acclimating them to the school regardless of their reason for visiting?

How you use your space communicates your values. What changes need to be made to communicate One School, Honest Talk, and Strong Systems? What improvements will allow your building to act as an agent serving your mission?

TIME

The last resource to consider is the one given equitably and that is time. We all have the same amount of it – it's how we use it that makes a difference. This topic is touched on in the section on meetings as we consider how to make better use of meeting time to move the school closer to its goals. The whole school Montessori method is predicated on everyone in the building optimizing their time in service of the big vision, so an honest appraisal of how time is spent in a day and in a week is a starting place. One school did this work and discovered an enormous amount of time was spent supporting struggling children who left the classroom and were having big feelings or were unreachable. The whole leadership team and the main office staff were constantly pulled off their other work to respond to classrooms where children were in need. Looking at this, they elected to commit to the nautilus approach, hiring a nautilus lead and training the full staff in the approach. This reallocation of funds to create a new position was a difficult decision but served not only the children and classroom adults but also the whole leadership team and office staff who were then able to attend to their own work.

Use of time has two main angles to evaluate: efficiency and effectiveness. Is it the most efficient use of time, and is it effective? In the previous example, time was not being spent efficiently or effectively. These are the first areas to tackle.

Next it will be important to look at those aspects that are one or the other but not both: for example, it's efficient to have children go right to class when they arrive late but not effective as now there is no record of tardiness; it's effective to spend the whole morning for multiple days with a student who is struggling yet not efficient as now other work, such as giving lessons, circulating to help others and observing are not happening. Creating a balance of efficient and effective use of time across all roles, all areas of work in the school will allow for successful implementation of Montessori across the whole school.

OVERVIEW

To take action, let's take a step back now and look at the whole (Table PV.1). Moving from whole to parts will support a steady implementation that allows for gradual changes in your school.

Table PV.1 Whole School Montessori Method Overview

One School	Calibrate		Organize	
	Weekly Meetings		Observation	
	Role Clarity		Professional Development	
	Appraisal Process		Family Engagement	
Honest Talk	Nourish		Validate	
	Fundamental Needs of the Montessori Educator		Language of Reverence	
	Reflective Coaching		Communication	
	Directive Coaching		Year End Reflection	
Strong Systems	Engage		Yield	
	Seamless Transitions		Onboarding	
	Student Portfolios		Record Keeping	
	System of Justness		Data Analysis	

Seeing the whole method on one page allows it to become manageable. The words that help us hold each component have a purpose:

Calibrate
Organize
Nourish
Validate
Engage
Yield

In addition to helping us remember how to bring the components to life, they are meant to convey us or carry us through to full implementation of the Montessori method across the whole school.

NOTE

1. Visit www.resilient-montessori.com for tools to support this process

Chapter 11
Steps to Building a Resilient Montessori School

But when through exceptional circumstances work is the result of an inner, instinctive impulse, then even in the adult it assumes a wholly different character. . . . Such is the work of the inventor or discoverer, the heroic efforts of the explorer, or the compositions of the artist, that is to say, the work of [those] gifted with such an extraordinary power as to enable them to rediscover the instinct of their species in the patterns of their own individuality. This instinct is then a fountain that bursts through the hard outer crust and rises, through a profound urge, to fall, as refreshing rain, on arid humanity. It is through this urge that the true progress of civilisation takes place.

—Maria Montessori, *The Secret of Childhood*

Congratulations on making it to this chapter! You have read about the many practices employed by thriving Montessori schools, and you are at the cusp of starting the journey yourself. You are about to embark on implementation, a fountain bursting "through a profound urge" so that "true progress of the civilization" may take place.

As you prepare to begin this method, remember that it emerged from the recognition of the ways successful Montessori programs relied on incredible people. At the origin story of many Montessori schools was at least one passionate visionary who saw what was possible for children and families and was committed to living into that ideal. Not only were they acting as a buffer to insulate the unique method of education within a larger district, but they were also holding the task of full implementation of the method. This fueled the school for as long as that person was there, yet once they left, the energy that drove the school and the cohesion that occurred around them was also gone. Unless they were replaced by someone equally passionate the school floundered, often activating a decline.

Many of the necessary ingredients were held inside the mind and heart of the person rather than belonging to the school community. Many of the systems and structures that allowed the school to function smoothly left with the person rather than being a foundational part of life in the school. For resilient schools to exist, there must be shared structures to serve all these unique programs, and they must be known by many people. This is the Montessori way.

IMPLEMENTATION RUBRIC

The whole school Montessori method then is built from identifying the critical aspects of the work that need to move forward regardless of the fast pace of every day in schools, regardless of the endless changes expected as a district school, regardless of the external pressures applied to keep the doors open.

The important point here is to implement this work in a way that will be lasting, meaning not people dependent, not dependent on you. The components shared in this book then belong to the community and need, from the very start, to be owned by them in the making.

Thus, to begin it will be important to get a baseline of where your school is now. The rubric shown in Figure 11.1 is included in its entirety with the resources.[1] It was developed to assist you in assessing your starting place. Given the One School vision, it's important to do this with your team so many perspectives are appreciated. Using copies of the rubric, have your team members fill it out individually without any conversation, circling the box that applies for each item. When that is complete, bring the different perspectives together on a fresh copy of the rubric that holds everyone's selections. In this way you will be able to see alignment (we all circled progressing for weekly meetings) as well as disparate views (we have a range of "Not yet" to "Progressing" for language of reverence) for where your school rests on the continuum.

Engage in a conversation, beginning with the divergent views, as you seek to understand the gap. Allow the discussion to shift perspectives until there is closer alignment. In the example of Language of Reverence, this may mean that the person who circled "Not yet" rightly names that the term hasn't been introduced to the community. The person who circled "Progressing" is aware that there is shared language being used by the primary team to discuss children having big feelings. The group decides to select "Started" and to introduce Language of Reverence as a new term and to create a chart of shared language together at the next staff meeting.

As far back as human history goes, tools have been created to assist us in our work, and this tool is meant to help you get started. The more people you ask to complete it, the wider a perspective you will get. In addition, it will spark many questions and conversations for those who are not yet familiar with the whole school Montessori method. This interest will then fuel your implementation.

IMPLEMENTATION PLAN

Based on the data you collect through use of the implementation rubric, you will be able to make a plan about which pieces you want to implement first. If you are opening a new school you may consider the plan laid out in Table 11.1. It stages the introduction of all three components (One School, Honest Talk, Strong Systems) from the outset with key aspects coming in one year at a time.

Table 11.1 Whole-School Montessori Method Implementation Plan

Year	One School	Honest Talk	Strong Systems
One	Role Clarity Observation Tools	Fundamental Needs Language of Reverence	Seamless Transitions Onboarding
Two	Appraisal Process Year-Long PD Calendar	Reflective Coaching Communication Tools	System of Justness Recordkeeping
Three	Weekly Meetings Family Engagement Calendar	Directive Coaching Year-End Reflection	Student Portfolios Data Analysis

If your team has the capacity to do more, focus on adding systems to start. Seamless Transitions, Onboarding, Recordkeeping, and System of Justness are all priorities to begin as you wish to continue. Likewise, Reflective Coaching ideally begins in the first year as an established part of your program.

In the end, selecting the areas you know you will be able to implement well to meet your communities' needs is an important driver. With some fully applied practices you will end the year stronger and ready to add the next layer. Your school will be in a better place if you do it slowly and well rather than attempting to begin too many new practices at once. Montessori is a patient method that chooses the long game over instant gratification and the implementation of the whole-school Montessori method follows that same wisdom.

COMMUNITY OF PRACTICE

You are now invited to join the revolution and a growing community of practice implementing the whole school Montessori method. The term community of practice originated from cognitive anthropologists and educational theorists Jean Lave and Etienne Wenger when they were studying apprenticeship.[2] It refers to a group of people connected through something they do, who work together to learn how to do it better. The practitioners engaged in this work are connected through their implementation of the whole school Montessori method. They continue to refine the method through its use, sharing ideas, resources, and strategies to build resilient schools. The work is too difficult to continue to do in isolation, and joining a community of other practitioners will fortify and strengthen you, your school, and the revolution.[3]

"This is the difference between the old and the new education. We want to help the auto-construction of man at the right time, so that mankind can go forward to something great. Society has built up walls, barriers. These the new education must cast down, revealing the free horizon. The new education is a revolution, but without violence. It is the non-violent revolution. After that, if it triumphs, violent revolution will have become forever impossible."[4]

Whole School Montessori Method Implementation Rubric

One School	Not yet	Started	Progressing	Implemented
Weekly meetings	There are no meetings that occur weekly.	Some meetings occur weekly though notes are not yet taken regularly.	Most meetings occur weekly A shared notes template is used in some meetings.	All meetings occur weekly: Individual lead teachers, Level teams, Leadership, Student support and Assistants- both classroom teams & level teams The shared notes template is used in all meetings.
Role Clarity	Roles & Responsibilities are not written and distributed.	Roles & Responsibilities written, not yet distributed.	Roles & Responsibilities written and distributed Some roles are regularly appraised.	Roles & Responsibilities written and distributed, regularly updated as roles change. There is an appraisal process for all roles including leader and coach.
Montessori Appraisal Process	There is not yet an appraisal process or tool.	There is an appraisal process & tool but they are not aligned with the method.	The appraisal process is adjusted using the conventional tool.	The appraisal process and the tool used are both aligned with the Montessori method.
Year-long PD Calendar	There is not yet a professional development plan.	Professional development is planned for the year but is not yet aligned to staff needs or distributed at the outset of the year.	Professional development is planned for the year without input from a staff survey but is distributed at the outset of the year.	There is a PD Calendar based on staff survey results and the needs of the educators which is distributed to everyone in August and reliably followed throughout the year.
Year-long Family Calendar	There is not yet Family Engagement.	Family Engagement opportunities are announced as they happen.	A Family Engagement series is distributed at the start of the year that is not reliably followed throughout the year.	A Family Engagement Calendar is created based on the needs of the community which is distributed in August and reliably followed throughout the year.
Shared Observation tools	There are not yet observation tools in use.	Various observation tools are used by some people without alignment or discussion.	Shared observation tools are used by some but there is no method for reviewing the data collected.	Everyone in the school competently uses shared observation tools and reviews the data collected to support the direction of the program.
Honest Talk	**Not yet**	**Started**	**Progressing**	**Implemented**
Fundamental Needs of the Montessori Educator	There is not yet an awareness of the needs of the educator.	There is a beginning conversation with slight adjustments made to meet the needs of educators.	The needs of the Montessori educator are openly discussed and are becoming more central in decision making.	The unique needs of the Montessori educator are openly discussed and decisions are made to amplify their work.
Reflective Coaching	There is not yet a trained Montessori coach.	There is a new coach beginning training who is starting to meet with educators without notes.	There is a trained Montessori coach who meets with some educators weekly, setting goals and keeping notes.	A trained Montessori coach meets weekly with educators who serves the community with skills in reflective coaching, allowing each person their own path.
Directive Coaching	There is not yet a trained Montessori coach.	There is a coach new to the role who is not yet having directive coaching conversations.	There is a trained Montessori coach who is finding their voice to engage in directive coaching conversations.	A trained Montessori coach observes and responds as necessary with directive coaching conversations in service of the school's mission.
Language of Reverence	Language of Reverence has not yet been introduced and there is not yet awareness of language being used.	Language of Reverence has not yet been introduced without shared replacement terms but beginning awareness.	Language of Reverence has been introduced and shared language is being used by some.	Everyone in the community understands Language of Reverence and has shared language that is reliably used.
Year End Reflection	There is not yet a process of reflection.	Year End Reflections are done by a select group.	The Year End Reflection process is followed by most but the information gathered is not yet fully put to use.	The whole community engages in the Year End Reflection process and the information gathered is used by leadership to make changes.
Communication Tools	There are not yet shared communication tools consistently used.	There are some shared communications tools used irregularly.	There are shared communication tools within the school that do not yet include families and are used variably	Communication tools are used to include everyone in the community and they are used reliably in a set cycle or process.

Strong Systems	Not yet	Started	Progressing	Implemented
Student Portfolios	Student Portfolios have not yet been started.	Teachers capture artifacts independent of an established Portfolio system or cover sheet.	Student Portfolios are intentionally created with student input using the cover sheet without a system for passing them to the next classroom.	Student Portfolios are developed and well maintained at every level by adults and students, with time designated for their passing as part of the Seamless Transition process, ultimately celebrated at the final conference,
Seamless Transitions	Transition skills are not articulated. Class placement is done without input from the teachers. Students begin in their new classroom the following year.	There is an awareness of transition skills without calibration. A class placement process is emerging that includes classroom adults. Students have some connection to their new class prior to the end of the school year.	There is a beginning list of what students should know by the end of each level. Class placement is done by the teachers with an emerging emphasis on the classroom communities. Students have a way to visit with families notified but not oriented	There is an explicit list of what students should know and be able to do by the end of each level with a process for placing them into new classrooms that balance the needs of individuals and the whole community with an intentional process for orienting both the students and their parents.
System of Justness	The school relies on a standard 'discipline policy'.	There is a beginning framework for supporting all learners that is used by some school based adults.	There is a framework for supporting all learners that is used consistently across the school with an emerging emphasis on Montessori instruction.	There is a comprehensive framework of practices at the school level supporting 1) Montessori instruction, 2) inclusivity and support for all learners, and 3) consistency and proactivity in attaching children to work.
Onboarding	There is not yet a transparent process for hiring or orienting new staff.	There is a transparent process for hiring with little to no orientation to no orientation or corresponding new people are hired.	There is a transparent process for hiring with an orientation process for only select roles in the school.	There is a transparent process for hiring and orienting new staff to the instructional methods, coaching culture, and overall community of the school.
Record Keeping	There is not yet a shared system for keeping track of lessons planned and presented without a shared system nor an expectation that all teachers are doing this.	All teachers are now keeping track of lessons planned and presented without a shared system or corresponding communication with families.	There is a clear, shared, regular system for keeping track of lessons planned and presented that most people are using regularly with some family communication.	There is a clear, shared, regular system for keeping track of lessons planned and presented to children that is accessible by teachers, administrators, and that produces regular family communications about children's progress.
Data Analysis	There is not yet a reliable system for reviewing data.	There are systems emerging for reviewing data that are not widely known or understood.	There are emerging systems for reviewing quantitative data at the school and beginning protocols for analyzing which data regularly.	There is a reliable system for reviewing quantitative data about student academics, culture, finances, and governance at the school. There is a protocol for analyzing this data regularly and a process for taking action to target areas for improvement.

Figure 11.1 Whole-School Montessori Method Implementation Rubric.

NOTES

1. To find all the resources go to: www.resilient-montessori.com.
2. J. Lave and E. Wenger, *Situated Learning: Legitimate Peripheral Participation.* Cambridge: Cambridge University Press. 1991.
3. Join the Community of Practice at www.resilient-montessori.com.
4. Maria Montessori. *The Absorbent Mind.* New York: Holt, Rinehart and Winston. 1995, p. 196.

Chapter 12
Resources to Support

Thus the earliest traces of man's life on earth are not his homes or houses, bones or remains, but the implements of his work. It may be said that man in his capacity as worker is responsible for all that is meant by evolution, progress or civilisation.
　　　　—Maria Montessori, *What You Should Know About Your Child*

The tools shared in this book were developed in public Montessori schools to bridge the gap created by situating a Montessori program in the public sector. They serve to hold and promote the method in large and small ways across the whole school. These have been piloted in schools like yours and further refined to offer you a starting point for your implementation. These tools, like those of early humans, are meant to continue to evolve and change to suit the times in which we live. They are also meant to save you time and energy in creating them on your own.

As such, the resources shared are available to you digitally by visiting www.resilient-montessori.com (password: Revolution). Here you will find all of the tools introduced in this book as well as some of those mentioned but not fully introduced. These tools are meant to allow you independence in the process of redesigning your school and implementing the whole school Montessori method. Feel free to take the tools, tailor them to your community, and use them with your school letterhead. As time is a valuable resource, let us not spend it re-creating something that already exists but rather share what we have already figured out. The tools were created to support the Montessori experience of children and adults and to serve as a start to the work of having shared tools that span our community and hold us together.

This chapter contains a checklist of all the tools introduced in the previous pages. It can be downloaded, printed, and used to keep track of your progress. It walks you through the chapters and serves as an outline for others in your building who you may wish to include in the process of implementation.

WHOLE-SCHOOL MONTESSORI METHOD CHECKLIST

ONE SCHOOL

Calibration Checklist

- ☑ Weekly Meetings
    - ☑ Weekly Meeting tool
    - ☑ Coaches Meeting tool
    - ☑ Curriculum Talk meetings protocol and tools
    - ☑ Information about Lesson Study protocol and tools
- ☑ Roles and Responsibilities
- ☑ Appraisal Process and Tools

Organization Checklist

- ☑ Whole School Montessori Method Year-Long School Calendar
- ☑ Observation Process and Tools
- ☑ Professional Development Process and Tools
- ☑ Family Engagement Tool

HONEST TALK

Nourish Checklist

- ☑ Fundamental Needs of Montessori Educator
    - ☑ Chart
    - ☑ Checklist
- ☑ Questions of Reflective Coaching
- ☑ Questions of Directive Coaching

Validate Checklist

- ☑ Language of Reverence Chart

- ☑ Communication Tools
  - ☑ Daily Staff Email
  - ☑ Daily Family Email
  - ☑ Staff Snapshot
  - ☑ Family Update
  - ☑ Staff Handbook Table of Contents
  - ☑ Family Handbook Table of Contents
- ☑ Year-End Reflection
  - ☑ Individual
  - ☑ Team

STRONG SYSTEMS

School-wide Systems Checklist

Engage Checklist

- ☑ Seamless Transition Overview
  - ☑ Sample Transition Checklist
  - ☑ Sample Transition Timeline
  - ☑ Class Placement Card Sheet
  - ☑ Sample Class Placement Family Letter
  - ☑ New World Seamless Transition Overview
  - ☑ Family Transition Observation Tool
  - ☑ Spring Focus List Primary
  - ☑ Spring Focus List Lower Elementary
- ☑ Student Portfolio System
  - ☑ Student Portfolio Cover Sheet
- ☑ System of Justness
  - ☑ RELATE
  - ☑ Information about Nautilus Approach
  - ☑ Information about Child Study

Yield Checklist

- ☑ Onboarding Overview
  - ☑ Hiring
  - ☑ Orienting
  - ☑ Onboarding Roles and Responsibilities
  - ☑ Interview Observation Tool
  - ☑ Interview Questions
- ☑ Recordkeeping
  - ☑ Family Conferences
    - ☑ Conference Format – Primary
    - ☑ Conference Format – Elementary
    - ☑ Conference Notes – Primary
    - ☑ Conference Notes – Elementary
    - ☑ Family Contact Log
  - ☑ Grace and Courtesy Checklist
- ☑ Data Analysis System
  - ☑ Data Review Process
  - ☑ Data Team Tool

Implementation

- ☑ Whole-School Montessori Method Implementation Rubric
- ☑ Whole-School Montessori Method Implementation Plan

With these resources you will be equipped to begin the work of building your resilient school. In spite of the myriad demands of running a Montessori school and the often conflicting priorities, you now have a road map for beginning. Regardless of who you are or what type of Montessori school you are in, at whatever stage of development it is in, this is a model that will help move the Montessori work forward.

References

Christensen, O. (n.d.). "Montessori Identity in Dialogue: A Selected Review of Literature on Teacher Identity." St. Catherine University. Available at: https://files.eric.ed.gov/fulltext/EJ1234685.pdf.

Debs, M. (2019). *Diverse Families, Desirable Schools: Public Montessori in the Era of School Choice.* Cambridge, MA: Harvard Education Press, 2019.

Dewey, J. (1897). "My Pedagogic Creed." *School Journal.*

Field, S., Kuczera, M., and Pont, B. (2007). "No More Failures: Ten Steps to Equity in Education." OECD.

Gopalan, M., and Nelson, A. A. (2019). "Understanding the Racial Discipline Gap in Schools." doi: 10.1177/2332858419844613.

Hammond, Z. (2015). *Culturally Responsive Teaching & the Brain: Promoting Authentic Engagement and Rigor Among Culturally and Linguistically Diverse Students.* Corwin.

Hirschfeld, L. A. (2008). "Children's Developing Conceptions of Race." In S. M. Quintana and C. McKown (Eds.), *Handbook of Race, Racism, and the Developing Child* (pp. 37–54). Hoboken, NJ: John Wiley & Sons.

hooks, b. (1994). *Teaching to Transgress: Education as the Practice of Freedom.* Routledge.

Ito, T. A., Larsen, J. T., Smith, N. K., and Cacioppo, J. T. (1998). "Negative Information Weighs More Heavily on the Brain: The Negativity Bias in Evaluative Categorizations." *Journal of Personality and Social Psychology* 75 (887–900).

Lave, J., and Wenger, E. (1991). *Situated Learning: Legitimate Peripheral Participation.* Cambridge, UK: Cambridge University Press.

Lillard, A. S. (2020). "Montessori as an Alternative Early Childhood Education." *Early Child Development and Care.* doi: 10.1080/03004430.2020.1832998.

Lorde, A. (2007). "The Master's Tools Will Never Dismantle the Master's House." *Sister Outsider: Essays and Speeches.* Berkeley, CA: Crossing Press, 110–114.

Malm, B. (2007). "Constructing Professional Identities: Montessori Teachers' Voices and Visions." *Scandinavian Journal of Educational Research.*

Montessori, M. (1949). *The Absorbent Mind*. India: Kalakshetra Publications.

Montessori, M. (1965). *Spontaneous Activity in Education*. New York: Schocken Books

Montessori, M. (1978). *The Secret of Childhood*, London: Sangam Books Limited.

Montessori, M. (1986). *The Discovery of the Child*. New York: Clio Press Ltd.

Montessori. M. (1988). *Advanced Montessori Method*, Vol.1. India: Kalakshetra Publications.

Montessori, M. (1989). *Education for a New World*. New York: Clio Press Ltd.

Montessori, M. (1989). *What You Should Know About Your Child*. New York: Clio Press Ltd.

Montessori, M. (1995). *The Absorbent Mind*. New York: Holt, Rinehart and Winston.

Montessori, M . (1997). *Education and Peace*. Oxford: ABC-Clio.

Montessori, M. (2007). *To Educate the Human Potential*. Amsterdam: Montessori-Pierson Publishing Co.

Montessori, M. (2008). *From Childhood to Adolescence*. Amsterdam: Montessori-Pierson.

Montessori, M. (2012). *The 1946 London Lectures*. Amsterdam: Montessori-Pierson.

Montessori, M. (2016). "Observation and Development from Dr. Montessori's 1946 London Training Course." *NAMTA Journal* 41:3.

Montessori, M. (2019). *Citizen of the World*. Amsterdam: Montessori-Pierson.

National Geographic. (1996–2021). "Lithosphere." Resource Library Encyclopedic Entry. Available from: https://www.nationalgeographic.org/encyclopedia/lithosphere/.

Nelson, L., and Lind, D. (2015). "The School to Prison Pipeline, Explained." Justice Policy Institute, February 24.

Olusegun, S. (2015). "Constructivism Learning Theory: A Paradigm for Teaching and Learning." *IOSR Journal of Research & Method in Education*, 5:1 (66–70).

O'Shaughnessy, M. (2016). "The Observation Scientist." *NAMTA Journal* 41:3.

Parker, P. (2018). *The Art of Gathering: How We Meet and Why It Matters*. New York: Riverhead Books.

Rosenberg, M. B. (2000). *Nonviolent Communication: A Language of Compassion* (1st ed., 3rd printing). Encinitas, CA: Puddledancer Press.

Singleton, G. (2015). *Courageous Conversations*. Corwin.

Index

Page numbers followed by *f* and *t* refer to figures and tables, respectively.